CH0079675Z

# Lord of the Pyrenees

## Gaston Fébus, Count of Foix
### (1331–1391)

The reign of Gaston III, Count of Foix and self-proclaimed sovereign Lord of Béarn, stands out as one of the rare success stories of the 'calamitous' fourteenth century. By playing a skilfull game of shifting allegiances and timely defiance, he avoided being drawn into the conflicts between his more powerful neighbours – France and English Aquitaine, Aragon and Castile – thus sparing his domains the devastations of warfare. Best known as a patron of the arts, and the author of a celebrated *Book of the Hunt*, Fébus – as he styled himself – also prefigures the eighteenth-century 'enlightened despots' with his effort to centralize government, protect natural resources and promote enterprise. But a sequence of mysterious tragedies – the abrupt dismissal of his wife, the slaying of his only legitimate son – reveal the dark side of the brilliant and enigmatic 'Sun Prince of the Pyrenees'.

RICHARD VERNIER is Professor Emeritus of Romance Languages and Literatures, Wayne State University. He is the author of *The Flower of Chivalry: Bertrand du Guesclin and the Hundred Years War*.

Gaston Fébus with huntsmen and hounds: the first page of his *Livre de chasse*,
Bibliothèque nationale de France, ms. fr. 619

# Lord of the Pyrenees

## Gaston Fébus, Count of Foix
### (1331–1391)

Richard Vernier

THE BOYDELL PRESS

© Richard Vernier 2008

*All rights reserved.* Except as permitted under current legislation
no part of this work may be photocopied, stored in a retrieval
system, published, performed in public, adapted, broadcast,
transmitted, recorded or reproduced in any form or by any
means, without the prior permission of the copyright owner

The right of Richard Vernier to be identified as the author of this
work has been asserted in accordance with sections 77 and 78 of
the Copyright, Designs and Patents Act 1988

First published 2008
The Boydell Press, Woodbridge

ISBN 978-1-84383-356-7

The Boydell Press is an imprint of Boydell & Brewer Ltd
PO Box 9, Woodbridge, Suffolk IP12 3DF, UK
and of Boydell & Brewer Inc.
668 Mt Hope Avenue, Rochester, NY 14620, USA
website: www.boydellandbrewer.com

A CIP record for this book is available
from the British Library

This publication is printed on acid-free paper

Designed and typeset in Lucida Blackletter and Adobe Jenson
by David Roberts, Pershore, Worcestershire

Printed in Great Britain by
CPI Antony Rowe, Chippenham, Wiltshire

# Contents

# List of Illustrations

# Preface

In a period that saw the known world ravaged by the Black Death, Christendom torn by the Great Schism, and two mighty kingdoms locked in the interminable duel of Plantagenets and Valois, historians of the Hundred Years War cannot be faulted for having paid only passing attention to the person and career of Gaston III, Count of Foix and Viscount of Béarn, commonly known as Gaston-Phoebus. In an imaginary group portrait of his famous contemporaries, with the likes of Edward III and Charles V at the centre, he would have stood in the second row, perhaps even at one or other end. Some better-placed members of the assembly, such as the redoubted Edward, Prince of Wales and Aquitaine, or the overactive King of Navarre, may have looked askance at this sometimes difficult neighbour; nevertheless, all his royal contemporaries would have thought it appropriate to acknowledge him at least with a more or less cordial, but still courteous nod.

As lord of disparate fiefs strung along the northern foothills of the Pyrenees, the twelfth Count of Foix was perhaps only a minor player in the power games of his time, but the strategic situation of his domains made him a pivotal one in the complex tugging between French Languedoc, English Aquitaine, Navarre and Aragon. Moreover, he was richer than some kings, and his wealth afforded him additional leverage in his dealings with his more powerful neighbours. Despite these claims to a significant part in the political drama of the late fourteenth century, Gaston-Phoebus (or more correctly, as he signed himself, *Fébus*) is most readily identified in his own country as one of the legendary folk heroes of the Midi, together with the historic Henri IV and the semi-fictional d'Artagnan. To a more rarefied public, he is known as the author of a *Book of the Hunt*, celebrated for its comprehensive cynegetic discourse and for the beauty of its illuminated manuscripts, in which the Count himself is portrayed as a regal but subtly unconventional figure. Recent research in early music has also revealed Gaston III as the patron of an important coterie of avant-garde musicians, corroborating Froissart's praise of his cultivated munificence. To this image of a picturesque yet peripheral character, the half-told stories of his private life add a touch of gothic mystery, of the sort that could not – and did not – fail to attract the attention of Alexandre Dumas.

There was, however, more to Gaston Fébus than the host of a lively provincial court and protagonist of his personal tragedy. His reign is remarkable as one of the rare success stories in a century particularly noted for calamities both natural and man-made. By reinforcing his diplomacy – essentially a skilful game of shifting allegiances – with a resolute show of defensive strength, Gaston III avoided being drawn into the Anglo-French conflict, and even managed to curb the activities of the lawless mercenary bands in his domains. His subjects were thus spared the ravages of warfare incessantly visited on most neighbouring lands, in periods of truce as well as of declared hostilities. In internal affairs, his efforts to centralize feudal government, rationalize finances, protect natural resources and promote enterprise and social mobility, might cast Fébus as a distant forerunner of the eighteenth century's 'enlightened despots'. At any rate, he is notable for the fact that, unlike many a contemporary magnate, he left to his heir not debts, but a considerable private treasure and a stable public economy. While not unique in his own time, Gaston Fébus is an idiosyncratic example of a new type of learned, pragmatic ruler emerging – if only just – from the feudal mould.

IN writing this book, I have had to rely almost exclusively on previously published sources, from such general histories as Jonathan Sumption's ongoing narrative of the Hundred Years War and Delachenal's venerable but still indispensable *Histoire de Charles V*, to the works of such regional historians as Charles Higounet and Philippe Wolff, or such specialized studies as Kenneth Fowler's *Medieval Mercenaries*. Various critical approaches to Froissart – especially those of Ainsworth, Dembowski and Zink – have been very helpful to my own always problematic reading of the *Chroniques*. Gunnar Tilander's annotated editions of the *Livre de chasse* and of the *Livre des oraisons*, and A. H. Diverres' presentation of Froissart's *Voyage en Béarn*, have proved to be priceless resources. I am indebted above all to the vast and thorough scholarship of Pierre Tucoo-Chala, whose 1959 doctoral thesis *Gaston Fébus et la Vicomté de Béarn (1331–1391)* was the first and remains to this day the most comprehensive study of the reign of Gaston III, and, indeed, the foundation of all *fébusien* studies. His subsequent contributions, including editions of many archival documents and the revised biography published in 1991 under the title of *Gaston-Fébus, Prince des Pyrénées*, have steadily increased the store of materials indispensable to an understanding, however tentative, of the enigmatic Count of Foix. While one may not always agree with the Béarnais historian's interpretation of his hero's motives and aspirations, it is undoubtedly thanks to the resources provided by Tucoo-Chala's indefatigable scholarship that one is able to differ with him. I wish to thank Jean-Jacques Castéret for making available to me his unpublished thesis and other articles on music at the court of Orthez, all of which have proved to be of great value in defining the impact of Fébus' patronage on contemporary cultural life. Last but by no means least, I wish to thank Matthew and John Keith Vernier for their respective contributions of photographs and line drawings. Unless otherwise indicated, all translations are mine.

# About Money

THANKS to several generations of scholars, it is no longer impossible to determine the modern equivalent value of medieval moneys. Given that the silver or gold contents of real coins – florins, ducats, gros, soldi, pfennig, etc. – at a particular time can be found in such works as Grierson's *Monnaies du Moyen-Âge* (Fribourg, 1976), their approximate current worth may be deduced on any given day from the market quotations for those metals. With the help of Spufford's *Handbook of Medieval Exchange* (London: Royal Historical Society, 1986), it is even possible to navigate the maze of equivalencies between the real currencies on the one hand, and moneys of account on the other (often referred to by similar names) issued or used by different countries, provinces and cities. In respect to the moneys mentioned in this book, it is perhaps enough to remember that in the mid-fourteenth century, the Florentine florin – later imitated by Aragonese florins of somewhat lesser value – was equivalent to 3 shillings sterling; French currencies were often devaluated through that period, and sometimes replaced with new issues: thus the *écu* went from 4 shillings to 2s 10d sterling, but the franc appears somewhat stabilized in the late 1360, at the rate of 4 shillings sterling. Unfortunately, Spufford makes no mention of moneys minted in Béarn, even though the Morlaàs silver coinage enjoyed wide circulation in Aquitaine, Languedoc and northern Spain, and Gaston III undertook to issue a gold florin in imitation of the Perpignan florin of Aragon.

The greatest challenge, however, is for the twenty-first-century reader to adjust to the vast disparity between the values of goods and services as perceived in their medieval and modern economic contexts. It is not easy to imagine an economy in which wind and water were the only sources of industrial energy, and wool – now hardly a critical commodity – was not only England's chief commercial export, but the staple of Flemish manufacturing wealth, and an object of contention between rival powers. Thus our distance from the everyday realities of medieval life makes any reading of relative values tentative at best, if not subjective. Was for instance Fébus' gift of 80 florins to Jean Froissart munificent or mean? The poet-chronicler appears quite satisfied with it – but then it is safe to say that he would have kept to himself any private disappointment. Perhaps the best measure of that parting gratuity is that it was equivalent to the pay of one Béarnais knight for a little over three months; or that it would have bought a riding horse, with possibly something to spare for a pack animal. It might seem easier to apprehend the gap separating the rich from the poor, to contrast for instance the sums – 100 florins here, 200 there – given to minstrels, or the enormous ransoms raised (ultimately by some form of taxation) on behalf of unlucky noblemen, with the plight of certain Béarnais peasants reduced to abandoning their home for lack of the 2 francs required to acquit themselves of the *annual* hearth-tax. But here again, our judgement is informed by anecdotal evidence taken out of its far from coherent context. All things considered, and despite the advances of scholarship since it was first given decades ago, Barbara Tuchman's well-seasoned advice to the reader 'simply to think of any given amount as so many pieces of money' is perhaps the most sensible and comforting one to be had.

# Abbreviations

*Chroniques*  Jean Froissart, *Chroniques*, in *Œuvres*, edited by Baron Kervyn de Lettenhove. 28 vols. Brussels: Académie Royale des Lettres et des Beaux-Arts de Belgique, 1867–77.

*Prince*  Pierre Tucoo-Chala, *Gaston Fébus, prince des Pyrénées.* Pau: J & D Éditions / Bordeaux: Deucalion, 1991–3.

*Vicomté*  Pierre Tucoo-Chala, *Gaston Fébus et la Vicomté de Béarn (1331–1391)*. Bordeaux: Imprimerie Bière, 1959.

*Voyage*  Jean Froissart, *Voyage en Béarn*, edited by A. H. Diverres. Manchester: Manchester University Press, 1953.

PART I

# The Making of a Prince

# Inheritance

O N 25 September 1347 one Acharias de Brunheys, 'gentleman', brought to the Count of Foix letters bearing the royal seal of France. He was much taken aback when, after reading the letters, the fifteen-year-old Gaston III informed him that he had come to the wrong place, at the wrong time. The envoy had travelled very far indeed, all the way to Orthez in the viscounty of Béarn (now the French *département* of Pyrénées-Atlantiques), only to be told that the royal summons would only be considered, and answered, after the feast of All Saints, when the Count would be back at his other seat in his county of Foix (modern Ariège). The weary, disappointed messenger returned no doubt as he had come, by way of Toulouse. His route sometimes ran parallel to the Pyrenees, and analogies may have occurred to him, between the reliability of certain far-flung allegiances and some elusive aspects of the great mountain range that shines one day high above the foothills, only to vanish the next day in a thin mist, itself almost invisible. And even when in clear weather those sharp peaks and glittering glaciers seem near enough to touch, their crystalline purity often conceals the imminence of a storm.

The looming, abrupt north face of the Pyrenees seems to confirm the opinion held so long by so many, that here ends Europe proper. While they are not the highest range on the continent – not rising above 12,000 feet – they stretch continuously from the Atlantic to the Mediterranean. Rivers rushing, as the chronicler Froissart put it, 'straight and hard' from the glaciers have carved short, deep valleys inhabited by fiercely independent folk, from the Basques in the West to the Catalans on the Mediterranean slope. To the rulers of France, the Pyrenees had meant nothing but trouble. Even in Merovingian times, after the Franks had expelled the Visigoths and pushed them into Spain, the foothills of Comminges had harboured the rebellion of Gundovald the Pretender, and suffered in consequence the massacre and razing of the ancient Gallo-Roman town where King Herod was said to have been exiled. In 778 the army of Charlemagne had suffered in the Roncevaux pass the humiliating attack and pillage of its baggage-train by the Basques – a minor episode, but from which would spring in the eleventh century the great epic of French knighthood, the *Song of Roland*. Indeed, the Pyrenean foothills, and the southern lowlands the French call 'le Midi', would long remain the promised land of heresy and rebellion.

The Midi had been conquered – if not subdued – in the devastating forty-year war that broke upon it in 1209. Under the nominal command of the Abbot of Citeaux and the military leadership of Simon de Montfort, the mission of the 'crusade' was to eradicate from the South the peaceful heretics called Cathars or Albigensians, and to punish by fire and sword the cities and feudal lords who had tolerated and even favoured them. By mid-century the Midi was in ruins: the Cathar stronghold of Montségur, near Foix, had fallen in 1244, and the burning of 200 men and women captured there signalled the end of overt resistance. Under the onslaught of land-hungry knights from the North, the old native dynasties – the House of Saint-Gilles in Toulouse, the Trencavels of Carcassonne – had been dispossessed, and many more of the local nobles murdered, driven into exile or at least reduced to poverty. In 1251 the processional entry in Toulouse of Alphonse de Poitiers, brother of King Louis IX, only solemnized an accomplished fact: the county and all its vassal dependencies now came under the direct sway of the French Crown, and were henceforth to be administered by royal seneschals answering to Paris. The new province, stretching from the fertile Garonne valley to the uplands of the Massif Central, was named Languedoc in acknowledgement of its linguistic difference: while the word for 'yes' was then pronounced *oïl* in most of the French dialects, the same word in the Midi was *oc*, hence the southern idioms were collectively known as *langues d'oc*.

Alone among the great local families, thanks perhaps to their sense of timing in both resistance and submission, the counts of Foix had managed to ride out the storm of the Albigensian Crusade and not only to keep but extend their domains. In 1214, from the eagle's nest of Foix, snug in its circle of mountains 50 miles south from Toulouse, Count Raymond-Roger had successfully defied Simon de Montfort, with a determination sustained by an entourage of Cathar sympathizers and outright 'heretics', including his own wife. His sister Esclarmonde had, indeed, publicly received the Cathar sacrament of *consolamentum*, and thus become one of the 'Perfects' venerated by many of the Count's subjects. But in the end his heirs had to make their peace with the King of France. Yet they had prospered: to the original county, stretching northward into the gently rolling hills of the Ariège valley, the House of Foix eventually added diverse rights, leases and other footholds in towns and fiefs – Mirepoix, Belpech, Cintegabelle, Auterive, etc. – that lay beyond its borders, in the French jurisdictions of Toulouse and Carcassonne, as well as other substantial lands and castles deeper into royal Languedoc, notably in the neighbourhood of Albi.

Through the complex workings of feudal marriages and legacies, the counts of Foix were also vassals of the King of Aragon for some fiefs in Roussillon and in Catalonia. For the Pyrenees were much more porous than the forbidding, abrupt view of their north face would lead one to expect. Two kingdoms straddled their high ridges: at the eastern end, the Crown of Aragon reigned over Roussillon, separated from Peninsular Catalonia only by the low fence of the Albères, while towards the Atlantic extremity Navarre stretched from the Ebro in Spain to the lowlands of the Basque country, north of the Roncevaux pass. And it was not by accident that two lesser, but still substantial feudal states also

# The Foix-Béarn Succession

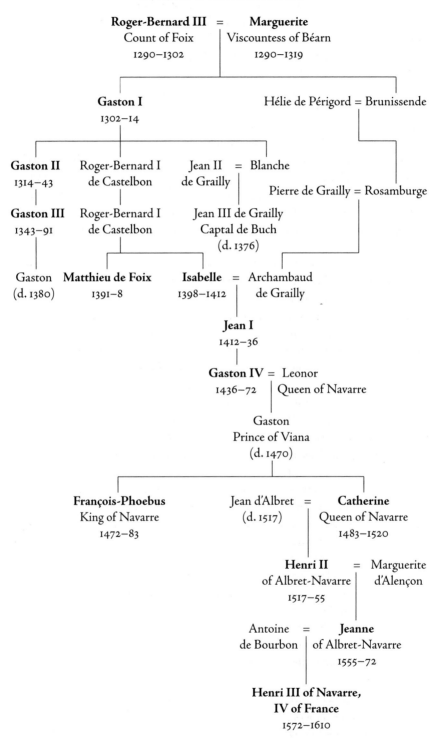

**Roger-Bernard III** = **Marguerite**
Count of Foix · Viscountess of Béarn
1290–1302 · 1290–1319

**Gaston I**
1302–14

Hélie de Périgord = Brunissende

**Gaston II**
1314–43

Roger-Bernard I
de Castelbon

Jean II = Blanche
de Grailly

Pierre de Grailly = Rosamburge

**Gaston III**
1343–91

Roger-Bernard I
de Castelbon

Jean III de Grailly
Captal de Buch
(d. 1376)

Gaston
(d. 1380)

**Matthieu de Foix**
1391–8

**Isabelle** = Archambaud
1398–1412 · de Grailly

**Jean I**
1412–36

**Gaston IV** = Leonor
1436–72 · Queen of Navarre

Gaston
Prince of Viana
(d. 1470)

**François-Phoebus**
King of Navarre
1472–83

Jean d'Albret = **Catherine**
(d. 1517) · Queen of Navarre
1483–1520

**Henri II** = Marguerite
of Albret-Navarre · d'Alençon
1517–55

Antoine = **Jeanne**
de Bourbon · of Albret-Navarre
1555–72

**Henri III of Navarre,
IV of France**
1572–1610

controlled some of the main trade and pilgrimage routes across the Pyrenees: several of the roads to Compostela via the Somport pass converged in Béarn, while Foix controlled the access to the Puymorens pass, the most direct way from Toulouse to the Catalan shrine of Montserrat.

The ramifications of feudal families throughout Christendom naturally favoured the odds of a nobleman inheriting a far-away fief or even a crown. Thus in 1234 a French prince, Count Thibaut of Champagne, inherited the kingdom of Navarre, sixty years after another trans-Pyrenean dynasty, the Catalan Moncadas, had come to rule the neighbouring viscounty of Béarn. Then, toward the end of the thirteenth century, Roger-Bernard III of Foix married the heiress of Béarn. Marguerite was only one of the several daughters of Gaston VII, last of the Moncade viscounts. To Guilhelma, an unmarried sister, he bequeathed some of the Catalan fiefs, and to Matha, married to the Count of Armagnac, the lesser viscounty of Gavardan. But the bulk of his domains in Béarn and Gascony were to be henceforth indissolubly joined in the dual lordship of Foix-Béarn. The rise of the House of Foix to greater wealth and power was proclaimed in heraldry by the quartering of their arms with the red cows emblematic of Béarn. It was perhaps inevitable that from then on the principal seat of the Count of Foix would be in Béarn. It has been suggested that Gaston VII Moncade may have imposed as a condition of his bequest that his son-in-law reside in Orthez.[1] Whether he did or not, the potential challenge to the succession may well have compelled Roger-Bernard to be conspicuously present and ready to defend his wife's inheritance. According to tradition, their son was given the dynastic name bestowed on the heirs of Béarn born in the viscounty. The fact that Marguerite de Béarn outlived both her husband and their son, and for a time even ruled as regent during the minority of her grandson Gaston II, may have also contributed to establish definitively the residence of the counts in Béarn. However, the heirs of the Moncades were clearly perceived as a new dynasty – the Foix-Béarn (hence Gaston I, rather than VIII). Chroniclers would always refer to them as counts of Foix, never viscounts of Béarn, although paradoxically the viscounty became the cornerstone of their ambitions. Whether expediency, fortuitous circumstances, or some long-range feudal strategy determined the transfer of the court of Foix-Béarn to Orthez, it is also possible that the counts appreciated a residence separated by six days' journey from the reach of the French royal officers in Toulouse. Moreover, while their orthodoxy was now unimpeachable, the descendants of Raymond-Roger may have felt somewhat uncomfortable in a land that the Inquisition continued to scour well into the fourteenth century, especially under the tenure of Jacques Fournier – the future Pope Benedict XII – as bishop of Pamiers.[2]

---

[1] Claudine Pailhès, *Gaston Fébus, le Prince et le diable* (Paris, 2007), 257–8.

[2] 1317–26. See Emmanuel Leroy-Ladurie, *Montaillou, The Promised Land of Error*, trans. Barbara Bray (New York, 1978).

Naturally, the partition arranged by Gaston VII Moncade pleased no one entirely. Successive rulers of Foix-Béarn, not content with the Catalan fiefs they eventually inherited from Guilhelma, nor with the Gavardan wrested from the Armagnacs, would inevitably strive to link their eastern and western lands, by acquiring or at least controlling such intervening domains as the counties of Comminges and Bigorre, and the lands of Couserans, Labarthe, Nébouzan, etc. Conversely, the counts of Armagnac felt that they had been cheated of Matha's fair marriage portion: bent on consolidating their lands along a north–south axis, they coveted the same prizes, and their rivalry, unabated by time, spilled over into every region where the two houses could find a pretext to square off.

T HE feud between two rich and powerful magnates – arguably the two richest and powerful in the Midi – presented serious problems as well as opportunities to their neighbours and nominal overlords, especially the kings of France and England, whose own rivalry had been simmering ever since the 1154 marriage of Duchess Aliénor of Aquitaine and Henry II, whereby the Plantagenets had become masters of nearly every province from the Channel to the Pyrenees. France had since then recovered Normandy, Poitou and other mid-Atlantic lands, but the core of Aquitaine – wine-rich Guyenne, and the busy maritime outlets of Bordeaux and Bayonne – remained secure, and for the most part loyal, Plantagenet fiefs. However, feudal custom decreed that, while he was sovereign in England, the Duke of Aquitaine was a vassal of the French King. Harking back to Charlemagne, the nominal overlordship gave the French monarch the right to interfere in the affairs of the duchy. This could be – and indeed became – an effective weapon, enabling the French judicial apparatus to intervene in disputes between the King-Duke and his own Gascon vassals. Not only could the English sovereign be placed in a humiliating posture, but a hostile or merely recalcitrant response on his part could be the pretext of a confiscation decree, which in turn would justify an armed intervention.

The conflict came to a head early in the fourteenth century, when a French dynastic crisis superimposed itself on the tensions stemming from perennial clashes of interests in both Aquitaine and Flanders. When the last of the Capetians in the direct line of succession died in 1328 without male issue, Edward III's claim to the vacant crown was founded on the fact that, through his mother Isabella, daughter of Philippe IV of France, he was the nearest male relative of the late Charles IV. The next nearest kinsman was the Count of Valois, head of a collateral branch of the Capetian dynasty. But Edward had no following among the French nobles. Following their lead, the Paris Parlement interpreted an ancient Frankish tribal custom excluding women from landed inheritance, to mean that a woman could neither inherit the throne, nor transmit rights of inheritance to her own male descendants. The Count of Valois was crowned.

However galling, the rejection of the English claim did not precipitate an open break. After much wrangling by lawyers for both parties, and despite Isabella's sour reply that 'the son of a king would not do homage to the son of a count', Edward did just that in 1329. There followed two more years of haggling over the exact meaning of his homage, eventually allowing the French *légistes* to have their way. But no conciliatory parchment was large enough to cover up the irreconcilable differences between the two crowns. Vital economic interests were at stake in Flanders and in Aquitaine, with England's revenue from the wool trade dependent on the Flemish textile industry, while Gascony thrived chiefly on the export of wine to the English market. Both parties did their best to undermine the other. With a view to a coalition, England courted the discontented Flemings and bribed the Holy Roman Emperor to appoint Edward his 'vicar' in the Rhineland. Meanwhile, France openly declared for the exiled David II of Scotland, promising military support for his embattled followers. Moreover, the threat of confiscation continued to hang over Aquitaine. It was decreed in March 1337 by Philippe VI's Great Council, and the *arrière-ban* – the formal mobilization of the feudal army, proclaimed a month later.

T HE first military actions of what would come to be called the Hundred Years War were neither spectacular nor promising for the English cause. In the North, Edward III, having revived his claim to the French crown, brought his army to Flanders in the summer of 1338 but, unable to hold his coalition together, made almost no headway. Meanwhile, the French fleet and its Genoese auxiliaries harried the shipping between England and Gascony, seized the Channel Islands, and conducted murderous raids on the south coast, notably on Southampton, Portsmouth and Hastings. Fears of a French invasion were laid to rest only by the ferocious sea-battle of Sluys on the coast of Flanders, when on 25 June 1340, the French fleet was destroyed or taken with appalling loss of life.

In Aquitaine the expected French offensive had failed to achieve any decisive success. The ambiguous outcome of two years of warfare in the Garonne valley and in southern Périgord resulted in part from the feuds among the great noble houses of the South West. While the counts of Armagnac and of Foix both served Philippe VI in Flanders, their enmity had not been diminished, and they both looked forward to the day when a truce in the Anglo-French conflict would enable them to resume their private war. The Armagnacs' fealty was put to the test when the dispute between their kinsman, the lord of Albret, and the Count of Périgord, entered a more violent phase. The French king, who valued the strategic importance of Périgord, took the part of the Count against the lord of Albret, whose loyalty was in any case rendered somewhat doubtful by the fact that his lands lay mostly in 'English' Gascony. These also lay in dangerous proximity to Béarn, and the capture of his town of Tartas by the troops of the Count of Foix in August 1339 may have tipped the scale of Albret's allegiances: together with his 200–300 vassals and an extensive clientèle of allies, he committed to the English side, and in the autumn campaign marched along with the seneschal of Bordeaux in a raid against the Toulousain.

It was more than possible that the Count of Armagnac would follow his kinsman of Albret, and he might well have, but for the fact that after three years of hard, enormously expensive warfare, the French had somewhat recovered from their earlier reverses in Aquitaine: the part of the duchy lying north of the Gironde was now in their hands, leaving Bordeaux on an exposed frontier. Edward III could never have made good the promises of territorial compensation made to Jean d'Armagnac. Moreover, the fortunes of war had favoured his rival of Foix-Béarn at the expense of the Albrets. Not only was there nothing to be gained by changing sides, but the best course for the Armagnacs was to try and gain the support of Philippe VI, at the time when the English threat was also receding on the northern front. On balance, the Anglo-French war had come to a draw, sanctioned in September 1340 by the truce of Esplechin.

As for the Count of Foix, although he was not seen to waver in his French alliance, his other title of Viscount of Béarn nevertheless exposed him to potential pro-English pressures. In theory at least, Béarn lay in the feudal dependency of the dukes of Aquitaine. In practice, the Moncade viscounts had been on the whole reliable supporters of the Plantagenets, but their successors, in keeping with the traditional allegiance of the counts of Foix to the French Crown, had reversed that policy. In doing so, they met with the disapproval and even open defiance of many Béarnais nobles, an attitude stemming in part from fidelity to a well-established tradition, but also rooted in economic and geo-political realities. While the county of Foix naturally looked to French Languedoc for its trade partnerships, the viscounty of Béarn depended on the markets of English Gascony, not only for its prosperity, but for its very economic survival: peaceful relations with the duchy were a concern of all, from the shepherds of the high valleys to the town merchants – some of whom had occasionally lent money to the King-Duke. For the nobles, the need for peace with the ducal administration was equally vital, and often more immediate, as many of them held fiefs in Gascony, lands and castles that open warfare would have exposed to confiscation. Relatively impoverished knights, and even some bourgeois, were also attracted by the prospect of regular remuneration in the service of the English king. The immediate entourage of Gaston II was not immune to such attraction: his half-brother, Bernard de Béarn, was from 1338 in the pay of Edward III. This did not bring him into direct confrontation with Gaston, but other Béarnais knights, invoking an overriding allegiance to the Duke of Aquitaine, did not shrink from taking the field against their other suzerain the Count of Foix.[3] On the other hand, even the counts had family ties in English Gascony, being cousins to the Graily lords – in Gascon 'Captals'

3 *Vicomté*, 50, 51.

– of the Buch country, south from Bordeaux. It is also worth noting (if only as an instance of the feudal absurd) that it was a Béarnais litigant who had in 1337 precipitated the confiscation of Aquitaine: unable to obtain payment of the debt owed him by Edward III, the baron of Sault-de-Navailles appealed to the Paris Parlement. This was the legal pretext Philippe VI needed to clothe his political decision, and the French high court obliged: the duchy was ordered seized like the property of any common debtor.

Although the truce of Esplechin was extended for four more years in September 1341, there was to be no peace, for the direct Anglo-French conflict found a surrogate outlet in the war of the Breton ducal succession. In the Midi, the Foix-Armagnac rivalry was in a dormant stage. The service of the Count of Foix to the French king had been rewarded with the viscounty of Lautrec in Languedoc, and the promise of the Basque viscounty of Soule, on the western border of Béarn – provided he could expel its Anglo-Gascon garrison. Why Gaston II chose that moment to go crusading in Spain has been sometimes explained as a move to renew the traditional Iberian ties of the Foix dynasty, a view perhaps supported by the betrothal of his nine-year-old heir to the daughter of King James III of Majorca. But the Count's decision to join the Castilian campaign against the Moors of Granada may have simply stemmed from a sense of his obligations as a knight and a Christian prince. Gaston II has been characterized as 'a ruthless and self-serving warlord', but he is also entered in chronicles with the epithet of 'le Preux' (the Hero).[4] And the crusading mystique still had a powerful hold on the chivalric imagination. It would fade only after the surrender of Moslem Granada had brought to completion the Spanish Reconquista, and the growing Ottoman threat had rendered the prospect of 'liberating' Jerusalem more chimerical than ever, but throughout the fourteenth century the idea of crusade was a constant preoccupation of every pope, and most kings.

Gaston II was only one among a galaxy of noble foreigners, such as the Earls of Derby and Salisbury, and Philippe d'Evreux, King of Navarre, who had come to help Alfonso XI of Castile take a key Moorish stronghold. Across the bay from Gibraltar, Algeciras was the port of entry of troops and supplies sent from Morocco to bolster the defences of Granada. Its capture was one of the steps necessary to isolate the last Moslem kingdom of Spain, but the two-year siege is also notable for one of the early appearances of firearms in Europe. It was not, however, to the Moors' bombards that Gaston II succumbed on 26 September 1343, but to the illness that overtook him in Seville, even as he considered whether to stay of to leave. On the same day, Philippe of Navarre also died in Seville, possibly of the same illness.[5]

---

[4] Jonathan Sumption, *The Hundred Years War*, 2 vols. (Philadelphia, 1990, 1999), I, 329.

[5] L. P. Harvey, *Islamic Spain, 1250 to 1500* (Chicago, 1990), 199–201.

'GEOGRAPHICAL dispersion and economic mediocrity' have been invoked as 'the essential characteristics' of the domains bequeathed by Gaston II to his twelve-year-old son.[6] These consisted in a feudal archipelago uneasily divided between several 'seas' of suzerainty – France, Aquitaine (*i.e.* England) and Aragon. Together, the two main 'islands' of Foix and Béarn covered less than 3,500 square miles, with a combined population gathered around fewer than 25,000 hearths, or about one-hundredth of those under the direct control of the French crown.[7] Although less overwhelming, comparisons with Castile, Aragon and English Aquitaine nevertheless point to the severe disparity of economic and military power between any of them and the untidy possessions of the House of Foix-Béarn.

This is not to say that the Count of Foix was of little consequence among the magnates of the Midi: as a potential ally, he was certainly valued as much as his neighbour the King of Navarre or his perennial antagonist the Count of Armagnac. Birth alone made him a full-share member of a cosmopolitan club of princely cousins: Gaston III could boast of family ties with the royal houses of Aragon and Majorca, and even, through his grandmother Jeanne d'Artois – a great-grandniece of Saint Louis – of Capetian blood. As a territorial lord his possessions, stretching for the most part along the northern flank of the Pyrenees, made him the vassal of three crowned overlords – France, England and Aragon. While this overextension was vulnerable not only to threats from potential or actual rivals (*viz.* Navarre and Armagnac), but also to pressures from his three suzerains, this same situation was not without its advantages, in that the potential adversaries could be used as counterpoises to one another. Moreover, the regional connections of the Foix-Béarn family ramified their reach far beyond the limits of their own lands. Their junior branch, descended from Gaston I, held the viscounty of Castellbó (Fr. Castelbon), directly south from Andorra, thus maintaining an active presence among the grandees of the Crown of Aragon, and an eastward-looking window on opportunities in the Catalan sphere of influence. North of the Pyrenees, the counts of Foix had been connected by marriage with the counts of Périgord and of Comminges, and twice with the 'Captals' of the Grailly family, lords of the coastal seigniory of Buch in Gascony.

With his far-flung domains, the young Gaston III undoubtedly inherited a multitude of problems, both external and internal. But he was also heir to the conscious efforts of his predecessors to assert a degree of defiance, if not of outright independence, vis-à-vis their nominal overlords. Despite the French kings' attempts to punish their 'usurpation', the lords of Foix had long styled themselves *Gratia Dei comes Fuxi* – Count by the grace of God. As for the viscounts of Béarn, they had since the eleventh century assumed the theoretically royal

[6] *Vicomté*, 44.

[7] *Prince*, 38.

prerogative of minting their own coinage, and while other seigniorial monies were steadily disappearing, their Morlaàs silver circulated throughout the Midi. Another recent fact also pointed in the direction of a traditional policy, and must have still been fresh in the minds of the young prince's mentors: although he was in principle his vassal in Béarn, Gaston II had not sworn homage to the King of England.

BEFORE leaving for his crusade, Gaston II had entrusted the regency to his wife, Aliénor de Comminges. Gaston III would officially come of age on his fourteenth birthday – 30 April 1345. Until then, and even for some years beyond, his mother and her advisers were chiefly concerned with the task of securing for the young prince the fealty of his far-flung vassals. But momentous events were taking shape in the wider world of great kingdoms. Their news would sooner or later reach Orthez, and make people wonder.

Only a few months after Gaston' majority, Edward III renounced the truce with France, and military operations, until recently confined to Brittany, resumed in both Aquitaine and Normandy. In concert with the Albret brothers, the Earl of Derby – the same Henry of Lancaster who had been a comrade-in-arms of Gaston II at Algeciras – led an altogether successful autumn offensive in the Bordelais, then into Périgord. Bergerac, commanding the lower Dordogne valley, was taken with other castles and towns, and a substantial French army utterly defeated at Auberoche. French losses were heavy and especially demoralizing as they included many great nobles and high-ranking officers killed or captured. The victors collected so much booty and ransoms that the profits from Bergerac alone enabled the Earl of Derby to rebuild his London palace – the Savoy – in the most lavish manner. By contrast, it was probably the lack of funds that prevented the French king's son – Jean, Duke of Normandy – in overall command of operations in the South West, from mounting a counter-offensive.

During that phase of the conflict, the young Gaston III appeared disposed to continue his father's policy of strong support for the French cause. On the occasion of the homage given at Orthez by one of his Béarnais vassals, he exhorted the latter to take up arms, and declared that he wanted to serve the King of France in his wars, 'as well as my lord Count, his father, had done, and even better'.[8] But this ringing declaration was followed by very limited military action. At the head of a small army in the King's pay, the Count of Foix was content to patrol his own lands of Marsan and Gavardan throughout the winter of 1345–6, without ever engaging the enemy. When the Duke of Normandy, before returning to Paris, gave the lieutenancy of Gascony to the Count of Armagnac, Gaston asked that his own domains be specifically exempted from the Lieutenant's authority. But, even though he obtained this concession, his

[8] *Ibid.*, 44.

pro-French zeal had already cooled, and he sent no troops to help Philippe VI face the latest English invasion.

In July 1346 Edward III had landed on the Cotentin peninsula with a strong army, and with the support of some leading Norman nobles who had fallen out with the Valois king, marched inland while meeting little opposition. After taking Caen, Edward continued towards Paris but, almost within reach of the capital, he turned northwards to avoid a pitched battle with Philippe, who had the advantage of a fresh force and superior numbers. The English army had only just crossed the Somme when it was overtaken by the French, and the first major land battle of the war was fought at Crécy on 26 August. At the end of the day the King of France was fleeing for his life, with only a few knights in attendance, and the royal standard abandoned on the ground. Scores of Philippe's great vassals, kinsmen and allies, lay dead on the field of slaughter. Shortly afterwards, Edward invested Calais, which the French king was unable to relieve.

News of the crushing French defeat could easily have reached Orthez within a fortnight: 'normal' travel, at the rate of 31 miles (50 km) per day's journey, was said to take twenty-two days from Sluys in Flanders to Saint-Jean Pied-de-Port in the Basque country, and a fast rider could have covered the distance in half that time. Together with English gains in Aquitaine, the event was bound to alter the balance of power in the Midi. Clearly, the Valois were in no position to oppose the Anglo-Gascon forces that now conducted devastating raids, north from Bordeaux into Saintonge and Poitou (the ancestral patrimony of Eleanor of Aquitaine), and eastward into Limousin and Quercy. Fears of imminent English attacks reached as far as Auvergne, and an epidemic of defections signalled a notable lack of confidence in the future of the dynasty.[9] Appointed royal lieutenant, the Count of Armagnac was not only given no troops, but his efforts to raise money and men ran repeatedly into contradictory orders from the King. Moreover, his own lands were now more than ever vulnerable to invasion, not only by English forces, but by his hereditary rival of Foix-Béarn.

In the event, the quarrel between the two counts was overshadowed by the reversal of fortunes in the larger conflict. The collapse of French military power, which seemed to presage the overthrow of the richest realm in Christendom, sent long psychological shock waves abroad. It stunned common folk, for in the popular imagination the King of France had remained the iconic successor of the invincible and mighty Charlemagne of epic legends. Some of the French crown's feudatories took a long, cold look at their allegiances. Among the most notable, the Count of Foix simply failed to appear when, on Whit Sunday of 1347, Philippe VI's vassals were summoned to Amiens to help prepare a counter-offensive. There was not much the King could do about the

---

[9] Sumption, I, 542–50.

passive disobedience of a nobleman who was for the moment out of his reach, except ask for an explanation, and reiterate the summons.

Such was probably the tenor of the letter written in Rodez on 19 September by Amadeus de Praelle, 'knight and seneschal', sealed with the royal seal and delivered six days later by Acharias de Brunheys to Count Gaston in the great hall of Castle Moncade in Orthez. From the minutes of the meeting, drafted by the Count's notary, we know that Gaston was being informed of the alliance concluded between the crowns of France and Castile: it was only wise, as well as courteous, that a frontier lord who held lands south of the Pyrenees, and who moreover was also a vassal of Aragon, Castile's neighbour and sometimes rival, should be made aware of the diplomatic situation. This was especially appropriate as Countess Aliénor, Gaston III's mother, was at that time negotiating on behalf of her son another 'Spanish' marriage, with a daughter of the Queen of Navarre.

The requests that came with this piece of news are not spelled out in the minutes, although it is likely that Gaston was again summoned to attend the King. But the answer – given almost thirteen months, to the day, after the disaster at Crécy – is unequivocally recorded:

> My lord the Count of Foix replies to the request presented to him by Acharias de Brunheys [...] that, as my lord Count is now in his own land of Béarn, which he holds from God and from no man in this world, and for which he is not required to do aught but what pleases him, the object of the request, namely the conventions, alliances and agreements made between my lords the Kings of France and Castile, is a new matter; that neither my lord Count nor any man of his council has heard of anything like it, and that at present there cannot be a plenary council to discuss the said requests; [the Count] says that the good alliances and conventions entered into by the said Kings please him very much and that he will make it known in his county of Foix, eight days after the next feast of All Saints, when he will have his plenary council with persons of his blood, and that there he shall have counsel and deliberations to give his agreement to respond to the letters of my lord the King of France and to the present request [...] and that my lord King must be satisfied with his reply, and he will do everything for the profit and honour of the King, to the best of his ability ...[10]

The King had little choice but to 'be satisfied'. On the surface Gaston's reply was couched in faultlessly courteous terms; he did not refuse to act on the royal request. He endorsed, albeit vaguely and provisionally, the Franco-Castilian alliance. And a more informed reply would be forthcoming, after the Count had heard the deliberations of his full council. The excuse implicitly given for

[10] *Prince*, 46–8.

the delay, that his advisers – including the 'persons of his blood' —could not be gathered at present, made good enough sense. The real issue, however, was not when, but where: the promised response would come only after Gaston had returned to Foix, which he held in fief from the King of France. Whereas, as long as he was 'sitting' at Orthez (to translate literally the Béarnais *sie*), he could not entertain the King's request, for he held 'his own land of Béarn … from God and from no man in this world', and therefore, while as Count of Foix he owed allegiance and service to the King, as Viscount of Béarn he did not. The first fully public declaration of Gaston III on external affairs clearly enunciated the policy he would pursue throughout his reign, the guiding principle of which was the independence, pure and simple, of Béarn.

The Seal of the House of Foix-Béarn

# ✦ 2 ✦

# Apprenticeship

WHEN he confidently asserted that, 'in his own land of Béarn', he answered to no overlord, Gaston III was only sixteen years old. If the self-portrait he was to pen long afterwards is to be believed, he was at that time barely emerging from a rather unpromising childhood. 'I was born', he wrote, 'most depraved and frivolous, so much so that my father and mother were ashamed of me, and everyone said: "This one will be worthless, and woe is the land of which he will be lord!"'[1] Even allowing for the fact that this self-deprecation was part of a penitential exercise, the young Count of Foix seems to have cut a far less heroic figure than his near coeval, Edward Prince of Wales, who at the same age had already distinguished himself on the field of Crécy. One year later the son of Gaston 'le Preux' was engaging in dilatory chicanery unworthy of a nobleman: such at least might have been the contrasted view of many contemporaries, imbued with the ideals and the prejudices of chivalry, and perhaps unable to perceive the risk inherent in defying a power in momentary disarray, but still capable of a dangerous recovery.

Nothing is known of young Gaston's upbringing, but the 'depraved and frivolous' disposition he confessed did not prevent him from becoming more learned and literate than was usual among men of his caste. He wrote, with a good command of the principles of rhetorics, in three languages: French, Latin and the somewhat fossilized *lémozi* of the Troubadour tradition. And it is likely that he also was fluent in several of the living Occitan dialects – Béarnais, Fuxéen, Toulousain, etc. – spoken in his scattered domains. The *Book of the Hunt*, written in the Count's mature years, is evidently the product of a mind long exercised in the empirical observation of nature. And, while his character was not altogether free of the irrational, impulsive violence then endemic in the feudal nobility, his career suggests that he had learned at an early age to reflect before making a move, whether diplomatic or military. On the whole, when he prayed for the 'sense and discretion' he would need to rule his land and his subjects wisely, his request seems to have been granted.

According to the chronicle of Esquerrier, Gaston's designated mentor (*gobernador*) was his distant relative Corbeyran de Foix.[2] His durable presence and his official duties at the court of Orthez are reminders of the ancient and complex ties of blood and fealty connecting the House of Foix with all the

---

[1] Gaston Fébus, *Livre des oraisons* (Stockholm/Paris, 1975), 27–8.

[2] Arnaud Esquerrier, *Chroniques romanes des comtes de Foix* (Nîmes, 1999), 52.

prominent families of the county – ties that, as relative newcomers, they did not have with the Béarnais nobility. However, much of the credit for the young prince's education and for his early training in statecraft belongs undoubtedly to his mother, Aliénor de Comminges. But even this remarkable woman would have been unable to accomplish her task without the support of a tight-knit, if somewhat unorthodox family. His grand and even royal connections notwithstanding, the heir of Foix and Béarn was nurtured at home among a less exalted, but more intimate family. The acknowledged and loyal bastards fathered by successive counts were often highly visible in the Orthez household: thus a son of Gaston I, Bernard de Béarn, called 'l'Aspois' (perhaps for maternal connection in the Vale of Aspe), is named as a witness to the audience at which the young Count evaded the French king's demands. Given that he held lands in Gascony and had openly served under the English banner, his influence in shaping his nephew's reply may be inferred. Nor was this Bernard the last 'bastard of Béarn' to appear in documents or chronicle. Throughout his reign Gaston III was well served by such illegitimate members of his entourage as his half-brothers Arnaut-Guilhem de Morlanne and Pierre de Béarn, lord of Labastide, as well as his cousins Pierre-Arnaud and Jean, descendants of Gaston I, also confusingly dubbed 'de Béarn'. Eventually, Gaston III's own bastards would have their own part to play in the drama of his last years.

The presence of openly acknowledged bastards in a royal or noble household was not a rare phenomenon in the Middle Ages, nor, indeed, until the advent of 'Victorian' – or more properly, bourgeois – morality. Illegitimate offspring suffered certain civil and canonical disabilities: they could not, in the normal course of events, inherit a fief or a crown, and they could only be received in the higher holy orders with a papal dispensation. But there was hardly any social stigma attached to their irregular birth, and public opinion even tended to regard the illicit progeny of a popular ruler as a kind of living proof of his bond with his people, as well as of his vigour. Thus in a later age, folk tradition credits another Béarnais prince, the *Vert-Galant* Henri de Navarre, with being more than figuratively the 'father of his country'. And if the wives, who on the other hand were held to the strictest standards of chastity, objected to their lords' extra-marital amours, they did so for the most part *in petto*, for whereas mistresses could easily fall from favour, the mother of a legitimate heir normally had the advantage of an unassailable position.

The Countess Dowager seems not only to have been on cordial terms with Bernard l'Aspois, but also to have relied on him and other irregular members of the Foix-Béarn family for advice and political support. Her pragmatic attitude is consistent with the circumstances of her marriage to Gaston II, a feudal union organized in 1325 by her uncle Bertrand de l'Isle-Jourdain, who happened to be the legal guardian of the fourteen-year-old bridegroom. Aliénor, one of the supernumerary daughters of the Count of Comminges, was then twenty-seven, an old maid by medieval standards. But she dismissed comments on the age disparity between herself and her intended with the remark that 'to marry the Count of Foix, she would gladly have waited for him to be born!'[3] For her part, and even though she was not likely to inherit Comminges, she brought as an intangible item of her marriage portion a valuable connection, and the prospect of a strategic alliance.

The sole surviving son of that oddly matched couple, the future Gaston III, was born on 30 April 1331. A first boy, also named Gaston, had died in infancy, and the heir of Foix-Béarn does not seem to have had any legitimate siblings, but was brought up with his half-brothers, Arnaud-Guilhem and Pierre, and a half-sister named Béarnèse. With her husband frequently away, serving Philippe VI in Flanders or in Gascony, Aliénor's must have been the dominant influence on their son's early years, and it is likely that she was given the authority to oversee his education. The testament dictated by Gaston II before leaving for his last campaign in Andalusia gives a measure of the trust and respect in which he held his wife: Aliénor was to be regent and guardian of young Gaston until he was fourteen – his legal majority. Furthermore, she was to continue and administer his private property until he was twenty-one. It was an arrangement fraught with opportunities for disputes and endless lawsuits between the Countess Dowager and the young Count, but nothing of the sort ensued: Aliénor managed not only to pay off the considerable debts incurred by her husband, but to acquire new seigniories. The accounts she rendered in 1351 to Gaston III were received without demur. Such harmonious rapport – by no means to be taken for granted in feudal society – may well be because Aliénor did not merely rule in her son's name, but she took pains to associate him to her activity, and thus guide him through the apprenticeship of government. Consequently, when Gaston III came of age, he was already well acquainted with the complex issues facing him as Count of Foix and Viscount of Béarn, Marsan, Gavardan, etc.

THE geographical dispersion of the Foix-Béarn domains was one of the chief problems, and by its nature perhaps the most intractable: disputes could eventually be arbitrated, fractious vassals cajoled or put down, but neither diplomacy nor force could abolish distances and other obstacles to communications. Not only did the inheritance of Gaston III stretch the whole length of the Pyrenees, from castles in Cerdagne to the edge of the Basque country, but its main components – Foix, Nébouzan and Béarn – were not contiguous. Communications between them were sometimes at the mercy of the elements: Jean Froissart, riding in November 1388 from Pamiers in the county of Foix to Orthez in Béarn, had to turn back from a broken bridge over the rain-swollen Garonne. The chronicler's party made a perilous ferry crossing and lost two days, but they were relatively fortunate in that they were travelling during a

3 *Ibid.*, 45.

period of truce, when the most dangerous bands of brigands had been eliminated or bought off.

Each of the two principal domains of Gaston III also extended along a north–south axis, and was made up of distinct regions with different, and sometimes conflicting, economies. The southern part of the county, high ridges bordering on Andorra, was a country of mediocre pastoral and agricultural yield, a region of subsistence economy. A curious, and typically Pyrenean anomaly was the mining of iron ore in some high valleys: according to a co-operative charter that was operative well into the nineteenth century, any and all of the inhabitants were guaranteed the right to extract a mutually agreed quota of ore, to cut wood in the surrounding forest and make charcoal for smelting. Given this remarkably equitable arrangement, the mines of Vicdessos were probably not a primary source of revenue for the counts. Nevertheless, the abundance of fuel and water near the mines favoured metallurgy, making Foix a principal exporter of iron to its Pyrenean neighbours. As for the gold occasionally found in the river Ariège, it must have brought more glitter than profit to the arms of Foix: no 'mother lode' seems to have been ever struck. North of the Plantaurel range, whose abrupt wall, parallel to the Pyrenees, formed a natural rampart to the counts' capital of Foix, lay the gently rolling landscape of a somewhat tamer Ariège, with the town of Pamiers, described by Froissart as 'a most pleasing city [...] situated in the midst of good and bountiful vineyards', whose wines indeed found their way to England, via Bordeaux. It is only 39 miles from Pamiers to Toulouse, and Mazères, where Gaston III would have his favourite residence in his eastern domains, lies even closer to the capital of Languedoc. This proximity, while sometimes politically uncomfortable, was no doubt one of the economic assets of the county, traversed as it is by the trade route from Toulouse to Catalonia by way of Andorra and Urgel. Industry was significantly more active in Foix: to implement his military building programme, Gaston III would eventually bring to Béarn brickmakers from the county. Not surprisingly, urban development was more advanced in Foix than in Béarn: while in 1385 Orthez and Morlaàs each counted respectively 436 and 304 *feux* (hearth), by the end of the century Mazères had 497 households, Foix 382, and Pamiers more than 2,000.[4]

Nevertheless, geopolitical factors had prompted the new lords of Foix-Béarn to move their seat to the westernmost frontier of their expanded domain. A casual glance at the map (see p. 76) may suggest that they regarded Béarn, augmented by the viscounties of Marsan and Gavardan, as the more important part of their heritage, at least in area. But more than size, the climates in which they developed their respective economies defined the disparity between these combined fiefs and the ancestral county. While north of the River Adour, Marsan and Gavardan offered little but the arid scrub and fly-infested

4 Pailhès, 258.

marshlands much feared by the pilgrims to Compostela, Béarn proper enjoys, thanks to the proximity of the Atlantic, a well-watered climate, much milder than that of the high country of Foix. Despite its relative poverty, the viscounty has been described as the most successful of several small (and mostly ephemeral) Pyrenean states comprised of both mountain and lowland districts. To his description of the land, Vidal de La Blache adds enthusiastically that 'one could not imagine a more favourable cradle than the Gave [de Pau] watershed, where such political centres as Nay, Lescar, Morlaàs and Pau flourished in turn.'[5] But, the great French geographer notes, the Béarnais state was firmly established only after the viscounts had acquired the western end of the plain, where Orthez and other castles controlled the confluence of the Adour, the Gave de Pau and the Gave d'Oloron.

This is not to say that Béarn was a rich country: indeed, none of the lands between Garonne and Pyrenees could fit that description, and Gascon poverty would long remain proverbial. In the fourteenth century the economy of the viscounty was largely based on agriculture, with revenue from livestock exceeding that derived from crop cultivation. Grazing on mountain pastures and lowland moors, sheep, goats and the cows celebrated by the arms of Béarn yielded such marketable commodities as wool, cheeses and leather. Herds of swine, sustained by the bounty of acorns in the forests that covered much of the land, provided most of the meat for domestic consumption. However, in Béarn as in Foix, hunting was not a seigniorial privilege, and so commoners as well as nobles could vary their pork-based diet with the occasional hare or partridge. Woodcraft was the chief industry, as abundant hardwood provided raw material for building timber, furniture, agricultural implements, and even plates and dishes.

As much – and arguably even more than – Foix, Béarn enjoyed a privileged situation astride ancient routes. Its first nucleus, the diocese of Lescar, occupied the site of the Gallo-Roman city of *Beneharnum* (hence the name of Béarn), on the imperial road to Spain over the Somport pass. Later, one of the several routes to Santiago de Compostela, the 'Via Tolosana', following the trade route linking Languedoc with the English-held ports of Bordeaux and Bayonne, brought pilgrims and merchants to the Somport, with resting stages at Morlaàs, Lescar and Oloron, while two other routes, the 'Podensis' originating from Le Puy-en-Velay, and the 'Lemovicensis', from Vézelay (via Limoges), converged towards the Roncevaux pass in Navarre, with stages at Orthez and Sauveterre-de-Béarn. Naturally, the mountain passes were travelled in both directions: bordering on Aragon to the south, and extending through Marsan and Gavardan, the viscounty benefited not only from the east–west traffic, but also as a trade corridor between the Iberian peninsula and English Gascony,

---

[5] Paul Vidal de La Blache, *Tableau de la géographie de la France* (Paris, 1979), 361. 'Gave' is the peculiarly Béarnais term for a mountain-born river.

as Béarnais merchants brought over the Pyrenees such diverse goods as Aragonese wool, Catalan olive oil, and the spices shipped to Barcelona from her
far-flung Mediterranean outposts. Proximity also made Gascony the market of
choice for the surplus of Béarn's livestock and agriculture, which could travel
almost to the gates of Bordeaux – only 49 miles from Captieux in Gavardan –
without leaving the Count's domains.

On the other hand, this south-to-north extension was in itself the cause
of certain internal problems common to countries that encompass several
regions with distinct and periodically conflicting economic needs. The physical
geography of Béarn, more so than that of the county of Foix, exacerbated the
classic antagonism between highlanders and lowlanders. Transhumance – the
seasonal move from summer mountain grazing to winter pastures in the piedmont – was a perennial necessity for the exclusively pastoral economy of the
high valleys, and the perennial grievance the lowland peasantry. In often violent
clashes, the men of Ossau and Aspe had gained control of vacant moorlands
in the regions of Pau and Orthez, to the detriment of adjacent farming communities. The viscounts' ability to prevent or punish such encroachments was
naturally hampered by the remoteness of the high country; moreover, their
judicial authority was limited by the *fors* – the traditional charters – granted by
their predecessors to the highlanders. In the lowlands, the obligations peasants
owed to the Viscount and other nobles were more or less severe depending on
their respective status as free men enjoying the privileges of the *fors*, *crestiaàs*
(*i.e.* 'Christians', an odd intermediate caste, perhaps descendants of lepers) or
serfs – the latter comprising in 1385 about a third of the rural population.

The highlanders, however, were constituted in communities, or 'syndicates' of
free men, that scarcely fit the mould of feudal society: with serfdom unknown
in those parts, and the land held in collective ownership, these fiercely cohe-
sive clans allowed the nobles little say in local governance. Their relation to
the central power of Béarn was defined by protocols emblematic of their independence, and sometimes frankly humiliating for the ruler. Thus for instance,
before entering the vale of Aspe, the Viscount was required to stop as soon as
his horse stepped in a brook marking the northern border of that district; he
could then proceed only after an exchange of hostages with the local elected
magistrates – the *jurats*. The high valleys even conducted their own external
relations: to settle or prevent conflicts about grazing rights and the often ill-
defined boundaries of summer pastures, the *jurats* of Aspe and Ossau met
regularly with their counterparts from neighbouring mountain communities
in Aragon and Navarre. Treaties and conventions were made at these *juntes*,
without reference to the respective sovereigns of the parties.[6]

The mountain folk were not the only beneficiaries of guaranteed franchises:
the diverse charters granted by successive viscounts since the eleventh century

---

[6] *Vicomté*, 129–30.

made up a complex body of feudal precedents, codified at the end of the thirteenth by Gaston VII, last of the Moncade dynasty. These *Fors de Béarn* in
effect spelled out the respective judicial, fiscal and military duties and prerogatives of the Viscount and of his subjects. Upon his accession, the new viscount
could only receive the oath of the communities after he had himself sworn
to 'uphold the *fors*'. Nor was this reciprocal oath a mere one-time ritual: the
implementation and oversight of the *fors* has naturally brought about the creation of representative bodies in the two estates of nobles and commoners. Of
these, the Cour Majour, in principle an assembly of all the nobles, functioned
as Béarn's supreme tribunal. A conflicted regency during the minority of Gaston II had given the burghers who dominated the commons the opportunity to
enhance their status: henceforth, the Court of Commons, albeit sitting sepa-
rately, would be called into session concurrently with the nobles' Cour Majour.
Any weakness, or a perceived vacancy of the seigniorial power, could be the
occasion for the two bodies to constitute themselves as Estates of Béarn and,
armed with the *fors*, to impose further limits on the authority of the viscount.

The regency of Aliénor de Comminges could well have ushered in such an
evolution. At his death Gaston II left not only an empty treasury, but the large
debts incurred in order to finance his military campaigns, especially the final
'crusade' in Andalusia, thus providing a legitimate opportunity for the *Cours* to
intervene. His periods of absence had probably delayed a necessary upgrading of the administrative system; last but not least, his pro-French policy had
antagonized both the commoners for whom Gascony was the most immediate
market, and the nobles of Béarn, many of whom (not excepting the viscounts)
had either fiefs or at least family ties in Anglo-Aquitaine. However, the first
challenge Aliénor had to fend off came from the brothers of her late husband.
Roger-Bernard had been given the viscounty of Castelbon in Catalonia, but it
was Robert, Bishop of Lavaur, who contested their sister-in-law's regency. He
was eventually silenced by Pope Clement VI, who ordered him not to leave his
diocese in French Languedoc. Whether Roger-Bernard was a party to Robert's
intrigues is a matter of conjecture, but the episode may have planted the seed of
Gaston III's lifelong enmity towards the Castelbon branch of the Foix family.

UPON his accession, Gaston II had waited at Orthez for his subjects to come
and exchange with him the customary oaths of fealty. But Aliénor could
afford neither the time, nor the appearance of passivity. Prompted perhaps by
warnings of other, impending challenges, she acted swiftly to present the new
Count of Foix to all the communities of Béarn that could be reached in the first
winter of his reign. Their journey was no classic progress, with solemn entrances
and prepared harangues, but a hastily organized circuit evidently undertaken
to affirm – and to a certain extent to dramatize – the mutual obligations of the
ruling family and their subjects. With a small retinue – a dozen or less – of
nobles, clerics and lawyers, Aliénor and her son left Orthez immediately after

the Christmas celebration of 1343; on 27 December they arrived at Morlaàs, the former capital of Béarn, and still the customary seat of the Cour Majour and of the Mint. A letter from the Viscount would normally have notified the inhabitants and summoned them to a pre-arranged time and place; in the event, they were roused by the town crier and called to assemble in the church of Sainte Foy – a still extant structure, whose modest dimensions give an idea of the population density in a fourteenth-century town of some importance. On 31 December the Viscount's party was at Lembeye, there to receive the notables representing several communities of the Vic-Bilh district of Eastern Béarn. On 1 January 1344, at Montaner. Here foul weather prevented some delegations from outlying villages reaching the improvised rendezvous; however, they caught up the next day with their overlord, on his way to Pau, and the oaths of fealty were exchanged in a roadside field, under pelting rain. On 4 January, after receiving the homage of the residents of Pau and several neighbouring communities, the travellers went on to Nay; the next day to Lescar, then to Monein, and so on. By their journey's end, on 24 January, Gaston III and his mother had stopped in twenty-one different towns and villages; in addition, they had met with delegations from fifty-one outlying communities, and thus they had exchanged the oaths, either directly or by proxies – with most of the people of Béarn. As for places that wintry condition had not allowed them to reach, such as the upper Ossau valley, the delegates had exacted the promise of a later visit to their village, where the mutual oaths would be properly reaffirmed.

With few local variations, the same ritual took place time and again. Whether addressing an entire community, or a delegation come to meet the seigniorial party, Aliénor would first address the assembly in her capacity as mother and guardian of the young Gaston III, announcing that she and her son had come to give the oath required of every new lord of Béarn upon his accession, and to receive in return the fealty of the communities. Gaston III would then speak, asking the assembly to swear fealty – to his mother *qua* guardian and regent, and to himself as Viscount of Béarn. The distinction was no mere minutia: the oath given to Aliénor was to be valid only for the duration of her guardianship, while the one sworn to the new viscount was given 'for his lifetime', as the 'natural lord' of Béarn: therefore Gaston III, when he had come of age, would need to renew his oath, but no similar *refresquiment* (literally: 'refreshing') was required of his subjects. Following these opening harangues, the Countess and her son took turns to swear on the Cross placed on top of the Gospels, to be 'good, loyal and faithful lords' to the particular community before them, to defend and protect it with all their might, and to defend and maintain its ancestral *fors*, customs and freedoms. The rulers also swore to be honest and fair judges 'equally to the rich man and to the poor', and to give both equal protection.

In return, the villagers then swore, first to Aliénor, for the duration of her guardianship, then to Gaston, 'for the time of his life', to be their 'good, loyal and obedient subjects', to defend their 'life and body', their lands and their seigniorial domains, and to give them protection and good counsel. Last but not least, the Viscount's subjects swore not to reveal any of the secrets that may have been entrusted to them, nor to take part in any subversive plot or conversation, but if they should happen upon such a conspiracy, to do their utmost to either make it fail, or to report it to the lord as soon as possible. The same rite sacralized the oaths from both parties: the Regent and the young Count swore with their hand on the Cross placed on top of the Gospels; their subjects would then swear while touching the same Cross and Book, jointly held in the hands of Aliénor and Gaston. In larger assemblies, it seems that the complete ritual was performed only by the notables, speaking for the community, but it is probable that, in the case of smaller delegations, each member would in turn kneel before the lord of Béarn.

The nobles renewed their fealty, either in groups, as was the case in Lembeye, or individually, in ceremonies separate from the commoners' assemblies. The formula recited was essentially the same for both orders, except that the word 'homage' (Béarnais *omenatge*) added to the oath sworn by the nobleman signalled the added dimension of his fealty: whether high baron or modest knight, he was not merely a subject of the ruler, but also his vassal – his lord's man, acknowledging specific military obligations. Moreover, a symbolic payment could be required of a nobleman: sometimes a small sum, fixed from the beginning of the grant, more often a decorative object – white gloves (of which Gaston III collected twelve pairs in Marsan alone), a white or gilded spear – or a falcon, it was in effect a token rent for a fief held ultimately at the pleasure of the overlord.[7]

After a scant three weeks' respite, the travellers left Orthez for a similar progress in the viscounties of Marsan and Gavardan: there, they were on the road until 31 March. The detailed records of later *tournées d'hommages* in Foix and Nébouzan have been lost, but there are surviving indications that the Count's party travelled in his eastern domains in May–June 1345, and again in January 1346. In Foix, where the dynasty enjoyed ancient ties with many of the seigniorial families, there was no need for his progress to be as exhaustive as it had been in Béarn. The chronicler Esquerrier states that Gaston 'was made Count in the year 1344', but other records indicate that it was on 3 January 1345 that, in the cloister of Saint-Volusien in Foix, he exchanged the oath of fealty with the communities and the nobles – including no doubt many 'persons of his blood' – of the county.[8] By then Gaston III, who had turned fourteen on 30 April 1345, had reached the traditional age of majority of a feudal magnate. Custom required that he should reiterate his oaths to the commons, and so

[7] Pierre Tucoo-Chala, *Livre des Hommages de Gaston Fébus (1331–1391)* (Saragossa, 1976), 14–25.

[8] Pailhès, 30.

there was yet another round of visits and ceremonies through Béarn, Marsan and Gavardan, lasting well into the summer of 1346. Thus was the young Count thoroughly initiated into an archaic style of government, in which the direct, personal relationship between ruler and subject was of paramount importance. This immediacy of contact was vividly illustrated by the ritual of the oath, the validity of which was signified by the hand *touching* the Cross and Book, and its perceived necessity by the insistence of the Ossalois and other delegates of remote districts, that the new lord in person come to visit each village and hamlet. Despite his own confession of a dissipated youth, the twelve-year-old Gaston seems to have been a diligent apprentice: he is reported absent from an assembly only once, on 15 January 1344, when the notary records that the Countess received the oaths alone, 'my lord being at the hunt'. Given the importance of that sport in the physical training of a knight, and anticipating Gaston's contribution to the literature on the subject, his absence from ceremonial duties may be excused.

ALIÉNOR'S decision to embark upon, and to carry through, those strenuous rounds of visits to all parts of the Foix-Béarn inheritance certainly went a long way to help restore a comital authority that had been seriously eroded under Gaston II, and it had laid the foundation for her son's further centralization of his government. No other proof of her efficiency is needed, but that the convening of the Estates of Béarn, which had seemed imminent in 1343, was postponed for the lifetime of Gaston III. But the problems facing the Regent did not stop at the frontiers of the Foix-Béarn domains. High on the list of urgent issues to be resolved was that of the young Count's marriage. Gaston II had not failed to attend to that essential piece of dynastic planning, but after his death, events had moved in such a way that a new start had to be considered.

The future Gaston III was only nine years old when his marriage to Isabella, daughter of the King of Majorca, was formally proposed and accepted. The kingdom of Majorca had been created by James I of Aragon 'the Conqueror' (1213–76) after he had wrested from the Moors not only the Balearic Islands, but also the mainland kingdom of Valencia. His testament provided for both of his two surviving sons: Peter III reigned over Aragon proper, Catalonia and Valencia, while his younger brother James inherited, together with Majorca and the Islands, all of the dynastic patrimony north of the Pyrenees, chiefly the county of Roussillon (now the French *département* of Pyrénées-Orientales) and the viscounty of Montpellier. The Conqueror had probably envisaged this division not as a dismemberment of his empire, but as a means to divide between his heirs the task of governing the disparate realms of the crown of Aragon, with their distinct ethnic composition, laws and customs. But in the event, his heirs soon fell to squabbling over the issue of the implied suzerainty of Aragon over Majorca. Distracted by other enterprises – such as the acquisition in 1285 of yet another kingdom, that of Sicily – Peter III was unable to prevent what had been created as an apanage to slip away from Aragon's control. With magnificent royal palaces in both its capitals of Palma de Majorca and Perpignan, the kingdom of Majorca flourished, and was increasingly recognized in the fourteenth century as an independent power.

The match appeared an advantageous one for both parties. First, it held the prospect of a strategic alliance stretching along the nearly entire length of the Pyrenees, in mutual defence against Foix's hereditary foe of Armagnac and any new Aragonese attempt to impose its hegemony over Majorca. The alliance would also facilitate trade, and the merchants of Foix and Béarn could perhaps look forward to privileged links, through the ports of Collioure and Maguelonne, with the Balearic Islands and their increasingly prosperous Mediterranean markets. Last but not least, Gaston II would surely have recalled how his forebears had come into the possession of Béarn: should the descendance of James III fail in the male line, a Count of Foix could well realize the royal dream of every great feudal magnate, and claim the kingdom of Majorca. Given enough time, these expectations – especially the most immediate one of mutual military support – were reasonable enough, but events were already moving too quickly for them to be realized. The new King of Aragon, Peter IV, was an activist monarch, determined to restore his dynastic rights over the outlying realms of the Crown of Aragon. Much of the energy of his embattled reign would be expanded in campaigns to put down uprisings in Sicily and Sardinia, but the goal of Peter's first enterprise was nothing less than the full reintegration of the kingdom of Majorca into the Aragonese empire. James III, who was Peter's brother-in-law as well as his cousin, made his task easier by refusing the homage that his predecessors had routinely given to the kings of Aragon, and flaunting the *de facto* independence of Majorca, whose successful maritime trade moreover impacted on the profits of Barcelona's shipping. Peter's carefully calculated legal processes culminated in February 1343 with the confiscation of Majorca, followed in May by a land and sea attack on the Balearic Islands and on Roussillon. James III was isolated from any potential allies: he had antagonized Philippe VI by disputing French suzerainty over Montpellier, and the Count of Foix was already engaged in his distant adventure, the Andalusian crusade. Defeated, he surrendered to Peter, then escaped and in November 1344 found refuge in the castle of Foix. Despite Peter IV's warning against interfering in what he termed the internal affairs of Aragon, the Regent Aliénor attempted to honour the engagements undertaken by her late husband and, as 'justice and alliance' required, to help the fugitive king of Majorca. But his cause was clearly lost: in order to raise a mercenary army, James III resorted to the desperate expedient of selling the viscounty of Montpellier to France. He was killed in 1349, shortly after landing in Majorca.

For all her manifestations of steadfast support for James III, Aliénor had to recognize that the prospect of a matrimonial connection with the deposed King of Majorca was no longer an advantageous one. She now turned her attention – and her not negligible diplomatic skills – to negotiating another royal marriage for young Gaston. She did not have to look very far to find an eligible bride-elect: her choice fell on Agnès, daughter of Queen Jeanne de Navarre and her late husband Philippe d'Evreux. The small kingdom of Navarre was not only the immediate neighbour of Béarn, but a connection with its ruling family also brought one with the most prestigious dynasty in Christendom, the royal house of France. Jeanne was the daughter of Louis X, one of the last Capetian kings of France. Her father had also worn the crown of Navarre, which had been in the possession of French princes ever since it had devolved in 1234 to Count Thibaut de Champagne. When Louis X died in 1316 without male issue, Jeanne was barred from succeeding her father on the dubious grounds of the 'Salic Law' but allowed, jointly with her husband Philippe d'Evreux, to inherit the throne of Navarre. In addition to their small Pyrenean realm, the couple held considerable domains in northern France: in addition to Champagne, which had remained in the patrimony of Thibaut's successors, the House of Evreux – an offshoot of the Capetian dynasty – possessed extensive and strategically important fiefs in Normandy and in the Île-de France.

To all appearances it was a marriage made in heaven: not only did it serve the political and economic interests of two neighbouring states, but it also sanctioned the ties of friendship between two families already bound by a common remembrance, for the fathers of both the prospective bride and groom had been comrades-in-arms, and had died on the same day while crusading in Andalusia. Moreover, France applauded a match that would make the Count of Foix a member of the extended royal family. After the rebuff to his envoy to Orthez in 1347, Philippe VI had not reacted to Gaston's show of independence – either because he could do nothing about it, or because he trusted that the young Count of Foix would in good time see the error of his ways and revert to his father's pro-French policy. Thanks in large part to Aliénor's conciliatory influence, the breach was partially healed in 1348, when Gaston did homage to France for his fiefs in Languedoc, and no more was said about the status of Béarn. Now the King showed his good will by bestowing on the young couple an annuity of 2,000 *livres*, and extending to Aliénor and Gaston an invitation to Paris, where the marriage was celebrated on 4 August 1349, with the whole French court in attendance.

This was for Gaston the occasion of an lengthy stay in and around the capital. For the first time, he was to come into close contact with the greatest in the land, surely a heady experience for the young provincial. He was also able to indulge his passion for the chase in the royal forests of the Île-de-France, in the company of the most expert huntsmen of the time. Moreover, he was the guest of a court renowned for its artistic and intellectual life – not the Louvre, but the Hotel de Navarre. Jeanne's residence was a repository of works of sacred and secular art, including the richly illuminated books she had commissioned. It was also the venue of the best and most progressive musical entertainment, for Jeanne had recently added to her household Guillaume de Machaut, whose masterpieces would set the standards of poetic and musical composition for several generations. The death of King John of Bohemia on the field of Crécy had deprived the great innovator of his long-time patron, but he was enthusiastically welcome at the court of Navarre, especially by the heir to the throne. Born in 1332, Charles II (as he was soon to be) was already acknowledged as a leader of fashion, and one of the cleverest and most seductive young princes of his time; of an age with his new brother-in-law just arrived from the provincial – not to say rustic – court of Orthez, he may well have been for the dazzled Gaston a model and a leader into the social uses of the capital. It is easy to imagine that it was at the Hotel de Navarre that the young Count of Foix acquired a taste for beautiful books, and an interest in the musical avant-garde. However, the year 1349 brought calamities as well as rejoicing: the Black Death, which had reached France in the preceding summer, continued to exact its toll. One of the victims was Jeanne de Navarre, who at her death had been unable to pay the whole amount of Agnès' dowry – a detail that would eventually have serious consequences. The same epidemic also took the life of the Queen of France, but Philippe VI soon filled the void by marrying Blanche de Navarre, a sister of Agnès de Foix and of Charles II. Gaston was now the brother-in-law of two monarchs, a somewhat short-lived conjunction, as Philippe VI also died in August 1350, only two months after the coronation of Charles II.

WITH the marriage of Gaston and Agnès, Aliénor's task was now complete, although she continued to manage her son's personal estates until his twenty-first birthday. Under her regency there had been peace, and some strained relations with greater powers – France and Aragon especially – had been eased; the patrimony of Foix-Béarn had been increased by, among other items, the purchase of the strategic seigniory of Lannemezan; and the Count's authority had been reaffirmed by several instances of arbitration imposed on contending parties, and sometimes harsh punishments for violators of the laws.[9] Under her guidance, Gaston III had become not only acquainted, but directly involved in the internal affairs of his diverse domains: he had visited practically every township and village in Béarn, exchanged with all his subjects the oaths of fealty, and learned at first hand the delicate business of administering justice, as he was sworn to do, 'equally to the rich and to the poor'. Documentary evidence shows that, when after a period of adventures he settled down to the business of government, he proved to be a diligent, if sometimes severe, lord and magistrate to all classes of his subjects.[10]

[9] *E.g.* the men of Ossau were assessed the exorbitant fine of 15,000 *sous* for their illegal transhumance in the lowlands of Morlaàs. See *Vicomté*, 55.

[10] See Pierre Tucoo-Chala and Jacques Staes, *Notaire de Prince* (Pau, 1996), *passim.*

In two areas, however, the young Count of Foix had had little or no experience: unlike many other princes of his own age, he had not yet had the opportunity to prove himself as a knight and defender of his domains; and at the time when his marriage brought him into close relationship with the royalty of France and Navarre, he was perhaps not prepared for the intrigues and power plays of a sophisticated and perilous court. But events were soon to remedy these shortcomings of his education.

✦　✦
✦

# Trials and Tribulations

GASTON III and his bride left Paris in late October or November 1349, after attending the funeral ceremonies for Jeanne de Navarre. For Agnès, who may well have lived most of her life until then in the elegant atmosphere of her mother's court, her loss must have been compounded by the prospect of a veritable exile to a distant, unknown land, among probably uncouth strangers, crowded in the relatively cramped quarters of the Château Moncade. And even though the Count of Foix would presumably not have set out without a strong armed escort, the journey itself would have been cause enough for anxiety. Although we do not know what route the couple took from Paris to Orthez, none was entirely safe. The more direct itinerary meant travelling through disputed regions on the fringes of Aquitaine, where hostilities had never subsided despite truce after truce renewed between England and France, and where local warlords were not always answerable to their royal masters. A longer route, down the Rhône valley, was still relatively free of brigand infestation: it would have afforded the opportunity of a visit to the Papal court at Avignon, before turning west to Montpellier and Toulouse. But then the country between Toulouse and Orthez – six to eight days' journey – was also a frontier of sorts, and indeed it was soon to be the theatre of fresh military action. At the beginning of December – not long after the young couple had arrived at Orthez – the Earl of Lancaster (the former Earl of Derby, who had taken Bergerac in 1345) launched a swift raid from Bordeaux, which brought him by the middle of the month within striking distance of Toulouse. The poorly defended capital of Languedoc was saved in part by the approach of forces raised by the Count of Armagnac. The Earl, choosing not to press his advantage, returned to Bordeaux.

Lancaster's *chevauchée* into Languedoc – the first of several English offensives in that direction – may come as a surprise, as fighting in the past few years had been localized in Poitou, Saintonge and Brittany. But the resumption of full-scale war had been anticipated since August, when the French government had decided to repudiate the latest truce. After Crécy, public opinion had expected, and the Estates General had bluntly demanded, a more vigorous prosecution of the war. There were plans to retake Calais, and even to invade England, for with the Castilian alliance, France could count on the most impressive naval force of the time. Although the Spanish fleet was severely mauled off Winchelsea on 29 August 1350, the threat to English shipping and to the Channel ports remained very real for decades to come. But the French plans for a counter-offensive had never come to anything. The ageing, ailing Philippe VI was widely blamed for being indecisive, and there were even murmurs of cowardice, aimed not only at the monarch, but at the nobles who were perceived as having simply scattered and run at Crécy – as some indeed had. The King's apparent lack of will to fight was not, however, the sole obstacle to a *revanche*, nor were his hesitations unjustified.

The bubonic plague, which had made its first appearance in Mediterranean ports in the autumn of 1347, had spread through the following winter from Provence west to Languedoc and Gascony, and north to Burgundy. Although it had reached the Île-de-France in 1348, the most intense mortality was recorded in the summer of 1349: it is then that the Queens of France and of Navarre were carried off, together with the Duchess of Normandy, wife of the heir to the throne, the Chancellor of France, and scores of other notables. By then the epidemic had already done its damage to government business: with many officers of the Crown dead, and survivors fleeing the cities, public administration had come to a virtual standstill. Moreover, the immense loss of life – estimates vary from one-third of the population to more than one-half in some regions – severely impacted public as well as private finances. The decimation of the agricultural work force translated into a corresponding loss of revenue, and the mortality among urban nobles and burghers resulted in a drastic shrinkage of the tax base. Better fed and better clothed than the peasants, and usually living outside the towns that were the crossroads of contagion, soldiers and country squires suffered relatively less. It was not as if the King could not find men enough: when the finances were adequate, France consistently fielded large armies. But, under the first two Valois especially, her armaments were often crippled, not only by financial crises, but by the ingrained prejudices of a military caste slow to recognize the differences between knightly sport and real warfare.

The disorderly charge of the French cavalry at Crécy had been symptomatic of a mindset in which reckless individual prowess was perceived at the same time as the duty and privilege of the knight, with the outcome left, as it were, to the judgement of God. This lethal insouciance was compounded by the nobles' contempt and distrust for the infantry. They viewed the town militias as potential rebels, the foreign mercenaries as likely traitors, and both as a common rabble wielding ignoble weapons, who could only get in the way of a hearty mêlée. To be sure, the cult of an anachronistic, if not semi-mythical, ideal of chivalry was also very much alive in England, where Edward III had ushered in a golden age of heraldic display with the foundation of the Order of the Garter, in imitation of the twelfth-century crusading orders of knighthood. But, in sharp and evidently successful contrast to their French counterparts, English men-at-arms did not deem it dishonourable to dismount and fight as heavy infantry, co-ordinating their action with the fire power of the yeomanry equipped with the dreaded longbow. The more able French commanders were not so backwards that they did not attempt to apply the lessons cruelly learned at Crécy and elsewhere, but the feudal ethos would continue to be a cross-purpose with the need for a profound re-education of the French nobility: after periods of successful applications of the new tactics, Poitiers first, then Agincourt, would signal sensational relapses.

At Jean II's accession, the failure of the spirit of chivalry, together with Philippe's indecision, was widely regarded as the primary cause of the defeats suffered under the previous reign. On this there was a consensus across social castes: the commoners demanded that the gentry fulfil more vigorously the fundamental obligation of knighthood to fight in defence of the realm, and the nobles clamoured for the pitched battles where they could show their valour and, not so incidentally, have a chance at capturing a richly ransomable adversary. In that respect the new king appeared likely to meet his subjects' expectations better than his father had done. Jean II, called 'le Bon' for the fine figure he cut both as a valiant knight and a magnificent prince, was impulsive, stubborn and so imbued with the spirit of chivalry that he would more than once make decisions more consonant with his personal honour than with the welfare of his kingdom. Not to be outdone by his English cousin, he wasted no time in founding his own order of chivalry, dedicated to the 'revival' of the lost virtues. More numerous and if possible more splendidly adorned than the Knights of the Garter, the Compagnie des Chevaliers de Notre-Dame de la Noble Maison – better known as the Order of the Star – received 200 charter members in January 1352, in a lavish ceremony followed by a gold plate banquet.

Meanwhile, the war was, on the whole, at a stalemate. In the North, plans for the recovery of Calais were thwarted by the English capture – in violation of a truce – of the key fortress of Guines. There were limited successes in Saintonge and Poitou, where companies of marauders were expelled from several strategic places. But in Brittany, Charles de Blois, the pro-French ducal claimant, had been severely defeated in 1347 at La Roche-Derrien, and was still England's prisoner. While he came temporarily to terms with Edward III, a French army was destroyed in August 1352 at the battle of Mauron, despite attempt to apply the tactics learned from the English. With its commander Guy de Nesle, one of the most promising French captains, eighty-nine members of the Order of the Star perished in that new disaster. In the Midi, the fighting mainly took the form of an inconclusive see-saw contest for the middle Garonne valley, a valuable stretch both for the control of the river traffic, and as a corridor of access not only to Languedoc but, through the tributary valleys of the Dordogne, the Lot, Tarn and Aveyron, to the uplands of Périgord, Quercy and Rouergue. It was in the course of these campaigns that the young Count of Foix not only made his military début, but also the unwelcome acquaintance of his hereditary enemy.

Whether so ordered by Philippe VI, or upon his own initiative, Count

Jean of Armagnac, whose lands were directly threatened by the English raid
of December 1349, had led a counter-offensive in the following spring, and
retaken most of the places garrisoned by Lancaster. Then, in the relatively quiet
summer of 1351, the lieutenancy of Languedoc was entrusted to the twenty-
year-old Charles de Navarre, whose star at the French court appeared to be in
the ascendant: not only was he, since the marriage of his sister Blanche – now
a queen-dowager – the new King's step-uncle, he had recently been betrothed,
with the promise of a magnificent dowry, to Jean II's eight-year-old daughter. It
was under Charles' banner that Gaston de Foix, then very much under the spell
of his glib and charming brother-in-law, is believed to have had his baptism
of fire. But the King of Navarre was not an enthusiastic soldier; he had business to attend to at court, where he would wed his child-bride on 12 February
1352. And so it is unlikely that either prince was on the southern theatre of war
when another of Gaston's relatives made a surprise appearance on the scene. In
December 1351 a band of Gascon adventurers led by Jean de Grailly, Captal de
Buch, seized the walled town of Saint-Antonin in Quercy, a position on the
Aveyron River from which they could threaten neighbouring districts – including some of the Foix domains in the Albigeois. The Captal was Gaston III's
first cousin, his mother being Blanche de Foix, a sister of Gaston II; but he was
also the son-in-law of the lord of Albret, and as the heir of the most prominent noble house in Bordeaux, a faithful vassal of Edward III. While he and
the other bands of freebooters who scoured much of the Quercy in that year
were acting without orders from the King-Duke (who could thus deny having
broken any truce), their encroachments nevertheless prepared the way for the
eastward expansion of English Aquitaine.

This time the response was more vigorous: in June 1352 a French army,
including an important contingent under Charles de Navarre, marched into
the Garonne valley, occupying Agen and several other strategic river ports.
They were confronted by a new English commander, the Earl of Stafford,
but neither side felt strong enough for a decisive action, and both armies
disbanded in September, their various contingents diverted to other operations in Bordelais and Périgord. But the lull between campaigning seasons
was again broken in October when a company of Anglo-Gascons (perhaps a
detachment from the garrison at Saint-Antonin) seized Lafrançaise, a fortified
*bastide* commanding the River Tarn as well as the road between Moissac and
Montauban, and only a day's march from Toulouse.[1] Fortunately for the hard-
pressed *capitouls* – the city magistrates – the Count of Foix was also within
reach, probably at Pamiers, and was able to bring reinforcements 'within days

---

[1] *Bastides* (from Provençal *bastida*, built-up place) were 'new' towns founded, chiefly in
the 13th century, by kings or great lords, for economic and/or strategic advantage. Often
fortified, they were usually built according to a geometric plan resembling the Roman
military camps.

of the news breaking'.² From that moment Gaston III was a major player in the events that were about to change the political shape of the Midi. And it is worth noting that, when he came to the rescue of the Toulousains, he was not so much fulfilling a feudal obligation to Jean II, but rather responding to the offer of a large remuneration from the *capitouls*. In entering such a contract he was certainly not unique, even among his peers, but this was only the first occasion in which the Count demonstrated the affinity for money that would earn him an enduring reputation for avarice. Then, as the King of France, whose attention was fixed on the invasion he expected from the north, could offer little more than the promise of relief in an indefinite future, the Toulousains opened their purse wider in order to recruit an army capable of eliminating the threat from Lafrançaise. Under the joint command of Gaston de Foix, his uncle the Count of Comminges and the Seneschal of Toulouse, this force invested the *bastide* early in November 1352.

It was a relatively brief siege: Lafrançaise fell in mid-January. The Count of Foix could now boast of having been played a significant part in a French success, and his actions since his return to the Midi seemed to signal a return to his father's policy of pro-French engagement. But within a few weeks Gaston III was back in Orthez, with no evident intention of returning soon to serve Jean II. This sudden cooling of his zeal for the cause of the Valois was no mere caprice. The timing of Gaston's actions suggests that its immediate cause was the appointment in January 1353 of the Count of Armagnac as the King's Lieutenant in Languedoc, a title that gave him a delegation of the royal authority over the vassals of the French Crown, not excepting the Count of Foix. Even as the heads of the two houses campaigned under the same banner, the old territorial rivalry between Foix-Béarn and Armagnac had never abated. If anything, it had been exacerbated since 1351 by a number of border incidents, and open warfare had been avoided only through the urgent mediation of both the King and the Pope. But in February 1353, while Jean d'Armagnac, in his capacity as King's Lieutenant, was laying siege to the Anglo-Gascon garrison of Saint-Antonin, Gaston III rekindled their private war. With a force of 200 knights and 2,000 foot soldiers assembled at Aire-sur-Adour in his viscounty of Marsan, he invaded the adjacent lands of Armagnac.

Even though he undoubtedly saw the elevation of his rival as a personal affront, Gaston had other reasons for distancing himself from the French cause. While he could confidently recruit troops in the county of Foix for French service, his Béarnais subjects were clearly manifesting their opposition to that policy. Some had in fact been enrolled in Stafford's army – and so had fought against their own lord in the campaign of 1352 – among them a number of prominent noblemen, such as Arnaud d'Aspe, a relative of the Count's uncle Bernard 'l'Aspois', and Lubat de Béarn, who had served as Lieutenant in Béarn

² Sumption, II, 98.

during the Count's absence from Orthez in 1344–5. Gaston III was well aware of the traditional turn of Béarnais interests towards Aquitaine, and mindful of the fact that his westernmost domain was also the most vulnerable to an attack from English Gascony. The outcome of the military operations in the Midi was by no means certain to favour France: it was simply prudent to avoid exposing Béarn to reprisals from Bordeaux. Thus Gaston could, with the clear conscience of safeguarding the interests of his subjects, withdraw from the service of Jean II, and concentrate his military resources on ravaging the lands of a neighbour who happened to be the King's Lieutenant.

Although this went a step beyond mere neutrality, there was little the King could have done to punish the Count of Foix or even stop him. Only after repeated attempts did Pope Innocent VI succeed in mediating a truce. But while Gaston agreed not to attack Jean d'Armagnac directly, the undertaking did not extend to the friends of his enemy, and he lost no time before invading the lands of the lord of Albret. These aggressions continued for almost two years; the King appointed a mediator, the Pope renewed his peace-making efforts, but it was probably through the influence of Aliénor on her son that a truce was concluded in August 1355. Meanwhile, Gaston had had to face trouble at home: on 19 October 1353 a disorderly mob had attacked the Count's Lieutenant for Béarn – his half-brother Arnaud-Guilhem – at his dinner in the Dominican convent of Orthez, and forced him to take refuge in the castle. The cause of that riot is unknown, but it had been quelled by nightfall, and the leaders arrested. Gaston did not return to Orthez until 16 November, a delay perhaps calculated to increase the anxiety of the townspeople. He then made the kind of entrance appropriate for a conquered city – or a rebellious one: the gates torn from their hinges, the offended lord and his escort in full battle armour. But to his subjects' undoubted relief, he did not exact the vengeance – summary executions, demolition of city walls – that usually followed the repression of urban tumults. Instead of such destructive measures, the ringleaders remained in prison, and the customary liberties of the city were suspended, but only pending payment of a large collective fine. In his moderation, Gaston III was showing his respect for the *fors* he had sworn to uphold, and by the same occasion he was also adding another substantial sum of money to his coffers. His pragmatism in this instance makes an interesting and even puzzling contrast to the apparent naïvety of his entanglement in the Franco-Navarrese feud – an imbroglio from which he was perhaps lucky to escape with his life.

BENEATH the surface of their apparently cordial relations, suspicion and resentment had never ceased to simmer between Jean II and Charles of Navarre. The marriage of Philippe VI to Charles' sister, the much younger Blanche, had angered Jean. Recently widowed himself, he may have had his eye on that famous beauty, but he also had cause to distrust the Navarre family:

after Crécy Queen Jeanne, Charles' mother, had as Countess of Angoulême negotiated with the English Seneschal of Gascony private agreements that amounted to a separate truce. As for Charles, he was the self-conscious bearer of dynastic grievances serious enough to be perceived as threats to the freshly installed – and so far none too successful – Valois.

Charles, like Edward III, was the son of a Capetian princess, the sole surviving child of Louis X. She had been denied the crown on the supposed authority of the ancient Frankish tradition that jurists would eventually develop as the 'Salic Law'.[3] The more immediate reason for prejudice against female succession may well have been the mutual jealousy of the great feudal magnates unwilling to let one of their peers rise to the throne as the husband of a reigning queen. To Charles de Navarre, the mountain kingdom he inherited was but paltry compensation for a great wrong, and he was quoted as joking bitterly that he would have been King of France – if only his mother had been a man! The sentiment of having been despoiled was heightened by the fact that Charles was also of Capetian royal blood in the male line, as the House of Evreux sprang from the third son of Philippe III 'the Bold'. Although, unlike the Plantagenet, Charles never overtly claimed the French crown for himself, he clearly expected a share in its wealth and its power proportionate to his place so near the stem of the dynastic tree. But, in spite of his status as a prince of the blood, he was kept away from the governing councils of the Valois court, and his fortune was relatively modest by comparison with that of other magnates – royal or not. His grievances were not all imaginary: neither the dowry of 100,000 florins promised upon his marriage with little Jeanne de France, nor the huge arrears of pensions owed to his mother and to himself had been paid. Moreover, he had not been given possession of some domains that were undeniably his by inheritance.[4]

To justify these defaults and outright spoliations, the Crown might have invoked the excuses of a depleted treasury and the urgent priority of military expenditures. Unfortunately, the extravagant generosity lavished on the King's favourite, contrasting with his parsimony towards his son-in-law, made a mockery of any such pretence. Descended from a dispossessed son of Alfonso X of Castile, Charles de la Cerda, commonly called Charles d'Espagne, had been made Constable of France in 1350 after the execution of his predecessor, which he was believed to have advocated. Raoul de Brienne had sold his strategic castle and county of Guines, near Calais, to Edward III in lieu of the ransom he owed the English king. This was arguably treason, but the secrecy surrounding his sudden fall, and his swift replacement by a young man of twenty-four who was the King's constant companion, gave rise to scandalous rumours about the nature of that relationship, and widespread resentment among the nobles and

---

[3] See p. 26 above.

[4] Sumption II, 108.

urban élites already disenchanted with the Valois government. No one hated
the Constable more intensely than the King of Navarre, who saw the florins
he had been promised, and domains that he considered to be his birthright,
given to the favourite. Their rivalry was brought to a head by the grant of the
county of Angoulême to Charles d'Espagne. This fief had previously belonged
to Jeanne of Navarre, who had accepted it as compensation for renouncing her
rights to Champagne; it had been a poor bargain, and near the end of her life,
Jeanne had been content to exchange Angoulême for some seigniories in Normandy and Île-de-France, nearer the domains of the House of Evreux. Nevertheless, her son regarded the county as part of his inheritance, of which he felt
he had been cheated.

It is only since the sixteenth century that historians have called Charles II
of Navarre 'the Bad', but contemporary chroniclers were already unanimous
in their assessment of his qualities as a dangerous mixture of charm, penetrating intelligence, and irresistible eloquence, all serving an ambition unen-
cumbered by scruples, and a murderous vindictiveness. When his objections
were brushed aside, and the grant of Angoulême to his hated rival confirmed
in 1352, he began to plot his revenge. He did not lack for allies and sympathizers. Within the royal administration a number of high officials were dismayed
by the 'excessive power of a weak monarch and the dishonesty of his powerful
friends', and ready to make common cause with Charles against the Constable,
whose greed and arrogance had made him almost universally hated.[5] At his
court of Evreux the King of Navarre was also in contact with some of the
most prominent noble families of Normandy, many of whom were nursing
grievances against both Philippe VI and Jean II. These personal feuds added
their own venom to the already bitter disagreements about the conduct of the
war, or the terms of a proposed truce, that divided the ruling élite. Charles of
Navarre kept quiet, but even as he seemed to be on most cordial terms with his
father-in-law, he was clearly preparing for an armed confrontation. In May 1353
he ordered his lieutenant in Pamplona to send a first detachment of Navarrese
troops to Normandy, and by the end of the year he had strong garrisons, not
only at Evreux, but also in his castles of Mantes and Meulan, which could control traffic on the Seine below Paris. He also recruited a number of soldiers of
fortune, including the Bascon de Mareuil, a squire from Béarn already notorious for his enormous strength and his brutality.[6] At Christmas, Charles and
his hot-headed brother Philippe came to the festivities at the French court
with the avowed intention of provoking a quarrel with the Constable. 'Gross
insults' flew, and Philippe drew his dagger in the presence of the King – in
and of itself an act of *lèse-majesté* that Jean, having separated the adversaries,

---

[5] *Ibid.*, 102.

[6] 'Bascon (i.e."bastard") de Mareuil' was the *nom de guerre* of Jean de Gasnoye, *alias* Jean
de Sault. One of Charles' ubiquitous henchmen, he was killed at the battle of Cocherel.

let pass with a mild verbal reproof. He would soon be made to regret his own restraint.

It is a measure of the Constable's hubristic self-confidence that, shortly after that incident, he was travelling in Lower Normandy without an armed escort. On 7 January he stopped for the night in L'Aigle, about 35 miles from Evreux, which he must have known to be filled with Navarre's troops. At dawn on the next morning, the inn was surrounded by armed men. Philippe d'Evreux and the Bascon de Mareuil, with a mixed group of Norman squires and Navarrese soldiers broke into the room where Charles d'Espagne was still in bed. Despite his pleas for mercy, and the promise to resign all his domains and leave France, he was butchered on the spot.[7] The Bascon de Mareuil had thrust the first sword. He then hastened to inform the King of Navarre, who happened to be just outside town, with many Norman nobles. These had not been invited solely for the pleasure of their company for, when the Bascon shouted, as soon as he was within earshot: 'It is done!' Charles was pleased to tell his somewhat dismayed guests that they would surely all be implicated in the murder, but that he would accept from the King no pardon that did not extend to all of them. Then, while Jean II and his court were in a state of shock, Charles brazenly proclaimed his responsibility for the murder. In letters addressed to the widest possible audience, from the Pope to the University of Paris and to the principal French cities, he went so far as to say that 'after he has reflected on it a while, [the King] should rejoice at being rid of such evil counsel.' At the same time, he was initiating contacts with England, writing to the Duke of Lancaster, whom he already knew, with messages to be forwarded to Edward III and the Prince of Wales. Hindsight makes it clear that, even when he waged open war against the Valois, he never intended to make a present of the French Crown to the Plantagenet, but for the next fifteen years he managed to blackmail both sides in the Anglo-French conflict with well-timed, alternating exhibitions of threats and promises.

Although contemporary chronicles credit Charles' pardon to the pleas of two queens dowagers – his sister Blanche and their aunt Jeanne d'Evreux, widow of Charles IV – it is also likely that Jean II was aware of the threat posed by an imminent alliance between his son-in-law and Edward III. Moreover, several of his advisers were sympathetic to Charles, or even in league with him. Thus within two months of the outrage, Jean II had agreed to a treaty whereby his son-in-law was to be granted vastly expanded domains in Lower Normandy, including all of the Cotentin peninsula, with the promise of more land grants, and letters of remission for himself, his brother Philippe and all those implicated in the death of the Constable. Whatever fears and pressures had made him give up his vengeance, the King could not fail to see that Charles would now control not only a rich province, but one that was uncomfortably close to

[7] *Chronique des quatre premiers Valois* (Paris, 1862), 25–8.

the capital. Still, he kept his thoughts to himself, and at the solemn assembly marking the reconciliation, it was the Cardinal of Boulogne who pronounced the pre-arranged formula of the royal pardon.

By the end of 1354, however, the improbability of this patching-up had been laid bare for all to see. While Jean II regained some control by dismissing those advisers who favoured too obviously the King of Navarre, Charles was still flirting with France's enemies. Most conspicuously his troops, led by the *alférez* – the hereditary standard-bearer – of Navarre, were fighting in Brittany for the English. In November, Charles, fearing an imminent arrest, fled to Avignon, ostensibly to ask for the Pope's intercession with the King – but in reality to renew his intrigues with Lancaster, who arrived soon at the papal court to represent Edward III at the peace conference sponsored by Innocent VI. This time, however, Jean II acted swiftly, ordering the immediate confiscation of all of Charles' possessions in France. Most of his towns and castles surrendered, but there were a few strategic exceptions: at the family seat of Evreux and at the fortresses of Mortain and Gavray, and most ominously at the Channel port of Cherbourg, the Navarrese garrisons held out for their master.

T HE news of the Constable's violent death must have reached Orthez within a few weeks. To the Béarnais commoners, these were only distant noises from another country, but to the Count and Countess of Foix, they were matters of immediate family concern. Fortunately, the pardon quickly granted to Charles relieved Gaston of the obligations that kinship, as well as common regional interests, might have dictated. However, he was undoubtedly disposed to make common cause with his brother-in-law. When the King commanded the counts of Armagnac and of Comminges to invade Charles' lands north of the Pyrenees, Gaston's resolve was made clear enough to deter any serious attempt at compliance, since in order to march into Basse-Navarre, they would have had to pass through Béarn. Then, almost unnoticed among the sensational events of that year, the Count of Foix seized the opportunity of an apparently trivial incident to reaffirm the doctrine of Béarn's sovereignty. One Pélegrin de Fosse, a Béarnais merchant bringing goods from Bordeaux, had been arrested in Montpellier as a presumably English subject, and his merchandise confiscated. Gaston III reacted as soon as he was informed, with a letter representing that the Béarnais was a subject of a sovereign – and neutral – country; therefore, his arrest and spoliation was an outrage to the lord of Béarn. Underneath his polite Latin rhetoric, the Count let the municipal officers of Montpellier understand that he reserved the right of reprisals against their own people – who were, as he well knew, subjects of the King of France.[8]

With the intrusion of Navarre, the Anglo-French conflict had now become a

---

[8] *Prince*, 61–2.

strange three-cornered game whose rules shifted with every one of Charles' new ploys. Nevertheless, the major moves were still those of the senior players, and in the first months of 1355 they showed every sign of being prepared to break a stalemate of several years. In February the peace negotiations at Avignon came to an abrupt end. Despite all of the Pope's efforts, the conference had never had a chance to succeed, for peace between France and England could be achieved only if one or the other surrendered an essential portion of its sovereignty: the status of Aquitaine, even more than the possession of the French crown, was the intractable issue. And it was in Aquitaine that Edward III decided that a new offensive should be launched. In April the Prince of Wales was appointed Lieutenant, and began to assemble his expeditionary corps. For his part, Jean II had been and was still more concerned – not unreasonably – with the threat posed to his capital by an enemy landing in Calais or Cherbourg. The King ordered accelerated preparations for defence, but the appointment of his son and heir as Lieutenant in Normandy, intended to restore royal control of that troubled province, and to boost the spirits of the Norman nobles still loyal to the Valois was of more political than military significance. In such real tasks as tax gathering, the authority of the seventeen-year-old Dauphin was constantly undermined by the ubiquitous presence of Navarrese agents and garrisons.[9]

In May, Jean II proclaimed the *ban* and *arrière-ban* – the mobilization of the feudal levies – while at the same time lending an ear to the renewed efforts of his family and of his closest advisers, all pleading for a reconciliation with his son-in-law. At that time Charles was in his capital of Pamplona. Under a variety of transparent pretexts, he had evaded repeated summons to appear before the Paris Parlement – the highest court of justice in the realm – to answer for his actions. The one excuse he could not very well invoke was that he was busy raising an army for a joint sea-borne invasion with an English force led by the Duke of Lancaster. The preparations went on under the wary eyes of English envoys, mindful of the double-crossing propensities of the King of Navarre. Even if he had no yet put in place the extensive news-gathering system noted many years later by Froissart, the Count of Foix could not possibly be unaware of his neighbour's not very secret activities, or unable to suspect the purpose of his armament. This throws a rather conspiratorial shadow on the letter to Jean II, in which Gaston adds his plea to those of the royal entourage, for an adjournment of the judicial proceedings against Charles. Whether he was mollified by their insistence, or because he sought to undercut the ambiguous Anglo-Navarrese alliance, the King yielded and on 1 June wrote to his

---

[9] The title of Dauphin, first borne by the future Charles V, had been the dynastic name of the lords of Vienne, in the Rhône Valley. In 1349 the last of their line had bequeathed his domain – the Dauphiné – as an apanage to the eldest son of the kings of France.

son-in-law, offering him a pardon if he would provisionally surrender his garrisoned towns and castles in Normandy to the Crown. But the royal messenger reached Pamplona too late: Charles and the Navarrese army had already boarded ships at Bayonne and other English-held ports in Gascony, and were sailing to Normandy.

The Navarrese fleet arrived at Cherbourg on 5 July. Charles was met on shore by English agents, but also by French emissaries bringing him the King's offer of a new treaty. Meanwhile Lancaster's invasion force, which had embarked on 10 July, was delayed by contrary winds, and forced to lie at anchor at Sandwich for a month or more: this gave the Franco-Navarrese negotiations time to come to fruition. Rumours of their imminent conclusion reached England, where the Duke, anticipating Charles' latest defection, gave up the attempt to cross the Channel. By the treaty signed at Valognes on 10 September, Charles agreed to the temporary surrender to French officers of the seven walled towns and castles he still held in Normandy – but the Navarrese garrisons were to remain in place, as a guarantee of his rightful ownership. For his part, Jean II promised to restore all of his son-in-law's domains after he had (again) asked for and received his pardon in a *lit de justice* – the full-dress judicial pageant before the Paris Parlement. The inclusion of the Count of Foix in the amnesty extended to the friends and confederates of the King of Navarre is the only indication of his presumed complicity in Charles' aborted enterprise, but nothing precise is known of the nature of his involvement.[10]

Soon, however, there were other definite signs that Gaston was moving from a neutral stance to more or less overt support of the English offensive in the Midi. The Prince of Wales had arrived in Gascony in late September at the head of an expeditionary corps of 800 men-at-arms and 1,400 mounted archers. They were augmented by the feudal levies of the Gascon nobility, making up together a strong but mobile force of between 6,000 and 8,000 men.[11] The army set out from Bordeaux on 5 October on a south-easterly route. By the end of the months, it had forded the Garonne 20 miles up-river (*i.e.* south) of Toulouse. The Prince only threatened the city, but his aim was not to settle down to a siege. He went on to attack Carcassonne, burning the unwalled *bourg* and by-passing the fortified *cité*, then on to Narbonne, where the army arrived on 8 November. The Prince's *chevauchée* had achieved its purpose: prosperous Languedoc, which had believed itself at a safe distance from the war, had been made to suffer its terror and its devastation. In its wake the English raid left not only burning crops and towns and hundreds of dead men, women and children, but also the vivid message to the local populace that the King of France had failed to protect them. After a few days within sight of the Mediterranean, the English army, beset by bad weather but unmolested by the French forces

[10] *Vicomté*, 71.

[11] Sumption II, 154, 175–6.

massed in Toulouse, started on its return journey. As it skirted the northern border of Foix, the Prince was the guest of Count Gaston on 17 November, at the Cistercian abbey of Boulbonne, about a day's ride south-east of Toulouse.

It was the first meeting of the two men, who spent the whole day together in mutually profitable conversation. Gaston's tacit co-operation was already an established policy. Many of his subjects – including his half-brother Arnaud-Guilhem – had enlisted, with his full consent, under the Prince's banner. He also authorized his subjects to provision the Anglo-Gascon forces, and it is not too far-fetched to suppose that the Béarnais merchants were expected to share the profits with their lord. In deference to the Count's benevolent neutrality, the Prince had given strict orders to respect his lands, and even some towns belonging to the French Crown – such as Belpech and Cintegabelle – were spared the usual burning, in consideration of some properties Gaston held there.

Treasonable as it was from the point of view of the French government, Gaston III's friendliness to the Prince of Wales can nevertheless be explained as a necessary recognition of the altered balance of forces in the Midi: the English *chevauchée* had sent shock waves of panic through the considerable length of Languedoc, and as far as Avignon. There was no relief in sight for the subjects of the King of France, only the promise of a new Lieutenant. A hostile attitude would have brought the Count of Foix nothing but the devastation of his lands—Gavardan and the northern Foix country – that lay in the path of the English army, and perhaps a direct attack on Béarn proper. And of course, Gaston had the satisfaction of seeing the domains of his Armagnac adversary ravaged – a task in which some bands of Béarnais had their share.

It is less easy to understand what the Count of Foix had to gain by being involved in another plot with Charles of Navarre. This time, nothing less was proposed than a coup with the connivance of the heir to the throne: on 7 December the Dauphin was to be met by Charles' agents at the bridge of Saint-Cloud, near Paris, and sent with a strong escort to Germany, where his uncle the Emperor would give him asylum. Charles' ultimate intentions are unclear, and so is the extent to which the Dauphin was aware of them. In the event, the plot was discovered almost at the last moment. The heir to the throne confessed all, and was instantly rewarded by being vested with the apanage and title of Duke of Normandy, and money to pay his debts. Jean II's military preparations had not progressed to the point where he could afford a confrontation with the 'Navarre party': another pardon was extended in January 1356 to Charles and his accomplices, including once again the Count of Foix. By some accounts, Gaston's part in the scheme was to organize the escape of the Dauphin to Germany, but although he could easily have been in Paris by the end of November, there is no firm evidence that he was actively involved in that cloak-and-dagger project.[12] Nor is there a credible account of his whereabouts on the day when the feud between the kings of France and of Navarre reached a violent climax.

Ever since the abortive Saint-Cloud conspiracy, Paris had been rife with more or less well-founded rumours of impending treason. Whether or not he had reasons to believe that, with or without the connivance of the Dauphin, Charles was hatching another plot in Normandy, Jean II decided to deal once and for all with the Navarrese. He gathered a detachment of 100 men-at-arms and, with his brother the Duke of Orleans, his son Louis d'Anjou and Marshal Arnoul d'Audrehem – a protégé of the Constable murdered by Navarre's henchmen – rode on 5 April to Rouen. The armed band burst into the castle's banquet hall as the Dauphin, in his capacity as Duke of Normandy, was dining with a number of his vassals. The gathering had been called by the Duke, who had been appointed Lieutenant in Languedoc, in order to prepare the defence of the province while he was away. Charles of Navarre and some of his officers were also his guests. In the affray following the irruption of the King and his followers, Charles was roughly seized, together with several of the leading Norman nobles. Three of these, who had been involved in all of Navarre's plots, and Charles' squire, who had threatened Jean with his dagger, were dragged to a Rouen fairground and summarily executed. The King of Navarre was taken to a succession of prisons, and finally shut in the formidable keep of Arleux in Cambrésis.

Whether Gaston de Foix was among the guests at that interrupted banquet is a matter of speculation. His presence in the entourage of Charles of Navarre would not have been extraordinary; he might also have come to Rouen to seek a rapprochement with the rather malleable young man who was to be the King's vicar in Toulouse. But, tempting as it may be to conclude that he was arrested with his brother-in-law, contemporary accounts of the day's events make no mention of the Count of Foix.[13] However, some chronicles report that he was imprisoned in the Paris Châtelet, and his protracted absence from Orthez, where his councillors appear to have acted in his name between March and July 1356, may be taken to support the probability of his detention. In the absence of any documentary evidence, the reasons for his arrest also remain obscure. It is not impossible to imagine that Gaston III was at least in the confidence of the King of Navarre. But his friendly attitude to the Prince of Wales during the English raid of the preceding year would naturally have angered Jean II. It is also possible that the King was punishing Gaston's refusal to give him homage for Béarn. Such at least is the uncorroborated explanation given by a fifteenth-century chronicler of the counts of Foix.[14] If that was the case, Jean II did not

[12] *Vicomté*, 71.

[13] *Chronique des quatre premiers Valois*, 50.

[14] Esquerrier, 52–3.

achieve the desired result. Moreover, excessive pressure on the Count of Foix would only provoke his Béarnais to join forces with the Navarrese, already at war with France since the arrest of their king. In the event, whether he was released, or simply allowed to escape, Gaston was freed, possibly by Midsummer: his first public appearance since March is recorded at Perpignan on 12 July. On that occasion, the Count of Foix did homage to the King of Aragon for his Catalan fiefs, and signed with him a treaty of mutual defence. He then returned to Orthez, where, two months later, the news of the massive French defeat at Poitiers may have made him wonder if he had escaped from one peril only to face another one.

✦  ✦
✦

# ✦ 4 ✦
## Fébus Revealed

AN English strategy for a decisive campaign was set in motion in the summer of 1356. The plan was simple: Edward III was to strike from the North, while the Prince of Wales, who only a few months before had demonstrated his ability to go far and fast, would march from Aquitaine. The French King would thus have to fight on two fronts, a predicament made even more acute by the open war now waged by Philippe de Navarre from his base in Cherbourg, and the doubtful loyalties of some vassals and neighbours – such as the Count of Foix – on the borders of Languedoc. In June the Duke of Lancaster's army was the first expeditionary force to take he field in Normandy. At the same time, reinforcements were sent from England to Bordeaux, and in early July the Prince of Wales began the southern thrust of Edward's strategy. His first move to La Réole, a key defence of the lower Garonne valley, seemed to presage another attack aimed at Languedoc, but in early August, leaving the lord of Albret to defend Gascony against the Count of Armagnac, the Prince led the bulk of his forces north through Périgord and Limousin. Striking deep into the French heartland, he rode towards Orléans, by-passing strongholds and sacking some profitable towns and abbeys on the way.

Meanwhile Jean II, who had been immobilized by siege warfare in 'Navarrese' Normandy, managed to extricate himself from that situation and to organize defences in the Loire valley. Moreover, the English plan for a junction of their northern and southern forces was meeting with various difficulties. The departure of Edward's army from England was thwarted by an Aragonese fleet under French contract; Lancaster, sent to meet the Prince instead, marched from Brittany, but was eventually unable to cross the Loire in Anjou. Up-river, the Prince of Wales prepared to attack Tours and thus take the bridge that carried the old Roman road. But the town was well defended, and on 10 September Jean II and the main French army crossed the Loire at Blois, only a day's ride from the English camp. Rather than be caught between the King and the defenders of Tours, the Prince of Wales decided to retreat south, but rather slowly, as he still hoped to be joined by Lancaster. The combined French armies of Jean II and the Dauphin followed, and came within striking distance of the English on 15 September, a few miles south-east of Poitiers. Their encounter was delayed by the intervention of two cardinals sent from Avignon with an offer to mediate a truce. Neither side was disposed to listen: the Prince of Wales did not know that his father had empowered him to negotiate, and the King of France, certain of a decisive victory, rejected any further talks. In their expectations, the

French command were not unrealistic: not only did they have a considerable advantage in numbers, but their troops were relatively fresh, whereas the English had been marching for more than a month, and were encumbered by the usual booty.[1]

The forces were arrayed on 18 September, a Sunday. There was a last, futile attempt at mediation, and the battle was joined at last the next day. The English held a strong defensive position with a wooded hill at their back – but they had been at their battle stations for twenty-four hours. They had slept under arms; they had no water, little food; and they knew that they were outnumbered. On the other hand, they could not be outflanked, and the terrain offered the French only a narrow front for a direct assault. The alternative proposal – to wait until hunger and thirst forced the English to abandon their position – was shouted down as cowardly. Once again, chivalry made a superior French force squander an overwhelming tactical advantage. Then, at the height of the mêlée, the Dauphin suddenly left the field, probably led away on orders from the King. He was followed, rather precipitously, by his two brothers, the young counts of Anjou and Poitiers, together with their uncle, the Duke of Orleans, and his men. With only his own division left, Jean II advanced on foot, only to be attacked from the rear by a mounted contingent led by the Captal de Buch. Fighting on with his youngest son, the fourteen-year-old Philip, Jean II was utterly overwhelmed, but would not surrender until he was assured that his captor was a knight.

It was a greater disaster by far than Crécy. The Duke of Bourbon, the Constable of France, one of the two marshals, and that exemplary knight Geoffroy de Charny lay among the 2,500 French men-at-arms killed. Fourteen counts, twenty-one barons and bannerets, and some 1,400 knights were taken prisoners – including the surviving Marshal. The booty in clothing, armour, horses and royal baubles, rich as it was, was dwarfed by the ransoms paid for the French magnates. But the worst was yet to come for France, and it would nearly bring about the fall of the Valois monarchy.

For the Count of Foix the news of the defeat and capture of Jean II meant that, for an indefinite and probably extended time, he had nothing more to fear from France. It did not follow, however, that he could feel quite secure: the military power to reckon with in the Midi was no longer controlled from distant Paris, but from Bordeaux, and no doubt with greater vigour. Sooner or later, the Prince of Wales would demand Gaston's homage not only for Marsan and Gavardan, but also for Béarn. But there would be a respite: the Prince was busy entertaining his royal prisoner, first at his Bordeaux palace, then in London, where he escorted him. A general truce was proclaimed until 1358. While

---

[1] Jean II had 8,000 men-at-arms and 3,000 infantry; the Prince had 3,000 men-at-arms, 2,000 archers and 1,000 Gascon foot soldiers. See Sumption II, 235–45.

peace negotiations continued, the Prince was unlikely to upset the delicate balance of forces on the borders of Gascony, and Béarn would be relatively free from English pressure.

From another perspective, the news of Poitiers also placed the Count of Foix in the situation of a man who has purchased the wrong kind of insurance policy. Never the most eager of vassals to any overlord, Gaston III had invoked the ravages of the plague of 1348 as an excuse to postpone his homage for the lands he held from the King of Aragon. An unspoken reason for that delay may have been a lingering sympathy for the cause of James III, the dispossessed King of Majorca to whose daughter Gaston had been betrothed, and who had been welcome at Foix as a fugitive from Peter IV's custody. James' death having dissolved that tenuous relationship, the Count of Foix had complied in 1350, and done homage to Peter for his seigniories in Roussillon and Catalonia. Six years later, recently released (or escaped) from Paris, and fearing an attack by the King of France – or at least by his Lieutenant Jean d'Armagnac – Gaston had returned to Perpignan to renew his homage and sign with the King of Aragon a treaty of mutual assistance for the defence of their respective domains. For Peter, faced with imminent war with his most powerful rival and namesake, the King of Castile, this was such a valuable addition to his forces that, upon receiving the news of the French defeat, he hastened to write to the Count to remind him of his treaty obligations.

Gaston III's response was, on the face of it, perfectly satisfactory: he would be at Peter's service 'in person and with his men, as must every loyal liege and ally'. But he also protested that he was at present unable to disburse his soldiers' pay, and asked for payment in advance of the monetary compensation stipulated by the treaty of Perpignan. The King rejected this demand in principle, but promised to pay his ally 5,000 florins if he would be in Aragon by mid-December, with at least 500 men-at-arms. Gaston replied that he would indeed march – but only when war was formally declared. In February he demurred again, asking this time for an increase of the rate of remuneration.[2] Peter replied angrily that 'in Aragon, it was not customary for a knight to ask for a pay increase before each muster', but nevertheless agreed to his ally's 'unchivalrous' condition. This only encouraged Gaston to more delays and haggling: first he argued that he could not leave Orthez until he had assurances that the Prince of Wales would not invade Béarn. Then, as that excuse was wearing rather thin, he disclosed that Pedro I of Castile had offered him a bribe of 2,000 gold florins if he would remain neutral. Badly in need of the Béarnais cavalry, Peter could only rage privately, and make his counter-offer. It was not until the end of March that Gaston entered Aragon through the Somport pass. Advancing

---

[2] The treaty of Perpignan provided that knights would be paid at the daily rate of 7 *sous* per man, 5 *sous* per horse, with a higher rate for the Count and his chief vassals. See *Vicomté*, 73, n. 21.

at a deliberate pace, he wrote at least twice more to the King, to complain of the cost of provisioning in Aragon, and to ask for yet another pay raise. The size of the Béarnais force – 1,000 knights, fully equipped and provided with remounts, and at least 600 infantry – suffices to explain why the irascible Peter IV was willing to put up with his ally's cynical demands, and even to levy and exceptional tax in order to meet them. The Count's army arrived at Saragossa on 18 May, six weeks after first entering the country, and only days after a truce had been concluded between Aragon and Castile. Before returning to Orthez in early June, Gaston managed to obtain one more boon, *viz.* the renewal of a privilege granted to the merchants of Oloron, of free transit through the realms of the Crown of Aragon.

Now twenty-six, the Count of Foix was showing remarkable business acumen, and a degree of calculating avarice generally deemed more characteristic of a low-born usurer than of a nobleman. To be sure, even great princes were not infrequently noted for their rapacity, but they usually tended to prey on their subjects, rather than on their peers. Young Gaston, however, showed himself capable of squeezing cornered magnates and defaulting burghers with the same dogged determination. Given this aspect of his character, it is therefore somewhat puzzling to see him embarked next on such a distant and usually unprofitable adventure as a crusade. By taking the Cross, Gaston III was not only following his father's example, but responding to the call of a pervasive and very current fashion. The idea of fighting the Infidel and of 'liberating' the Holy Land would live on in Christendom for at least another century, with kings and dukes periodically pledging themselves to one grand expedition after another. A few eventually got under way, some with such ephemeral victories as the futile capture of Alexandria in 1369, but most ended in failure, or worse. The only lasting success would come in 1492, with the surrender of Moslem Granada to the rulers of Castile and Aragon. But in 1357 Gaston sailed, not to Syria or Africa, but to East Prussia.

After the fall in the thirteenth century of the Christian kingdoms and principalities in Palestine, the knightly monks of the Teutonic Order had chosen as their new field of enterprise the marshlands and forests of the Eastern Baltic, sparsely inhabited by a variety of pagan tribes. Their repeated attempts at subduing them were only sporadically successful, and when they attacked the Orthodox Russians in 1242, the knights suffered a crushing defeat at the hand of Alexander Nevsky. Nevertheless, by the mid-fourteenth century the Order controlled at least the coastal regions of modern Estonia and Latvia, as well as East Prussia. From their many great strongholds, they periodically launched 'crusades' against their eastern neighbours, even after some of the native princes had received baptism. Like the erstwhile Latin lords of Outremer, the Grand Master regularly called for knights from all of Catholic Europe to join the Order's fight against the 'infidels'. In the best aristocratic circles, the annual crusade of the Teutonic Knights had acquired the 'must do' cachet of a blessed safari. The Grand Master Winrich von Kniprode knew how to give noble volunteers the opportunity to show off their prowess, and also the entertainment of memorable hunts in primeval forests where they may well have thought themselves transported to the enchanted groves of Arthurian romance. Among those guest champions were some of the most celebrated knights of the century: the first Duke of Lancaster, Henry of Grosmont, and eventually his grandson Bolingbroke – the future Henry IV – the Earl of Warwick, the French Marshal Boucicaut, and many more.

To accommodate all potential participants, the Grand Master organized two seasonal campaigns. Gaston de Foix elected to take part in the winter 'crusade', and prepared to leave Béarn in the autumn of 1357. Why he should have made up his mind to embark on that adventure can only be understood in the context of his faith and of his social caste. Like most of his contemporaries, Gaston's belief in the teaching of the Church was literal and unquestioning. The evident fervour of his *Livre des oraisons* suggests that his devotion was as intense as it was personal. The prospect of the remission of sins, promised to those who took the Cross, would have been incentive enough, but the call of chivalry must have been equally strong. Until then the young Count of Foix had led armies, more often than not under a lucrative contract, but he had not performed the individual feats of arms that ensured initiation into the select club of knights mentioned in chronicles: the relief of Toulouse in 1352, and the more recent excursion into Aragon, had been mere troop movements. It is even probable that Gaston had not yet been knighted: perhaps he expected to be dubbed by the Teutonic Grand Master.[3] It was indeed high time for the son of Gaston II, called 'le Preux', to prove himself no less worthy than his father. All in all, a crusade promised what every gentleman – whether squire or belted knight – longed for: the opportunity for individual prowess, together with salvation of the soul. And, if those lofty aspirations seem somewhat austere, stories of fabulous hunts in unknown lands had probably reached Gaston's ears, and whetted his appetite for an adventure that would be at once holy, glorious and great fun.

For his part, the King of Aragon was taken aback by what in his view amounted to his ally's desertion. He had every reason to fear a resumption of hostilities with his powerful neighbour – and indeed the 'war of the two Pedros' would go on for another nine years. Throughout the summer of 1357 Peter IV pleaded with Gaston to postpone his crusading plans. But the Count could be neither threatened, nor bribed, nor swayed by a cardinal's plea, and he was even deaf to the taunts of the Catalan envoy who rudely denounced Gaston's 'crusade' as a mere pretext to evade his vassal duty.[4] His indifference to that

---

[3] *Chronicon Galfredi Le Baker de Swynebroke*, ed. E. M. Thompson (Oxford, 1889), 135.

[4] *Vicomté*, 76.

public rebuke gives a glimpse of the curious juxtaposition of rashness, obstinacy and pragmatism that would govern some of his most fateful decisions. As it were, his enthusiasm for the Nordic adventure was somehow buttressed by the cool-headed calculation that, given the imminence of war with Castile, Peter's threats could be safely dismissed. Gaston must also have felt that he could leave Béarn without fear of an English aggression: not only would the Count travel with his cousin Jean de Grailly, the same Captal de Buch who had contributed so much to the victory at Poitiers, but the Prince of Wales was too imbued with respect for the conventions of chivalry to harm the property of a crusader. It is also worth noting that, in an age of hazardous travel, when one did not set out on a distant journey without first putting one's affairs – both spiritual and material – in order, Gaston left for the Baltic without making his will. Perhaps a measure of his self-confidence (bordering, one might say, on hubris), this was a serious omission, all the more so when seen retrospectively, as the Count of Foix never got around to correcting it before death surprised him in his sixty-first year, still intestate.

The expedition set out in October. In addition to the Captal and his retinue, Froissart reports that Gaston led sixty lances (*i.e.* at least 180 men). For an overseas adventure, of which the Count was this time underwriting the expenses, this was a respectable number, even if it did not represent, as another chronicler asserts, 'all his nobles'. The muster of that company shows only names from the county of Foix: this may reflect a lingering reluctance – either on Gaston's part, or of the Béarnais – to deprive the viscounty of any of its armed forces.[5] The crusaders boarded ship at Bruges, where Gaston borrowed 24,000 gold *écus* from the Flemish merchants, and may have arrived in East Prussia at the onset of winter. Little is known of their voyage, or of the subsequent campaign against the 'pagans', but a chapter of Gaston's *Livre de chasse*, devoted to the reindeer, states explicitly that he and his party were the guests of King Magnus Eriksson for memorable hunts in Sweden and perhaps Norway. Whether his feats of arms earned him admission to that inner circle of Baltic crusaders, the quasi-Arthurian Order of the Table, with the right to hang his shield in the great hall of Marienburg Castle, remains a matter of speculation.

The Count's crusade was, however, something to celebrate in his country, and his lieutenant in Béarn lost no time in doing so: in commemoration of that adventure, he gave the name of Bruges to a *bastide* founded near Pau during his lord's absence. Gaston himself, according to the historiographers of the House of Foix, marked the occasion by exhibiting for the first time the defiant motto '*Toquey si gauses*' (in Béarnais: 'Touch [me] if you dare') and the war cry '*Fébus aban!*' ('Fébus go forth!'). More unusual, and thus especially significant, was the adoption of a *nom de guerre* that would eventually become at least as familiar as his given name. For the chronicler Miégeville, writing in the fifteenth

[5] *Ibid.*, 77.

century, the event warranted putting some verses in the mouth of the late
Count:

> When I made to Prussia the voyage
> Against Saracens to defend
> Of Christians the lawful rights,
> *Fébus* I called myself.[6]

This self-bestowed name had nothing in common with the more or less
descriptive, flattering or derogatory epithets (the Fair, the Long, the Good, the
Bad, etc.) routinely added by historians to the name of rulers, either in their
lifetime or after their death. Gaston III himself chose to be known as Fébus, a
name that would eventually become his official signature and appear not only
on lapidary inscriptions, but also on coinage from his Morlaàs mint. As a gesture, its adoption is akin to that of a conqueror crowning himself. Fébus is the
Béarnais spelling of Phoebus, one of the several names of Apollo, the sun god
of the classical Antiquity. As for its meaning, the etymology of the name (from
the Greek verb meaning 'to shine'), and the perceived (albeit anachronistic)
analogy with the emblem chosen three centuries later by Louis XIV – the 'Sun
King' – suggest an explanation in terms of physical vanity. Froissart notes that,
contrary to current fashion, Gaston III always went bareheaded, with his hair
floating free down to his shoulders; and in a surviving motet in praise of the
Count of Foix, the entrance of the 'illustrious prince' is pointedly illuminated
by his 'blond curls'.[7] While it is virtually inescapable, this 'visual' interpretation
does not exclude an allusion to another aspect of the myth of Apollo: the sun
god Phoebus was the twin brother and male counterpart of Artemis-Diana,
goddess of the moon – and of the hunt. Celebrated for his victory over the giant
serpent Python, Phoebus-Apollo may be seen as one of the pagan forerunners
of the dragon-slayers of Christian legend, the Saint George and Saint Michael
hailed as the heavenly patrons and models of chivalry. Textual evidence shows
that the Greek god's cynegetic avocation was not unknown in the fourteenth
century: his initial exploit is celebrated in the ballade 'Phiton, Phiton, beste tres
venimeuse', composed in honour of Gaston.[8] The dedication of a contemporary treatise on venery ('Gasses [de la Buigne] made this work / For Phebus
Duke of Burgundy') also proves that the mythological name was occasionally
bestowed on other champions of the chase.[9] By a not so strange coincidence,
it was to that other Phoebus, Philip of Burgundy, that Gaston would also offer
his *Livre de chasse*.

---

[6] *Ibid.*, 69.

[7] 'Ecce princeps occurit inclitus / Flava caput tectum cesarie.' From the anonymous
motet 'Inter densas', in Castéret, 'Musique et Musiciens à la Cour de Gaston Fébus'
(unpublished thesis, Paris: Université de Paris-Sorbonne, 1992), 155.

[8] *Ibid.*, 124.

[9] *Vicomté*, 108–9.

Unlike their Occitan counterparts (*e.g.* Esquerrier and Miégeville) French chronicles of the time ignore the name of Fébus, and usually refer to Gaston only by his title. The exception of a reference, in a diplomatic document, to the death of 'Gaston de Foix, named Fébus', is the only tenuous evidence that it was acknowledged in the world at large.[10] Whether he had on his own conceived the idea of assuming this solar persona, or been prompted by a courtier's erudite flattery, the simultaneous adoption of the war cry *'Fébus aban!'*, the selective substitution of Fébus for his given name as a signature, as well as its epigraphic use, all mark the intensity of Gaston's attachment to his self-image – and raise one more question about a complex, and ultimately enigmatic, character.

Fébus and the Captal returned to France in June 1358, riding this time through Germany by different routes. According to Froissart, they met again in Champagne, at Châlons-sur-Marne, in time to find themselves caught in a civil war. Since the disaster at Poitiers, France had been sinking into political chaos, and was now on the brink of a bloody revolution. With the King in English captivity, the eighteen-year-old Dauphin had assumed the lieutenancy of the realm. For the next four years – until Jean II secured his own release at the enormous cost of the treaty of Brétigny – he faced an unprecedented combination of threats to the kingdom and to the monarchy itself. While he managed to stave off the overthrow of the Valois dynasty, he was powerless to stop the ravage of his country. In 1361 the great humanist and diplomat Petrarch would thus try to put into words his horror at the plight of a kingdom he 'could scarcely recognize as the same one [he] had previously visited':

> Everywhere were dismal devastation, grief, and desolation, everywhere wild and uncultivated fields, everywhere ruined and deserted homes [...] everywhere remained the sad vestiges of the Angli and the recent, loathsome scars of defeat. [...] Paris itself, the capital of the kingdom, is disfigured with ruins up to its city gates, quakes with fires, and shudders at its wretched misfortune ...[11]

The 'loathsome scars of defeat' refers of course to Poitiers. 'From that time on', wrote Jean de Venette, 'all went ill with the kingdom, and the state was undone.' The worst scourge of all was the endemic violence unleashed throughout the land, as bands of soldiers left unemployed by the truce turned to looting and extortion for their livelihood. Countryside and city suffered alike, the Carmelite chronicler reports, as brigands 'despoiled the inhabitants of country villages in their own houses', and the citizens of Paris razed 'many handsome and splendid dwelling, both within and without the walls', in order to strengthen

---

[10] *Ibid.*, 108, n. 6.

[11] Francesco Petrarca, *Letters on Familiar Matters*, vol. 3, trans. Aldo S. Bernardo (Baltimore: Johns Hopkins University Press, 1985), 242.

the city's defences with new ditches and ramparts. For that state of affairs Jean de Venette squarely blames the Dauphin: 'Yet Charles, duke of Normandy, the king's eldest son, who was bound by hereditary right to defend the realm and to rule the state, applied no remedy.' Peasant-born himself, the same chronicler is equally blunt as he reports class animosities nearing their flash point: 'The nobles despised and hated all others [...] They subjected and despoiled the peasants and the men of the villages. In no wise did they defend their country from its enemies. Rather did they trample it underfoot, robbing and pillaging the peasants' goods.' [12]

The Dauphin's inability to protect the land and its people was in large part due to an empty treasury. To remedy this, the Estates-General, an occasional assembly of the clergy, the nobility and the commons, were convened in 1356, 1357 and again in 1358. Inevitably – given the commons' distrust of the nobles and of the royal bureaucracy – they quarrelled about the means of national recovery. Soon, they were ripe for manipulation by less disinterested parties, chief among these the agents of Charles of Navarre. The difficult relations between the Dauphin and the Estates were further complicated by orders from the absent King, often at cross-purpose with the efforts of the Paris govern-ment. In an attempt to relieve the pressure on the royal finances, the Dauphin had ordered in December 1356 a devaluation of the coinage. Coming on the heels of a defeat widely perceived as the result of cowardice – if not outright treason – on the part of the princes and nobles, that measure was, to the class most immediately affected by it, *i.e.* the urban bourgeoisie, further evidence of treason in high places. The fuse for the forthcoming explosion burned slowly for months, but dangerous sparks suddenly began to fly when, in November 1357, the King of Navarre escaped from prison. What followed was a three-cornered contest of deceit and violence involving Charles, the Dauphin and a powerful revolutionary faction led by Etienne Marcel, provost of the mer-chants of Paris. Under pressure from the indefatigable dowager queens, and the strong Navarrese party at court, the Dauphin was persuaded to pardon his brother-in-law and promise to restore all of his domains; for his part, Charles of Navarre used his vaunted eloquence to woo the Parisian crowds and, with sly hints at his dynastic rights, to position himself as a possible guarantor of a *coup d'état*. In what appears like a grim rehearsal of a later revolution, a series of violent incidents culminated in February 1358 with the irruption into the royal palace of a mob led by Etienne Marcel. The two marshals who were with the Dauphin were hacked to death in his presence. The terrified young prince, wearing 'for his protection' the crimson and blue hood of the Parisian insur-gents, was forced to pardon the murderers, and to accept, with the tutelage of Marcel, the title of Regent – which the rebels perhaps hoped would drive a wedge between him and the King his father. Although he was not in the city

---

[12]  *The Chronicle of Jean de Venette*, trans. Jean Birdsall (New York, 1953), 66–7.

at that time, Charles of Navarre was one of the chief supporters, and the chief beneficiary, of the Paris revolution, as Marcel forced the Dauphin to grant him more money and territory, including the county of Bigorre and other lands situated between Béarn and Foix. About one month later the Dauphin-Regent left Paris under pretext of presiding over the provincial Estates convening at Senlis. In reality he began to raise the forces needed to regain control of Paris and counter the threat posed by Anglo-Navarrese bands. The occupation of two strongholds at Meaux and Montereau, both up-river from Paris, put him in a position to blockade the capital, as waterways were then the principal avenue for the movement of all freight and victuals. The Dauphin then installed his wife, their small daughter and other royal ladies with their retinues, in the presumed safety of the so-called 'Market' of Meaux – in fact a fortified suburb of the town. But it was there that, while he was away in Champagne, they became the target of an unexpected and terrifying threat.

The peasant revolt known as the Jacquerie erupted at the end of May.[13] What sparked it at that precise moment is not known for certain, but the root causes of anger in the rural population are easy enough to identify. As Jean de Venette soberly noted, the villagers had borne the brunt of wars, famines, requisitions, and pestilence; now they were defenceless prey to bands of brigands from which the nobles – their natural protectors – were incapable or unwilling to shield them: often enough the seigneur, his own house looted and ruined, had then joined the marauding *routiers*. According to Froissart, the uprising began with a spontaneous gathering where rumours and pent-up anger combined to ignite a near-panic, and turned into a radical resolve: 'They said that all the nobles of the kingdom of France, knights and squires alike, shamed and betrayed the kingdom, and that it would be a good thing to destroy them all.'[14] The mob set out 'without further counsel and with no weapons except iron-tipped staffs and knives' and, growing as it marched, attacked the nearest manor, killing the resident knight, his wife and children 'little and big alike', and burned the house. There followed the all-too familiar recital of atrocities to be expected of collective rage: arson, rape, torture and even cannibalism. Spreading quickly to districts north and east of Paris, the uprising did not remain altogether 'without counsel': leaders emerged, who made overtures to the rebellious bourgeois rebels in Paris. Their collusion might have led to a true revolution, but for the vigorous reaction of Charles of Navarre, who lost no time in leading the nobles against the peasant mobs. But it lasted long enough for a large band of Jacques to converge on Meaux, together with some of Etienne Marcel's less savoury partisans. On 9 June the town's mayor, a sympathizer of the Paris rebels, opened the city gates and welcomed the Jacques with food and wine.

---

[13] 'Jacquerie' is derived from 'Jacques Bonhomme', the generic term of contempt for French peasants.

[14] *Chroniques*, VI, 45.

The royal ladies were besieged in the market, with a garrison inadequate for a prolonged defence.

Froissart's version, according to which the Count of Foix and the Captal de Buch had heard of their predicament while at Châlons, is doubtful, as the attack of the Market was quite unexpected. More probably, they happened to stop at Meaux, on their way home, to present their respects to the ladies. They also happened to travel at the head of at least forty lances. It was the assailants' turn to be surprised, as the gates of the fortress opened wide, by a furious cavalry charge 'with spear and sword'. Caught with their backs to the Marne, hundreds of the Jacques were either cut to pieces or drowned, although Froissart's report of 7,000 dead rebels is probably exaggerated. The victors then burned the town and killed many of the local citizens, including the mayor, for having made the rebels welcome. At Meaux and elsewhere, the uprising was put down as ferociously as it had dealt with the gentry, but much more thoroughly, and thousands of peasants perished for the thirty to sixty nobles actually slain in the Jacquerie.

The affair at Meaux, more carnage than combat, was nevertheless celebrated as an exploit. Gaston and the Captal had performed the duty of knighthood, regardless of feudal allegiances, and rescued ladies from mortal peril. Their gesture, under the unfurled banners of chivalry, was also a manifestation of class solidarity transcending political divides, but in no way erasing them. Jean de Grailly, a steadfast vassal of the Prince of Wales, went on to join the Anglo-Navarrese forces in Normandy. Fébus, having by this prowess secured a respectable place among the famous knights of his time, went home. Although some chronicles name him among those who helped the Dauphin regain control of Paris that summer, dated documents indicate that he was probably in Foix by the end of June, and in Béarn in October.[15] The rift between the Count and the French government was growing wider, and there was no reason for him to help the Valois monarchy in its hour of need.

Their mutual grievances undoubtedly included such incidents as the probable participation of the Count of Foix to the plots of Charles of Navarre, and his subsequent arrest, but the root cause of their estrangement was, as it had been for the past six or seven years, the ever closer alliance between the King – and now the Dauphin – and Gaston's hereditary enemy. While Philippe VI had attempted to keep on good terms with the two most powerful of his southern vassals, his successors had had little choice but to rely on the Count of Armagnac, whose interests clearly converged with those of the Crown, since the defence of his lands coincided with that of Languedoc. The domains of Foix-Béarn, on the other hand, lay largely on the fringe of the French defensive perimeter, and some beyond it altogether. The evasive attitude adopted

[15] *Vicomté*, 388.

by Gaston de Foix soon after Crécy contrasted sharply with the unwavering support of Jean d'Armagnac, whose appointment as the King's Lieutenant in Languedoc was only logical – if only because he was the more experienced leader of the two. In December 1357 the Dauphin, who had been vested before the defeat with the nominal lieutenancy, now conferred it on his brother, the eighteen-year-old Jean, Count of Poitiers, but with his godfather the Count of Armagnac as his mentor. It was thus during Gaston's winter adventure in East Prussia that his rival was able to obtain the recognition by the French Crown of Armagnac's rights in Bigorre.

The county of Bigorre, coinciding roughly with the modern *département* of Hautes-Pyrénées, belongs to the same natural environment as neighbouring Béarn. The Gave de Pau, for instance, flows from the glaciers of Gavarnie, past Lourdes, before irrigating the piedmont of Béarn, and only a local antiquarian could detect the nuances between the speech, customs and artefacts of the two countries. At the death of the last Countess of Bigorre in 1251, the Viscount of Béarn and the Count of Armagnac had both laid claim to her inheritance. In addition to the intrinsic value of the county, its situation athwart the road between Foix and Béarn had made its possession even more desirable, since the reunion of both lordships under the same ruling house. In the event, the French Crown had gained direct control of Bigorre, but the counts of Foix and Armagnac had never abandoned their respective claims. The dormant dispute was revived in 1357 when a tentative treaty, intended to secure the release of the King of France, proposed among other concessions the transfer of Bigorre to Edward III. Neither this clause, nor the subsequent cession of the county to Charles de Navarre, came to be implemented. But, upon hearing of what might transpire in London, Jean d'Armagnac had remonstrated with his pupil the Count of Poitiers who in August 1358, in his capacity of Lieutenant-General in Languedoc, ordered the Seneschal of Bigorre to prevent anyone taking possession of the county without the prior consent of the Count of Armagnac. This implicit recognition of Armagnac's right of intervention was naturally unacceptable to the Count of Foix. In January 1359 Gaston III wrote to the Dauphin to complain of the actions taken by the counts of Poitiers and of Armagnac. Protesting, however, of his devotion to the French Crown, he offered his alliance, in exchange for the lieutenancy of Languedoc, the control of Bigorre and 500,000 florins.[16] This bold diplomatic move was not unconnected with Gaston's political manœuvres in Languedoc, where the Estates had convened to discuss an exceptional tax to underwrite the defence of the province. There was in that assembly a strong party favouring the Count of Foix. To the men of Toulouse in particular, he was more than neighbour, since he also held fiefs in the seneschalsy; he may also have been more or less consciously perceived as the standard-bearer of the Midi's perennial spirit of defiance, in contrast to

[16] *Ibid.*, 83.

Jean d'Armagnac's 'collaboration' with the French Crown. The delegates from Montpellier and eastern Languedoc, remembering perhaps his veiled threats at the time of the Pélegrin affair (see p. 38 above), were less friendly to the Count of Foix, and despite his intrigues, declined to elect his Toulousain candidate for treasurer general of the province. A measure of Gaston's concern is his offer of 100,000 florins to defray the expenses of the Count of Poitiers' eventual return to Paris – in effect, bribing the current King's Lieutenant to resign his office. For once in his life Jean de Poitiers did not take the kickback, and the Dauphin endorsed his brother's decisions favouring the Count of Armagnac. Diplomacy, bribery and intrigue had failed. Gaston resorted to armed intimidation. His hired bands of Anglo-Gascons and Navarrese began to ravage the Toulousain countryside, and then seized Auterive, on the most direct route between Toulouse and Catalonia. The Count of Poitiers denounced Gaston III as a rebel, and decreed the confiscation of his properties. Pope Innocent VI also intervened, to no avail, as the news from the north assured the Count of Foix of impunity.

More than three years after the battle of Poitiers, Edward III and the Dauphin had not yet been able to agree on conditions for the release of the King of France. While Jean II was ready to acquiesce to demands amounting to the cession of the western half of France, the Estates General of 1359 rejected the terms as utterly inacceptable. Edward III decided to settle the issue with one final blow, and in November, together with the Prince of Wales and the Duke of Lancaster, led a large army out of Calais: riding first through Picardy and northern Champagne, he headed for Reims, the traditional venue for the coronation of the kings of France. If his intention was to be crowned there, it was frustrated, largely by the banal difficulty of provisioning his army during the mid-winter siege of Reims, and afterwards by the war of slow attrition waged by the Dauphin. With the French refusing to do battle, while defending the walled towns, the English marched in a wide arc south of Paris, through country emptied of provisions. They were within reach of Normandy, and perhaps relief from hunger, when on 13 April 1360 the army was caught in the open plain of Chartres by a thunder and hail storm so murderous that some took it as a signal from Heaven to sue for peace. At any rate, the expedition had failed to achieve a military decision. The preliminaries of a peace treaty were signed on 7 May.

Meanwhile in Languedoc the Count of Foix had routed the city militia under the very walls of Toulouse, and set fire to the suburbs on the left bank of the Garonne, before retiring to Béarn. But he too had failed to achieve any substantial gain. Now, as the clauses of the treaty of Brétigny became known, they signified a radical alteration of the political map in the Midi. The centrepiece of the agreement was the creation of a Greater Aquitaine, adding to Gascony many of the provinces that Duchess Aliénor had held – or claimed – at the time of her marriage with Henry II Plantagenet: Poitou, Saintonge, the county of Angoulême, Limousin, Périgord, Quercy, Rouergue and, of most immediate concern to the Count of Foix, Bigorre. His adversaries were even more directly affected: Jean de Poitiers was not only losing his apanage, he was also summoned to serve, with his brother Louis d'Anjou, as one of the noble hostages to be held in England pending the payment of three million gold *écus* for the King's ransom. As for the Count of Armagnac, his lands now passed under the suzerainty of Edward III, but it was only with great reluctance that he eventually did homage to his new overlord, and the timing of his daughter's marriage with the Count of Poitiers, celebrated before the young prince's departure from Languedoc, was surely intended to proclaim his continued attachment to the French monarchy. Possibly because he understood that his greater peril would now come from the English ruler of Aquitaine, Gaston agreed to the mediation proposed by the Dauphin. The treaty he signed at Pamiers on 7 July did not directly address the territorial disputes underlying the Foix-Armagnac conflict, but a commission of jurists would be given the task of examining the respective rights of the two parties in Bigorre. Should the findings go against him, the Count of Foix was to be compensated with grants of properties in Languedoc. More immediately, the belligerents were to give back most of the towns they had taken, letters of remissions would be issued to exonerate Gaston III and his followers and, as a reward for their 'good will', the Estates of Languedoc would pay Fébus and Jean d'Armagnac indemnities of 200,000 florins each.

It became evident soon enough that neither of the two adversaries expected, or even desired, a lasting peace. The Count of Armagnac and his nephew the lord of Albret agreed 'never to make peace with the Count of Foix, *nor with his son*', without each other's consent.[17] This oath, exchanged before Gaston III had a legitimate heir, is a clear indication that his antagonists were preparing for a long dynastic struggle. Their conjunction made Béarn and Marsan vulnerable to attacks from the home base of the Albret clan in western Gascony, as well as from Armagnac on their eastern borders. For his part, Fébus was making the most of an opportunity to recruit from a vast pool of mercenary manpower. Thousands of soldiers of fortunes, idled by the cessation of Anglo-French hostilities and the reconciliation – however temporary – of Jean II and Charles of Navarre, continued to ravage almost every province of France. A royal army, sent to destroy them in April 1362, suffered a humiliating defeat at Brignais, in the Rhône valley. Far from being a leaderless rabble, the 'Companies', as they styled themselves, were highly organized, professional enterprises led by elected but seasoned captains. After Brignais, the French government negotiated with the chief warlords a treaty providing for their employment in Spain, where they would serve Peter IV of Aragon in his protracted war against Pedro I of Castile. The expedition was to be led by Pedro's half-brother and bitter rival, the bastard of Castile Enrique de Trastamara. However, an explicit clause of

---

[17] *Prince*, 102. Italics mine.

the treaty allowed the Companies to remain north of the Pyrenees in the event
of war between the counts of Foix and Armagnac offering them employment
closer at hand. While awaiting the promised advance payment, the Companies
assembled in September in the vicinity of Pamiers and Mazères in the county
of Foix, a logical staging area for crossing into Catalonia via the Puymorens
pass. It was also very convenient for Gaston III, who enlisted the most important of these bands. Although chroniclers often called them indifferently 'English', only one of the captains recruited by Fébus, John Amory, was an English-
man; the rest were an assortment of Gascons (Petit Meschin and Bertuquin)
Béarnais (Espiote) and German (Hazenorgue).[18]

Until the final outbreak there were various attempts at mediation, by the
Dauphin, the Pope and, repeatedly, by the King of Navarre, who is known to
have met with his brother-in-law at least twice – in December 1361, and again
on the occasion of the birth of a son to Gaston and Agnès, in September 1362.
Hardly ever moved by altruistic motives, Charles had probably no desire to
see either Foix or Armagnac dominant, or so exhausted that neither would be
able to check the expansion of English might in the South West. Conversely,
both counts may have been anxious to seize the opportunity – the delay in
the implementation of the treaty of Brétigny – for their show-down, while
there was time to act without interference from one of the suzerain powers. In
October Fébus wrote to Jean d'Armagnac a downright unctuous 'dear brother'
letter, warning him in veiled terms that his coalition, which now included
the counts of Comminges and Pardiac, the Viscount of Fezensac and a host
of lesser barons, was being watched. The Count of Armagnac replied with a
formal challenge, and the armies clashed near Launac, about 15 miles north-
west of Toulouse, on 5 December 1362.

Not surprisingly, the chroniclers of the House of Foix-Béarn, writing much
later, report that Fébus met the enemy with a relatively small force ('petita gent'
in du Bernis' chronicle), but better trained and devoted to him ('mas bona
gent, habila en armas et a lui fizels').[19] Although the Armagnac party, which
included so many of the Gascon nobility, had probably the advantage of numbers, it was an already obsolete feudal host of mounted knights trusting in their
courage and the shock of a frontal charge. Having left his Béarnais subjects to
defend their own country, Gaston's army was made up only of the men of Foix
– knights and town militias – and the mercenaries. But, while he deployed a
smaller cavalry, his infantry included a contingent of archers, skilled hunters
from the mountain districts of the county. The battle was over in half a day: it
appears that Fébus applied the English tactics co-ordinating the movements
of various corps, tactics familiar at least to the hired auxiliaries. The rout was
complete, and the haul of prisoners spectacular. The roster was headed by Jean

[18]  Kenneth Fowler, *Medieval Mercenaries*, I (Oxford, 2001), 64.

[19]  *Ibid.*, 65.

d'Armagnac, the counts of Comminges and Montlezun, Arnaud-Amanieu d'Albret, his brothers and his cousins, and dozens of lesser lords and captains.

There is no doubt that the ransoms he collected after Launac were the foundation of the fortune he is known to have hoarded in the Moncade Tower of Orthez. While the total reported by Froissart ('ten times one hundred thousand francs') may be dismissed as a rhetorical flourish, more sober accounts agree on a minimum of 600,000 florins, equivalent to more than 2 metric tons of gold. The most heavy ransoms were those of Jean d'Armagnac (300,000 florins) and his nephew the lord of Albret (100,000 florins), followed by that of the Count of Comminges (50,000 florins). It is estimated that the minimum amount demanded from a mere knight was 1,500 florins.[20] The amounts were not negotiated, but unilaterally fixed by the Count of Foix, who moreover refused to honour the convention then current and let his prisoners free on parole. They were assigned residences in Gaston's castles at Foix, Pamiers, and Mazères, where they promised to remain until 'the fourth day after Easter' of 1363. But even after a peace was solemnly proclaimed at Foix on 14 April, the leading members of the unlucky coalition were kept as guarantors of the full payment of all ransoms. Despite further intercessions by the Pope and the King of Navarre, Jean d'Armagnac was able to discharge his debt only in 1365, by the 'sale' to Fébus of two strategic seigniories between Bigorre and Comminges.

At the time of the battle of Launac, Gaston Fébus was thirty-one years old – no longer a youth, by medieval reckoning, but still very much in his prime. He had survived a period of imprudent entanglements and far-away adventures, and now found himself the richest lord in the entire Midi. He was also showing undoubted political restraint by resisting the temptation to exploit his victory for territorial gains that could have put him on a collision course with Edward, Prince of Wales, and now Prince of Aquitaine. It is a recurring fact of history that territory ceded almost always becomes disputed territory, whereas money paid is written off as a definitive loss. Barrels of florins, on the whole, were easier to keep and defend than expanded frontiers; moreover, their acquisition had drained the treasury of Gaston's adversaries as surely as the loss of lands, and more discreetly. In the aftermath of Launac one can already discern the guiding principles of Fébus' future policy of unobtrusive, but effective regional dominance. Last but not least, the birth of an heir – named Gaston, in accordance with the custom of Béarn – less than three months before the decisive battle, now promised the dynastic stability that was craved as much by his subjects as by the Count of Foix himself.

Given these circumstances, Fébus' abrupt dismissal of his wife seems to defy all rational explanations. His stated grievance was the failure by Navarre

[20] *Ibid.*, 67, and *Vicomté*, 90–2.

to pay the outstanding balance of Agnès' dowry. In view of the enormous wind-fall he was about to reap, this was, as Pope Urban V would bluntly put it, a mere pretext.[21] Why Gaston III chose the moment of his triumph to humiliate not only the mother of his newborn son, but also his dangerous brother-in-law Charles of Navarre, remains an unanswered question. However it may be explained, the deed was done with a degree of discourtesy that suggests deep-seated rancour, and motives more intimate than a stale dispute over money owed since 1349. Shortly after Christmas 1362, while Fébus was still in Foix, his half-brother Arnaud-Guilhem was sent to Orthez with the mission of con-veying to Agnès her husband's order, and escorting her to Pamplona. Ostensi-bly the Count merely dispatched his wife to Navarre, with mission to retrieve the unpaid dowry – but she was told not to return without the money. Agnès understood well enough the definitive reality of her exodus: she had already packed her personal jewels and other valuables when Arnaud-Guilhem gave orders to unload the pack mules. In a deposition given in 1391, she recalled having managed to take away, besides her underclothes, only one tapestry, a fur coat and a dozen silver cups.[22] Her newborn son remained at Orthez in his father's custody. As a consequence of the *de facto* repudiation of Agnès, the child would remain the only legitimate son of the Count of Foix, sole direct heir 'of his body'. Given the high rate of infant mortality then prevailing, it was at best a tenuous hope, at worst a gamble all of one piece with Gaston III's life-long failure to make a last will and testament. And, of course, no one could have foreseen then that, as the consequences of Gaston's callous decree matured in the shadow of larger events, the boy would be one day the protagonist of their tragic dénouement.

---

[21] *Vicomté*, III, n. 19.

[22] *Prince*, 113.

Fébus' signature

# PART II

# The Accomplishment

# ✦ 5 ✦
## Challenges and Designs

IT was an impulse natural to feudal magnates to try and achieve as much political and legal independence as they could exact from their royal over-lords. The eventual triumph of centralizing monarchies would make such centrifugal proclivities appear as retrograde movements against the flow of history – provincial obscurantism and feudal greed impeding for a time the formation of the indivisible national state. However, the resurgence in the twentieth century of many regional *particularismes* hitherto believed extinct, suggest that the wish to be master in one's own house was by no means the monopoly of medieval nobles, and that their resistance to royal hegemony could sometimes reflect their subjects' desires for a measure of self-governance and a distinct cultural identity. It remains to be seen whether we can read in Gaston III's external relations the grand design that has sometimes been suggested.[1] But it is safe to say that his policy did not greatly differ from those of other territorial seigneurs, and that his aims were not at variance with the needs and aspirations of at least his Béarnais subjects.

The ransoms from his victory at Launac had made the Count of Foix one of the richest – if not *the* richest – lord between Gascony and Languedoc. Should he want to do so, his new found wealth of ready cash could now afford him the means, military and political, to tip the balance between the greater contending powers of the region. But as he counted his florins, he showed no haste to align himself with either France or England, although both claimed him as a vassal. From the beginning of his reign, his attitude towards them had indeed been ambiguous. While his father had served Philippe VI in far-away Flanders, Gaston III had only discharged his liege obligations to the King of France insofar as that service also coincided with his own regional interests, whether patrolling his lands of Marsan and Gavardan with troops paid by the French treasury, or buying political capital in Languedoc with a neighbourly rush to the defence of Toulouse. Moreover, he had clearly enunciated, as early as 1347, the conviction that he held the viscounty of Béarn 'from no man in the world', and he continued to style himself, like his predecessors and in usurpation of royal prerogative, Count of Foix 'by the grace of God'. Relations with the Valois had been further strained by Gaston's perceived complicity in the treasonable activities of his brother-in-law Charles of Navarre, and his own private war against the Count of

---

[1] *Vicomté*, 301–16.

France, Aquitaine and the Iberian Kingdoms

Armagnac – then the King's Lieutenant – had brought them very near the breaking point.

Towards England, Gaston III had maintained a correct, sometimes even friendly, but always circumspect posture. His helpful neutrality during the Prince of Wales' *chevauchée* of 1355 had been prompted in part by prudence, in part by the interests and opinions of his Béarnais subjects, but also by the opportunity to ravage the lands of Armagnac. After Poitiers, however, the Count of Foix had been quick to perceive the new danger posed for him by a shift in the balance of military power in the South West. Despite the cordial appearances of their meeting of November 1355, he did not trust the Prince of Wales. To be sure, the English army had scrupulously respected the lands of Foix-Béarn, and even refrained from burning towns in which the Count held some property. But Gaston III understood that the Prince's restraint was dictated by the tactical needs of the moment: far from his home base in Gascony, he could ill afford to alienate a willing source of provisions, let alone risk provoking a hostile reaction. When, shortly thereafter, the King of Aragon required the Count's service as vassal and ally in his war against Castile, and Gaston invoked a potential English threat to Béarn as the excuse for delaying his intervention, he was not entirely disingenuous. In 1357 he would also seek assurances of the Prince's peaceful intentions before embarking on his voyage to Prussia. More recently, if the troops mustered for the campaign leading to the battle of Launac included none of the feudal levies from Béarn, that was because their paramount duty was to be the defence of the viscounty against both the real threat from the Armagnac foe, and the potential one from Anglo-Gascony.

But after Launac the Count of Foix could no longer avoid dealing directly with the issue underlying those apprehensions. He was undoubtedly aware of Béarn's historical ties to the duchy of Aquitaine, and equally of the fact that his predecessors had steadily whittled down that allegiance. Upon his accession in 1314 Gaston II had not done homage to the King of England; in 1354 a detailed survey of Edward III's possessions in southern Gascony, while it covered Marsan and Gavardan, did not include a single village in Béarn.[2] Although this omission might have been taken as a tacit abandonment of the King-Duke's claim of suzerainty, Gaston III could not, and clearly did not, expect that the issue had been put to rest. But if his refusal to acknowledge the French king as his overlord in Béarn was also meant to be heard in Bordeaux and in Westminster, he could not have foreseen the French defeat at Poitiers nor the extent to which it would alter the political map of the South West.

Signed in May 1360 and ratified in October, the treaty of Brétigny effectively recreated the Greater Aquitaine that Duchess Aliénor had bequeathed to her Plantagenet heirs: to the Gascon hinterlands of Bordeaux and Bayonne were restored Poitou and Saintonge, Périgord and Quercy, Angoulême, Armagnac and, next door to Béarn, the county of Bigorre. On every side the viscounty was now surrounded by English possessions. But the application of the treaty on the ground was far from immediate, as many cities and territorial lords were reluctant to transfer their allegiances to the English Crown. The Count of Armagnac would not do homage to Edward III until 1363; after he was captured at Launac, it was to his former suzerain, the King of France, that he turned for mediation. Nevertheless, Edward's deputies proceeded in newly ceded districts with the formal transfer of sovereignty. Thus, while Sir John Chandos was dispatched to receive the submissions of Agen and of the contentious citizens of Cahors and Rodez, Adam de Houghton came to Tarbes in January 1362 to take possession of Bigorre, and soon thereafter informed the Count of Foix that he

[2] *Ibid.*, 93.

was empowered to receive his homage. Some six weeks later, Gaston replied that he did not consider it proper for a lord of his standing to swear his fealty to a mere envoy, but that he would gladly proceed with the ceremony of homage when King Edward made his progress in Aquitaine. This somewhat disingenuous concern with etiquette (some years later, Fébus would see nothing wrong with delegating his cousin Pierre-Arnaud to convey his homage to the King of Aragon) not only postponed the issue to a yet unknown future date, and at the same time kept it vague enough to avoid specific reference to Béarn.

The Count of Foix was only one of the many new vassals of Edward III who showed reluctance to acknowledge his suzerainty. The naming of the Prince of Wales as Prince of Aquitaine, serving notice that there would be in Bordeaux a reigning Plantagenet, was intended in part to address that problem. The effect, however, was not immediate, as almost a whole year passed before the Prince, invested on 19 July 1362 with all the powers of the Crown, arrived in Aquitaine. In the interval Gaston III had defeated and captured scores of his Gascon subjects; under French auspices he had also concluded a peace treaty with the Count of Armagnac, and he had collected the first instalments of his sudden fortune in ransoms. It must have been quite clear to the Prince that this was not the best moment to try and force the issue of the homage for Béarn. Nor was Gaston, despite his new-found wealth, ready for an open break. He temporized: while Froissart's account of a supposed meeting at Tarbes is highly suspect, the Count at least showed his good will by allowing the lord of Albret – then still his prisoner – to travel to the Prince's court for the ceremony of homage. But for himself, he invoked legalistic scruples, saying that he could swear fealty to Edward only in the presence of French Crown officers empowered to release him from his allegiance to their King.

The Prince of Wales granted this new request, and so the invitation to attend him at Agen on 12 January 1364 was one that the Count, having run out of excuses, could no longer put off. But before leaving Orthez, he ordered his secretariat, on 1 January, to make an apparently minor change in the redaction of official acts: from now on, Gaston III – and his successors – would be styled, not *vicecomes Bearni*, but *dominus Bearni*. This was not an insignificant detail. The titles of count and viscount had originally been those of royal officers; but even after they had become hereditary, they were still perceived as denoting a nobleman's place in the feudal hierarchy, and the dependence of his fief on the pleasure of an overlord. But, while the Viscount must have held the viscounty from an earthly suzerain, the lord – *dominus* – of Béarn held it, as he had already indicated in 1347, 'from God and from no man in this world', and therefore owed no allegiance for it to any duke, prince or king. The meaning was clear. Nevertheless, should anyone find the Latin formula obscure, the same change was soon found in acts recorded in the vernacular, with *senhor* replacing *vescounte* de Béarn – an even stronger affirmation, for in old Béarnais, the word *senhor* denoted ownership, rather than nobility: a mere peasant could be *senhor de l'ostau* – lord of the house. An occasional flourish referred to Gaston III as *lo senhor senhoreyant en Bearn* (literally: 'the lord lording in Béarn'), and the Morlaàs mint followed suit, with coins bearing the formula *Gratia Dei Dominus Bearni.*[3] The timing of this bureaucratic directive marks it as the equivalent of occupying the high ground on the eve of a battle. Significantly, it is also at that time that the Count began to sign official documents with his chosen cognomen Fébus, a practice that would soon become routine. Gaston was indeed preparing, not for a frontal assault, but for yet another legalistic manoeuvre.

The event itself was minutely recorded by the Prince's notary. On the appointed date the Count of Foix duly appeared at the Dominican convent in Agen, and there, before a distinguished array of witnesses – the Constable of Bordeaux, the Chancellor of Aquitaine, the Duke of Brittany, the Earl of Warwick, etc. – Sir John Chandos presented him to the Prince of Wales, a purely ceremonial introduction, since the two men were already personally acquainted since November 1355. Next Chandos announced that the King had delegated the Prince to receive homages on his behalf; he then asked the Count to declare himself the liege of Edward III. The stipulation of homage liege, involving heavier and more specific obligations than the homage simple, was a departure from the traditional feudal relations between the dukes of Aquitaine and their Gascon vassals, and it clearly signalled Edward's intention to bind them more closely than ever before to the English Crown. It was then the turn of the French Crown officers to formally release the Count from allegiance to the King of France for his fiefs in Gascony. And at long last Gaston III, kneeling unbelted and bareheaded, placed his hands between the hands of the Prince of Wales, declared himself the liege of King Edward, received the ritual kiss from the Prince, and swore to uphold his fealty.

The ritual was repeated, the Prince now receiving the homage to himself as Prince of Aquitaine. In neither of the two ceremonies had there been a specific enumeration of the fiefs Gaston acknowledged he held from his English overlords. Perhaps he hoped that the issue would not be raised then and there, and that he could later, and from a safer distance, reiterate his position with regard to Béarn. But the Prince and his advisers knew very well what the elusive Count was about, and before he could make his exit, Chandos asked pointedly 'if he had done this homage for the viscounty of Béarn'. This time there was no further evasion. Or so it seemed, but Fébus again parried the thrust: his homage was given for the viscounties of Marsan and Gavardan; concerning 'the land of Béarn', he would do 'what he must reasonably', when and if he was given satisfactory proof (*en fourme suffisante*) that he held it from any man. It was a masterful move: while refusing homage for Béarn, the Count seemed to leave an opening for further negotiations, and the burden was now on the Prince's lawyers to produce documentary proof of Béarn's dependency, proof

[3] *Ibid.*, 95, 109–10.

that Gaston surely knew would not be easy to find. It was also a calculated risk, but if the Prince was irritated by this unexpected turn of events, he probably could not avoid at least a moment of doubt about the status of Béarn. Whether, as Froissart relates, it was Chandos who advised against any precipitous reaction, the Count of Foix was allowed to withdraw unmolested, and lost no time in riding back to Orthez.

This was not quite the end of the affair: in a letter dated 18 July 1365 the Prince summoned Fébus to his court. The Count, remembering his arrest of 1356 at the French court – a misadventure perhaps not unconnected with the issue of homage for Béarn – may have feared for his safety. The Prince reiterated his invitation to discuss 'important business', and provided a safe-conduct for the Count and a retinue of 200 knights. Fébus then pleaded 'a sick leg' that kept him at home, a lame excuse if ever there was one, and utterly mendacious. The Prince made it clear to his 'most dear and faithful cousin' that he did not believe a word of it, but nevertheless dispatched a physician bearing a renewed invitation. Fébus, who naturally had recovered before the doctor arrived at Orthez, thanked Edward for his attention, but did not budge. According some sources, Gaston may have eventually met the Prince, after ensuring that English hostages be sent to Orthez to guarantee his safety. If the interview took place, it did not produce the desired result, for in December 1365 Edward III wrote to Charles V, asking him to use his authority to make the Count comply with the terms of the treaty of Brétigny. Nothing suggests that the King of France, who had no such obligation, might have done so. As for the search of the English royal archives, it had failed to turn up the desired proof of Béarn's vassal status. Having reached an impasse, the Prince of Wales commanded Gaston III to give homage for Béarn 'as Madame Marguerite had done to the seneschal of Gascony in 1290'.[4] By the end of the year, the imminence of the French intervention in Spain, which in effect made the Peninsula a surrogate battlefield of the Anglo-French conflict, would have given pause to the Prince of Aquitaine, and made him reflect that the time was not the best for a war with a recalcitrant and by no means defenceless vassal.

In the next century Gaston III's refusal to do homage for Béarn to the Plantagenets was embellished with several anecdotes. He is said to have sent the Prince a letter illustrated with the mocking sketch of three figs. A more decorous variant was cited in 1428 by the reigning Count of Foix in a memorandum of his house's long-time devotion to the French Crown: it tells how Fébus had presented himself before the Prince, wearing a robe adorned with fleurs-de-lis. To the Prince's query: 'Cousin, are you French then?' the Count then replied: 'I am within as I am without', and opened his robe to show the lining similarly decorated. In fact, far from such needless provocations, the tone of Gaston's

---

[4] Reference to the daughter of Gaston VII Moncade, Viscountess of Béarn in her own right, and wife of Roger Bernard III of Foix. Cited in *Prince*, 122.

letters to his 'most dear and redoubted lord' is downright ingratiating, and almost chatty when, as he promises to come, he suggests that the Prince gather 'all of Chandos' hounds and as many as you can have, and I shall show you something of my knowledge [of the hunt]'. But, apocryphal as they are, these stories suggest that public opinion, and that of his successors, regarded Gaston's resistance to English pretensions as an accomplishment worth celebrating with an occasional flourish. For that matter, the Count did not just wait for the applause of posterity. Almost certainly commissioned by Fébus, two Latin motets from a manuscript probably compiled between 1360 and 1365 praise him with sometimes obscure political allusions. But the words of *Febus mundo oriens* are crystal clear: 'the flourishing Count / Shows himself to be French / And the false discourse perishes / That called him English.'[5]

Gaston III was certainly not 'English'. But to say that he 'showed himself' 'French' somewhat stretches the truth. In the past decade he had consorted with both of Jean II's most dangerous enemies – the Prince of Wales and the King of Navarre – and waged war on the King's Lieutenant. Now, while personally estranged from Agnès and her family, his attitude towards the Navarrese party was at best ambiguous. After the King had denied his claim to Burgundy and seized the duchy, Charles II had taken the offensive, using troops made available by the Anglo-French truce. With the connivance of Edward III and his son, Navarrese reinforcements sailed from Gascony to Charles' bases in Normandy. There, a few days before the coronation of Charles V, an Anglo-Gascon Navarrese army, led by Fébus' cousin Jean de Grailly, suffered a crushing defeat at Cocherel, with the Captal himself taken prisoner. Undaunted, Charles of Navarre pressed on with the preparation for an attack on Burgundy. On its north-easterly march from Saint-Palais, where it was mustered, the army led by the King's brother Louis de Navarre must have traversed, if not Béarn proper, at least Marsan and Gavardan. Fébus' duty to spare his subjects the hazards of warfare might have been invoked for allowing the Navarrese free passage. Harder to justify was the fact that the hiring of leading mercenary captains had been negotiated at Orthez in April–May 1364 under his auspices.[6] On the other hand, there is at least one piece of evidence to suggest that, as he met with his brother-in-law at Saint-Palais, the Count of Foix attempted to broker a reconciliation between the kings of France and of Navarre.

MORE prudent than the young Gaston of 1347, the mature Fébus was nevertheless determined to uphold the principle of Béarn's independence from any earthly suzerain. Knowing that the Prince of Wales would not tolerate his defiance much longer, his dilatory manœuvres entailed a degree

5 '... comes floreus / Ostendit se Guallicum / Perit sermo felleus / Em dicens Anglicum.' In Castéret, 95–9, 150.

6 Fowler, 99; Sumption, II, 515.

of calculated risk, but he may well have taken it with the conviction that time was on his side. Propagated by minstrels, the protestations of his pro-French sentiment suggest that Gaston probably shared the view held by the Valois, that there was nothing final about Brétigny. Having only agreed to that treaty in order to secure the release of Jean II, they were by no means resigned to the loss of French sovereignty over Greater Aquitaine, and the issue of the juridical status of the principality remained unsolved after the accession of Charles V. While the new King resisted the pressure to resume the war prematurely, he appointed his brother Louis d'Anjou, the most vocal leader of the war party, as his Lieutenant in Languedoc. From his court in Toulouse the energetic Duke could be counted on to undermine the Prince's efforts to control his new and often reluctant subjects, and to prepare for the eventual resumption of hostilities.

At the end of 1365, however, that day was only the hope of a vague future. The Prince of Wales, having helped them pay off their Launac ransoms, had received the homages of the Albrets and of Jean d'Armagnac. Fébus was now isolated, and hemmed in by enemies who would be only too glad to obey their overlord in any action against him. But events beyond the Pyrenees gave the Prince of Aquitaine no time to deal with the recalcitrant lord of Béarn. At Christmas, the Breton captain Bertrand du Guesclin – the victor at Cocherel – and other *condottieri* in French service were feasting at Barcelona as guests of Peter IV. The ostensible purpose of their Iberian expedition was a 'crusade' against the Moors of Granada. The real one was to employ as many as possible of the mercenary companies that had been ravaging France since they had been idled by the truce. Less well publicized was the fact that Du Guesclin's mission was to depose Pedro I 'the Cruel' of Castile, and install on his throne his half-brother Enrique de Trastamara, a bastard of Alfonso XI. Unaware of this, the Prince of Wales had given to several of the most prominent English and Gascon captains, who were his vassals, permission to join Du Guesclin's army. Indeed, chivalry required the Prince to allow them to take up the Cross, and to facilitate the purging of brigands from the beleaguered French countryside. The view from Westminster was more realistic: the principal misdeed for which Pedro was to be 'punished' was his abandonment of the French alliance, and the long-range political goal of the 'crusade' was to ensure the restoration of that pact by Don Enrique, a long-time client of the French King. Edward III ordered his son to recall the English captains who marched with Du Guesclin, but by the time the Prince could act on his father's instructions, it was too late: on Easter Sunday Enrique de Trastamara had been crowned at Burgos. By the end of May 1366 Pedro had fled from Seville. A fugitive unwelcome in Portugal, he made his way to Galicia where, only pausing long enough to massacre the archbishop and the dean of Santiago de Compostela, he sailed in mid-summer for Bayonne.

Anxious no doubt to redeem his earlier blunder, the Prince received the deposed monarch with all due honours and started negotiating terms for an English intervention to restore Pedro to the throne of Castile. On 23 September the treaty of Libourne committed the Prince to the invasion, while Pedro promised to defray the costs and pay him 550,000 florins. Edward would also be granted the county of Biscay. Charles of Navarre was also a party to the treaty: his military contribution, and more importantly free passage through his land, would be rewarded by the cession of Guipuzcoa and other Castilian territory – and 200,000 florins.[7] Even before the treaty's conclusion, the Prince had begun to recruit forces for the forthcoming campaign: the English garrison in Gascony was augmented with mercenaries, archers from England, and contingents led by Edward's Gascon vassals, chief among them the lord of Albret and the Count of Armagnac. From his nearby vantage point of Orthez, Fébus did not look on that armament without some misgivings, which he shared with the King of Aragon. Peter IV, who had lent his support to the dethroning of Pedro I, also had cause to fear an Anglo-Castilian-Navarrese alliance, but he made no move to try and forestall the English intervention. Meanwhile, some at least of the English-led mercenary bands had been recalled from Spain to Gascony. This was another potential threat to Fébus, as their shortest route to Dax, where the Prince was mustering his army, would take them through Béarn. Froissart reports that Chandos, who had been delegated to supervise the operation, asked the Count to allow their passage 'through a corner of his land', probably the westernmost district, between Sauveterre and Orthez. Whether this alleged request for Fébus' permission amounted to a tacit recognition of Béarn's independence is debatable, but what follows makes it clear that, at least for the moment, the Prince was not yet ready to use force against him. After obtaining assurances of the companies' good behaviour during their transit through Béarn, Fébus graciously consented. In fulfilment of his vassal duties as Viscount of Marsan and Gavardan, he also sent a token contingent to the Anglo-Gascon host, and even came to Dax to greet the Prince and his brother John of Gaunt with 'a great deal of curtseying and fair semblance'.[8] Then, instead of joining the expedition, he returned home to organize the defence of Béarn.

For the present, however, and probably for sound strategic reasons, the viscounty remain unmolested: the army, under the nominal command of Pedro I, entered Spain through the Roncevaux pass in February 1367. On 3 April the Trastamara usurper and his allies were routed at Najera. While many of his

[7] P. E. Russell, *The English Intervention in Spain and Portugal in the Time of Edward III and Richard II* (Oxford, 1955), 63–9. The author notes (66, n. 3) that the grant of Biscay to the Prince of Wales violated the traditional privilege of the Basques to choose their own lord.

[8] *Chroniques*. VII, 149. No translation can quite render the discreetly sardonic flavour of Froissart's 'grand chère et grant révérence de bras et semblant'.

noble Spanish followers were taken, together with Du Guesclin and the French Marshal d'Audrehem, Don Enrique was led to safety by the Aragonese knight Pedro de Luna – the future cardinal and anti-pope Benedict XIII. His stay in Aragon was brief: fearing that Peter IV might want to ingratiate himself with the Prince of Wales by betraying him, Enrique slipped away and arrived at Orthez towards the end of May. Fébus received him graciously, but was glad to provide his embarrassing guest with the means to move on to Toulouse, where he was welcome by Louis d'Anjou. It may be a testimonial to Fébus that, when the Count had as much cause as the King of Aragon to fear an English attack, Enrique trusted him to honour the obligation of chivalry to a fugitive.

It was to be expected that when he returned from Castile that summer the victorious Prince of Wales would try, before disbanding his army, to resolve by force his differences with the Count of Foix – and Fébus clearly expected it. True to the defiant motto *Toquey si gauses* (Touch me if you dare), he took unprecedented measures to make the viscounty ready for any eventuality. The orders issued from Orthez between May and July amounted to a general mobilization. Every able-bodied man was to ready himself for a muster at Orthez on 15 August, with arms and mounts; equipment would be provided for those who had none; the sale of horses abroad was prohibited; ready or not, corn and hay were to be harvested and stored in walled towns; livestock were also to leave their summer pastures for the safety of fortified places. In every village the bailiffs were to organize a twenty-four hour watch, and the men of the high valley communities were charged with surveillance of the mountain passes and trails 'so that no suspicious or foreign person, *such as those who have been to Spain and are returning hither*, may enter the country.'[9] One could not have pointed more explicitly to the Prince's army as the potential enemy.

Even for a fresh, combat-ready force, the Béarnais hedgehog would have been a hard one to approach, let alone swallow. But the English army returning in August was no longer the mighty host that had mustered at Dax in January. After their great victory at Najera, Don Pedro had been unable – and probably unwilling – to raise the half-million florins pledged to the Prince, or even to help meet the campaign expenses. He had gone on to Seville, leaving his allies to manage as best they could with promises of forthcoming payment. Hardly recovered from the hard winter campaign, the army had then suffered the torrid Castilian summer, foraging for dwindling supplies of food in notoriously poor and increasingly hostile country, while waiting for the restored king to honour his word. Famine and dysentery took such a heavy toll that, according to some reports, only one fifth of the original army was able to return to Gascony. The Prince himself had fallen ill, of an ailment from which he would not recover. Such were, in Froissart's estimation, the circumstances that spared Fébus and Béarn a war that had, only a few months before, appeared inevitable:

---

[9] *Vicomté*, 102. Emphasis mine.

the Prince 'was often tempted to make war on those lords of Upper Gascony, and would have done so in the season when he went to Spain, if the voyage had not broken him, and then, more and more, he had so much to do, that he could not cope.' From the chronicler's remarks, the issue thus resolved by default was quite clear: '... the Count of Foix wanted to keep his people free, and he said that by right they were his, belonging neither to the King of France nor to the King of England.'[10]

The *de facto* abandonment of the English claim of suzerainty over Béarn was not the only consequence of that disastrous campaign, nor the most damaging for the Greater Aquitaine envisaged after Brétigny. In Castile, what had been accomplished at Najera was soon dissipated: no sooner had the Prince returned to Gascony than Enrique de Trastamara again entered Spain with 400 lances. The Pretender enjoyed at least the passive support of Fébus: not only his troops had been allowed to gather in the county of Foix, but the largest contingent was led by a 'Bastard of Béarn' who is generally believed to have been the son of a precocious Gaston III (see Appendix). If he was, it is quite possible that the mercenaries he led had been recruited with Fébus' florins. The Trastamara reconquest gained momentum after Du Guesclin, ransomed at last, joined Don Enrique with fresh troops in July 1368. Then, less than two years after Najera, the defeat, capture and murder of Pedro at Montiel in March 1369 effected a definitive change of régime in Castile, and bought France a strategic ally.

In Aquitaine the days of the principality were also numbered. Even during the Spanish campaign, there had been signs of disaffection. The Count of Armagnac and the lord of Albret, who had hoped that rich rewards in Castile would help restore their fortunes devastated by the ransoms after Launac, had quarrelled with the Prince and gone home. Also cheated of his expected reward, unable to pay his troops, Edward then attempted to raise funds by imposing an unprecedented hearth tax on all his subjects. The measure met with immediate opposition in Gascony: already hard pressed, Jean d'Armagnac refused to allow collection of the Prince's *fouage* in his lands, and many other seigneurs followed his lead. With a greater display of arrogance than he could afford, the Prince threatened confiscation of fiefs. The Gascon lords, making the most of the juridical limbo in which the treaty of Brétigny had left Aquitaine, appealed to the King of France as the Prince's nominal suzerain. After collecting opinions from the foremost legal authorities in Christendom, Charles V agreed to hear the appeal, and summoned the Prince of Wales to appear before the Paris Parlement. Thus the charade of 1337 was re-enacted: in May 1369 the herald called the Prince's name. His failure to respond was duly recorded, and the duchy was declared confiscated. A month later, Edward III revived his claim to the French Crown. But war in the Midi had started long before those ceremonies.

---

[10] *Chroniques*, VIII, 313.

Throughout the next decade the Count of Foix reacted with his now accustomed mix of firmness and caution to a radically altered balance of power. A new pragmatism – clearly displayed in the appointment of the low-born Du Guesclin as Constable – now informed the renewed French will to fight. With the royal dukes of Burgundy and Berry sharing in the leadership, Poitou and Saintonge were all but completely recovered by the end of 1373. Famous casualties included John Chandos, killed in 370, and the Captal de Buch, taken prisoner again in 1372. Charles V having refused him ransom, Fébus' cousin and once his fellow-paladin would die four years later in a Paris dungeon. The Prince of Wales had gone home to England in 1371. In July 1373 his brother John of Gaunt, Duke of Lancaster, who had been made the King's Lieutenant in Aquitaine, led a grand *chevauchée* from Calais, hoping perhaps to provoke another Poitiers or Crécy, but Charles V's orders to avoid battle was obeyed, and the English army, harried by skirmishers, was drawn ever deeper into hostile and depleted country, until only a sorry troop of dismounted knights reached Bordeaux in December. Lancaster, having accomplished nothing, found an already diminished Aquitaine, now more than ever on the defensive.

Since the resumption of hostilities, Louis d'Anjou had been busy dismantling the outer perimeter of the principality. After regaining control of its easternmost regions – Rouergue and Quercy – as far as mid-way down the Garonne valley, the Duke turned southward, and by July 1370 he had occupied most of the county of Bigorre, with the exception of the two strongholds of Mauvezin and Lourdes. Bound as Charles V's Lieutenant by very precise instructions, Anjou placed the county in the hands of vassals and allies of the Count of Armagnac. For his part, the Count of Foix had clearly seen that Armagnac's leadership of the Gascon revolt against the Prince of Wales signalled a resurgence of the adversary he had crushed at Launac. Although the control of Bigorre was of paramount importance to the security of Béarn, Fébus was anxious to avoid a direct confrontation with Louis d'Anjou. This did not, however, prevent him, as early as 1369, from enlisting bands of marauders for raids into the lands of Albret and Armagnac. His adversaries paid him back in kind, notably with incursions in the viscounty of Marsan. This petty warfare, while it amounted to little more than arson and cattle-rustling, was serious enough for the populations subjected to it, and for the Pope to mediate a truce signed only after five years of mutual ravages.

The provenance of some troops fielded by the Count of Foix is symptomatic of the discrepancies in a complex and sometimes absurd web of formal allegiances and contractual obligations. The mercenaries known as the Companions of Lourdes held that castle in the name of the King of England, but their captain was a kinsman of Fébus, Pierre-Arnaud de Béarn, the son of a bastard of Gaston I. Contrary to the dramatic anecdote in which Froissart relates his premature death at the hand of Fébus, there can be little doubt that Pierre-

Arnaud was a trusted lieutenant of the lord of Béarn. Operating under the guise of an 'English' garrison, and more often as independent freebooters, the Companions' connection with Fébus long remained deniable, but as a permanent exception to the Franco-Armagnac control of Bigorre, and a base for raids into the lowlands, Lourdes certainly served his designs. Mauvezin, the other fortress commanding trade routes through the county, belonged to another of Fébus' cousins, Roger-Bernard de Castelbon, but it was garrisoned by Béarnais troops under the command of Raymond l'Aspois (Froissart's 'Raymonnet de l'Espee'). The Viscount of Castelbon had not joined the other seigneurs of Bigorre in their revolt against English rule, and thus Mauvezin, like Lourdes, was held in the name of Edward III.

Left to his own devices, the Duke of Anjou might have come to mutually acceptable terms with Fébus. He was in a position to evaluate the military and economic strength of the Count of Foix, as well as his popularity in the region. But Louis' efforts to convince his brother the King of the need for a more balanced policy in the Midi were countered by the successful lobbying of the Armagnac-Albret party at court. That clan had effective support from the Duke of Berry – Jean d'Armagnac's son-in-law – and Armagnac's nephew Arnaud-Amanieu d'Albret gained another foothold in the royal entourage by his 1372 marriage with Marguerite de Bourbon, a sister of the Queen of France. Anjou was sharply ordered to break off his unauthorized negotiations with the Count of Foix. Fébus responded in August by attacking several Armagnac towns in a swift march from Béarn to Foix, a pointed demonstration of his military capabilities. Another truce was mediated by Pope Gregory XI and signed shortly before the death of Jean I d'Armagnac on 15 May 1373. Meanwhile, Louis d'Anjou, determined to gain complete control of Bigorre, was gathering his forces for attacks on Mauvezin and Lourdes. After a brief but spirited resistance, the Béarnais garrison of Mauvezin surrendered for lack of water. At the end of June, Louis had moved on to Lourdes. The castle proved impregnable by assault, and the Duke lacked not only the resources, but the time for a prolonged siege: by then Lancaster had begun his circuitous *chevauchée* through the whole length of France, and Charles V recalled his brother to the defence of lands north of the Garonne. Before leaving Bigorre, Louis concluded a truce with the Companions of Lourdes, whereby they promised not to molest French subjects.

It may well have been the Duke's intention, after taking Lourdes, to seek an armed showdown with Gaston III, and perhaps to impose a settlement of that perennial cause of instability in the sub-Pyrenean region, the Foix-Armagnac rivalry. Such was at any rate the eventuality against which Fébus once again mobilized the defences of Béarn. Many years later his retainer Espan de Lion would thus remember that 'in that season, the Count of Foix greatly feared the Duke of Anjou, for he saw him so near and did not know what he had in mind.' Froissart's travelling companion then recites the list of contingents despatched to various garrisons (including Espan himself, to Mont-de-Marsan with 200 lances) and concludes: 'there was no castle in all of Béarn that was not well provided with soldiers, and [the Count] remained in his castle of Orthez, close to his florins.'[11] (The last phrase, evoking a miserly dragon crouching on his hoard, may well be an interpolation by the chronicler.) But the Duke, hastening to Périgord, had no time and perhaps no great desire for a direct confrontation with Fébus. Nevertheless, after skirting the eastern border of Béarn on his northward march, he vented his ill-humour on lightly defended Marsan.

Louis d'Anjou's campaign in Bigorre had only achieved half its object, with the capture of Mauvezin. The castle was now granted to the new Count of Armagnac, Jean II 'the Fat', who was also given the provisional lieutenancy of Languedoc during the Duke's absence. This was more than Fébus could swallow: the affront of the raid in Marsan gave him a pretext for breaking a fragile truce and renew his own incursions into Albret and Armagnac territory. But Lourdes remained under the command of his kinsmen, whose promise with respect to the King's subjects could scarcely be taken seriously. Moreover, the castle was still nominally English, a circumstance that would soon provide Fébus with the opportunity to demonstrate the superiority of purchasing power over military might.

Early in 1374 the Duke of Lancaster had sufficiently recovered from his dismal *chevauchée* across France to plan another English venture in Spain. Married to Doña Constança, eldest daughter of the murdered Pedro I of Castile, John of Gaunt now claimed that crown as his wife's inheritance. His financial resources were inadequate to provide for both the defence of Aquitaine and an expedition against the Trastamara usurper, but it was at that juncture that the Count of Foix showed himself most obliging. While we do not know who initiated the negotiations, Fébus and the Pretender met at Dax on 19 March, there to sign two joint document. The first was a loan agreement, whereby Fébus advanced 12,000 florins to John, and received as security the castle of Lourdes: thus by a simple commercial transaction, Gaston III acquired *de jure* title to a stronghold whose garrison was already in his *de facto* control, and to some extent reversed the effects of Louis d'Anjou's campaign in Bigorre.

The second treaty appeared even more portentous, for it was nothing less than an alliance that was to be sealed by the marriage of Gaston's heir to Lancaster's daughter Philippa. Fébus was also to assist the Duke in his 'conquest of Spain [*i.e.* Castile] against Henry who now holds it'. In this text, as in the first one, John of Gaunt was given the titles of King of Castile and León. Moreover, it was stipulated that the agreement was subject to the approval of Edward III, 'our lord the King of France and England'.[12] The financial clauses of the treaty – Philippa's dowry, and the retainer due to the Count for his military

---

[11] *Voyage*, 29–30.

[12] *Prince*, 141–2.

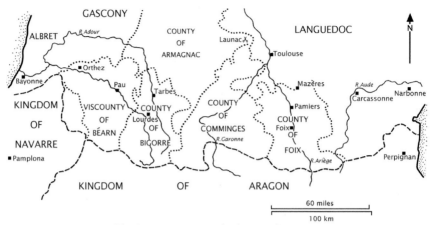

The Pyrenean states in the fourteenth century

intervention – were naturally most advantageous for Fébus, and so clearly
spelled out that it is hard not to take the treaty of Dax at face value. On the
other hand, it is equally hard to believe that Fébus was in earnest: not only his
relations with Enrique II of Castile were – and remained – most cordial, but
given the overall military situation, it would have been a singularly ill-chosen
moment for him to really support Edward III's claim to the French Crown.
And it is symptomatic of England's diminished expectations that in the Dax
documents, Fébus is styled 'by God's grace [...] lord of Béarn', rather than 'viscount' – a tacit abandonment of any claim to his homage in that capacity.

It is, of course, possible that Gaston was hedging his bets against another
reversal of French fortunes: Crécy and Poitiers, still fresh in men's minds, had
shown that such a catastrophe was always possible. But his rapprochement
with Lancaster, short-lived as it was, served above all to remind the French government that to persist in antagonizing the most powerful seigneur in the Midi
would be unwise – precisely the point that Anjou had tried to impress on his
brother the King. In the event, when military operations resumed later in 1374
Fébus maintained his neutral stance. After failing to enlist Peter IV of Aragon
in a joint attack on Castile, Lancaster sailed home to England. Louis d'Anjou,
who had resumed his lieutenancy in Languedoc, campaigned briefly in the Garonne valley, but failed to support a Castilian attack by land and sea on Bayonne,
soon withdrawn in disarray. Meanwhile, Fébus' only move was to take effective
control of the Basque valley of Soule, on the western frontier of Béarn. Nominally a part of the duchy of Aquitaine, that viscounty had been promised in
1338 by Philippe VI to Gaston II – if he could conquer it. Thirty-five years later,
the English garrison of Mauléon was withdrawn, leaving the country open to
marauding bands of *routiers*. Fébus simply offered the inhabitants his protection – at cost, plus 4,000 florins: all profit to him, as his obligation consisted in
putting his troops in control of Mauléon Castle.

B Y the summer of 1375 Fébus had achieved only mediocre territorial and strategic gains: the protectorate of Soule and a tightening of control over Lourdes. But, partly thanks to his diplomatic footwork, partly thanks to ambient circumstances, the pressure from France had begun to ease, and the moment of greatest danger from that quarter had passed without any serious harm to the lands of Foix-Béarn. The peril had been very real, and the prospect far more ominous than it had been at the time of the confrontation with the Prince of Wales. The object of that contest had been clearly defined, and the issue might in the end have been resolved, after some exercises in brinkman-ship, by a face-saving compromise. But the estrangement between Fébus and the Valois was more deeply rooted in unforgiven wrongs, the kind of festering grudges more common within families than between strangers. By no means a forgiving man, Charles V had, of course, good reasons to distrust and detest his brother-in-law the King of Navarre, and it was not unreasonable for him to doubt the loyalty of Navarre's other brother-in-law, the Count of Foix. For his part, while protesting that he was 'French', Fébus gave the appearance of at least passive complicity in the repeated treasons of Charles de Navarre – and what was one to make of his transactions with Lancaster? Moreover, he did not conceal his bitter resentment of the royal favour shown his hereditary enemy of Armagnac, especially in the matter of the lieutenancy of Languedoc.

After the expected invasion of Castile failed to materialize, the focus of the Anglo-French contest shifted away from the South West. The humiliating and costly reverses suffered since 1369 had made the war increasingly unpopular in England. With Edward III sinking into senility, and the Prince of Wales dying, Lancaster, now the effective leader of English policy, agreed to the peace nego-tiations which opened officially at Bruges on Easter 1375 (in fact, lower-level parleys had been mediated by the Pope's envoys since January 1374). Through the years 1373 and 1374, the Midi had been hard hit by epidemics; a cycle of bad weather had led to crop failures and famine in Languedoc – all of which may account in part for the desultory character of warfare in the region. At any rate, French military efforts during that period were more vigorously applied to the consolidation of gains in Poitou and Limousin, and the reduction of stubborn English strongholds in Brittany and Normandy. Last but not least, the Duke of Anjou seems to have at last convinced Charles V of the need for more balanced relations with the counts of Foix and of Armagnac. The King's tacit agreement allowed him to sanction the situation in Bigorre by simply not reacting to it, and to turn his attention to a grand enterprise of his own. Like his English counterpart John of Gaunt, Louis d'Anjou craved a royal crown. Deprived by the birth of the future Charles VI of the prospect of succeeding his sickly brother, he envisaged the conquest of other, more or less chimerical thrones. First, a kingdom of Lombardy was promised by the Avignon papacy as a reward for Louis' support against the Visconti of Milan. But the more recent object of his attention was the kingdom of Majorca. Thirty years after his father had been evicted by Peter IV, the last direct pretender, son of the dispossessed Jaume III, died in February 1375, having bequeathed his 'rights' to his sister Isabella, Marchioness of Montferrat, who in turn sold them to the Duke of Anjou for 12,000 florins in cash, plus a life annuity of 5,500 francs.[13] Historians have argued about the Marchesa's ability to inherit (the 'Salic law' again), and her right to dispose of her brother's claim, but the realm itself was firmly in the grip of the King of Aragon. Papal mediation failed to settle the dispute altogether, but the expiration of the Anglo-French truce in 1377 required Louis once again to lead an offensive in Aquitaine. Not only war with Aragon was avoided, but Peter IV agreed to a French alliance against England. The third party to that treaty was the Count of Foix.

Although Fébus would not renew his homage to the King of France in the lifetime of Charles V, the treaty of Tarbes sealed his political reconciliation with France. However, it had only been achieved after one more flare-up of the dispute with Armagnac, the brief but in some ways conclusive 'War of Comminges'. Straddling the upper course of the Garonne south from Toulouse, the county of Comminges bordered on the Foix-Béarns' lands of Nébouzan: its acquisition would have been for Fébus a major step towards the consolidation of his domains along an east–west axis. Conversely, the county lay directly in the path of the Armagnacs' southward expansion. On 15 October 1375 Pierre-Raimond II de Comminges died, leaving the county to his young daughter Marguerite. The Count of Armagnac immediately offered to 'defend the rights of the little girl', a protection sealed by her betrothal to his son. Through his mother, Aliénor de Comminges, Fébus could claim some rights of succession as the only male heir in sight, but he may also have proposed a matrimonial alliance between his son and heir Gaston and the 'little girl'. To emphasize his kinship with the House of Comminges, he chose that moment to fulfil his mother's last wish and also display his military might: the small but imposing army escorting Aliénor's mortal remains from Béarn to the convent of Salenques in Foix could not pass unnoticed as it travelled through Comminges in February 1376. Fébus then met with the Dowager Countess, but failed to advance his suit. In the confused period that follows, it is unclear whether the initial hostilities came from him or from his rival, but throughout that spring and summer, the Armagnacs scored some minor successes in Nébouzan and in Foix. In August Fébus launched an attack from Béarn into western Armagnac, but a diversion by Armagnac forces struck hard at neighbouring Marsan, capturing the town of Cazères-sur-l'Adour, an important store of Fébus' provisions and armoury.

The Count of Foix wasted no time before laying siege to Cazères, but before any decisive engagement could take place, Louis d'Anjou had mediated a truce that effectively put an end to the 'War of Comminges'. On 12 November the Armagnacs agreed to evacuate Cazères, and negotiations began towards a

---

[13] Roland Delachenal, *Histoire de Charles V*, 5 vols. (Paris, 1909–31), V, 47.

lasting settlement of the ancient dispute. While it is an important episode of
the Foix-Armagnac feud, the siege of Cazères has caused perhaps more ink to
be spilled than its military significance warrants. This is almost entirely due
to Froissart's second-hand account in which, recalling from memory (or perhaps from misread notes) his conversation with Espan de Lion, he situates the
action some 90 miles to the east, at Cazères-sur-Garonne, with the picturesque
finale of the Count of Armagnac and his garrison forced to leave the town one
by one through a narrow breach, and then ransomed for 200,000 francs.[14] All
the known facts, however, point to Cazères in Marsan as the site of the final
event of that war. Moreover, Jean II d'Armagnac, much less warlike than his
father, was probably not there in person, as the truce was signed by his vassal the Count of Pardiac. Lastly, it was not for ransoms, but as a 'war indemnity' included in the subsequent peace treaty, that Gaston III was paid 200,000
francs.[15]

That settlement was reached at Tarbes in the last days of January 1377,
when Fébus, meeting with Louis d'Anjou, agreed to the Duke's arbitration of
his dispute with the Count of Armagnac. In return for his pledge of alliance
with France against England, which would entail losses of income from his
fiefs liable to confiscation in English Gascony, Gaston III was granted financial compensations in cash and annuities. Lastly, the reconciliation of the two
regional rivals was to be sanctioned by the marriage of young Gaston, heir of
Foix-Béarn, with the daughter of Jean II d'Armagnac. This is not to say that the
terms of the treaty pleased everyone. There was in Armagnac such a residue
of resentment against Fébus that the Duke felt the need to demand oaths of
observance not only from Count Jean and the Countess of Comminges, but by
a number of their vassals. Louis, who had hoped to rid Bigorre of the 'Companions' of Lourdes – a menace to the whole region, and an embarrassing lapse
of the royal authority – was also frustrated in that matter. Fébus balked at
helping him expel the garrison, but instead offered his mediation: for a fee to
himself of 40,000 francs, he would persuade the Companions to evacuate the
castle in exchange for an indemnity of 20,000 francs. Whether Anjou agreed to
that bizarre scheme and paid the money is doubtful, for the Companions were
still in possession of Lourdes two years later, when Fébus signed with them a
profit-sharing agreement.

Evidently hoping for further concessions, Fébus was in no hurry to ratify
the treaty of Tarbes. Nor was he in danger of any serious pressure from the
French government: Charles V and his lieutenants were then too busy preparing for a resumption of the war with England. Through the summer of 1377
Louis d'Anjou would be wholly engaged in the recovery of Périgord, a campaign that brought him within striking distance of Bordeaux. The death of

[14] *Voyage*, 10–13.
[15] *Vicomté*, 309–10.

Edward III and the accession of Richard II, almost coinciding with the expiration of the truce of Bruges, were the occasion of renewed efforts by the English government to find friends on the frontiers of beleaguered Gascony. They
found the King of Navarre ready once again to turn against the Valois. For
his part the Count of Foix entertained an English embassy led by Richard II's
lieutenant in Aquitaine, and there was also intense diplomatic activity between
the courts of Orthez and Pamplona. The tenor of the negotiations between
Fébus and Charles of Navarre has not been divulged, but the fact that most of
the exchanges – and possibly face-to-face meetings – took place in 1378, may
in itself be a clue, for that was the year of Navarre's 'great treason' that delivered the port of Cherbourg to England. Although it seems that Fébus only
listened, without acquiescing to any move hostile to France, the mere appearance of rekindled friendship with his brother-in-law would have been enough
to underscore the fragility of the political balance in the sub-Pyrenean region.

For that matter, instability was by no means confined to the Midi. Christendom as a whole was shaken in that same year by the onset of the Great Schism.
Pope Gregory IX had died only one year after bringing back the seat of the
Church from Avignon to Rome. The election of his successor, Urban VI, gave
rise to contention between the 'national' factions in the college of cardinals. A
party of rebels – mostly made up of French and pro-French cardinals – elected
a kinsman of the Valois, Robert de Genève, who returned to Avignon as Clement VII. The contest – sometimes a scramble, often a cynical haggling – for
the obedience of bishops and the recognition of kings, divided Europe along
predictable lines: France and French allies supported the anti-pope of Avignon,
while England and her friends upheld the Roman pontiff. However, some rulers – most notably Peter IV of Aragon – held neutrality as the only moral
course, but also as an opportunity to keep some of the Church revenues, as it
were, in escrow. It was, as we shall see later, not one that Fébus would miss.

Despite great advances in the South West, France was also passing through
a difficult period. The latest treachery of Navarre had seriously hampered the
complete recovery of Normandy, where Du Guesclin was unable to recapture
Cherbourg. Charles V's ill-advised attempt to annex Brittany united the nobility of that duchy in the defence of Breton independence. In the central and
southern provinces, petty warlords and their mercenary bands had for years
occupied strongholds from which they ransomed and pillaged, unchecked by
royal officers. That situation was especially scandalous in Languedoc, where
the King's Lieutenant – Louis d'Anjou – while levying taxes ostensibly for the
defence of the province against the brigands, was in fact using his office as a
base for his own foreign quest after an elusive crown. In 1379 a new round of
unbearable taxation provoked riots throughout the province, culminating in
October with the bloody 'Great Rebellion' of Montpellier.

Although a superficial glance at the political map might suggest only mediocre gains, the delay between the treaty of Tarbes and its ratification at Orthez

on 20 March 1379 had been on the whole favourable to the Count of Foix. If Fébus can be said to have entertained a 'grand design', its goal was undoubtedly the acquisition of the lands separating Foix and Béarn, in order to forge a single, continuous state – albeit a feudal one, each of whose components may have had a different juridical status. Outright possession of Comminges, and especially of Bigorre, was essential to the realization of that project – or so it seemed. But, after several wars, Fébus had failed to conquer either county. By the peace of Orthez, he recognized as valid the marriage, imposed against her mother's will, of Marguerite de Comminges to the heir of Armagnac, and renounced his own claim to the county. As for Bigorre, Froissart reports (from another one of Espan's tales) that it was offered to Fébus, but that he found the attached condition of homage liege to Charles V unacceptable, and therefore refused the county. While it is, at least in part, psychologically plausible, the story is uncorroborated, and makes ultimately little sense, for whether or not he had renewed his homage, Gaston III was already the King's liege man for the county of Foix and various seigniories in Languedoc.[16]

The chronicler adds that the Count 'retained the castle of Mauvezin' as a freehold and 'his heritage of old'. And indeed, the peace of Orthez granted Fébus Mauvezin and the neighbouring lordship of Goudon as his hereditary possessions. He also received, but for his lifetime only, the castle and land of Saint-Julien de Comminges, which in practice constituted a western extension of the county of Foix into the Upper Garonne valley. As for Bigorre, Fébus would soon tighten his effective grip on that county, and so close the widest gap between Béarn and his eastern possessions.

But first, the rituals of reconciliation between the Houses of Foix and Armagnac were dispatched in the briefest possible time. On 3 April – two weeks after the signing of the treaty of Orthez – the two counts, meeting on the border of their respective domains, shared the Eucharist and exchanged the kiss of peace. On 19 April young Gaston de Foix and Béatrix d'Armagnac were married in a rather low-key ceremony. Last but not least, the dowry of 100,000 francs promised by Jean d'Armagnac was paid in full by 24 April. Then, when it might appear that the last page had been turned on that chapter of history, Fébus chose to put his connection with the Companions of Lourdes to the most profitable use. As the Duke of Anjou had been increasingly busy elsewhere – the previous year in Périgord, now in Brittany – the freebooters under the command of Pierre-Arnaud de Béarn had resumed their exactions in the lowlands of Bigorre. The Count of Foix, who since 1374 held the mortgage on their eyrie, offered to the communities most exposed to their activity a protection that the King's seneschal was clearly unable to provide. On 8 July the first Béarnais garrison – invited by the inhabitants – was installed at

---

[16] *Voyage*, 51–3. Neither Delachenal nor Tucoo-Chala makes any mention of this purported 'offer.'

Bordères-sur-Echez, a village (and now a suburb) near Tarbes, in exchange for
a small retainer to the Count of Foix, and the upkeep of the troops. Similar
agreements were then signed with at least twenty-six other towns and villages.
If the contract with Tarbes, signed on 27 November, is typical, the compensation required by Fébus was modest ('480 francs in gold'), with some quaint,
and possibly symbolic, provisions: 'three lengths of silk, seventy-two torches, or
their price in cash …' [17] But the retainer paid by the communities of Bigorre was
not the real object of the operation. The goal Fébus had achieved was military
control of the county, and he had achieved it without even the appearance of a
challenge to the King's authority, for each one of his garrisons was installed pursuant to a private contract in which the Count acted as nothing more than the
provider of a security service. To fulfil his part of the bargain, Fébus negotiated
a pact with the Companions, compensating them for the booty they would be
denied with, in effect, a kick-back from the payments he collected. Many of the
*routiers* decided to migrate to other theatres of action. In the end, all the parties
directly concerned could deem themselves satisfied: Pierre-Arnaud de Béarn
went on to serve his cousin as his lieutenant in Marsan, the lowland towns and
villages were at last free of the threat from Lourdes, and Fébus occupied the
long desired county of Bigorre. With only a few narrow stretches of territory
yet to be brought under his control, the object of his 'grand design', – joining
Foix and Béarn in a single continuum – was after all within his sight.

[17] *Prince*, 172.

# 6

# Governing Wisely

WHATEVER the ultimate goal of Gaston III's territorial expansion may have been, his policy of armed neutrality in the Anglo-French conflict, together with successful resistance to claims of both English and French suzerainty over Béarn, had effectively preserved his domains from the then endemic ravages of war. To be sure, the perennial feud with Armagnac brought some enemy incursions, particularly into Marsan and Foix, but the most dangerous foreigners – Edward of Wales and Louis d'Anjou – refrained from attempting an invasion of Béarn. During his devastating *chevauchée* of 1355 from Bordeaux to Narbonne, the Black Prince spared not only the Count's possessions, but also French towns such as Belpech, where Fébus had only a house. The time came when he would have been more inclined to punish Fébus for his evasions, but English power in Aquitaine was by then waning, Béarn was poised for a strong resistance, and an invasion might well have turned into a rout. A few years later, when the balance of forces in Aquitaine was altered and Fébus had reasons to fear a French attack, Louis d'Anjou also hesitated. Then, as more urgent tasks required his presence north of the Garonne, the turbulent Duke moved on without breaching the Béarnais border.

More dangerous perhaps than the various royal armies, which could at least sometimes be stopped or diverted by diplomacy, mercenary companies idled by lengthy truces between the 'regular' belligerent powers were one of the major scourges of the century. And yet the well-organized bands of freebooters who terrorized so many provinces of France and Italy seemed to have for the most part left Gaston's domains alone. Even though his city of Pamiers in Foix was one of the chief mustering places for companies seeking employment, and Béarn lay in the path of troop movements between Spain, France and Aquitaine, neither region suffered the kind of vicious treatment meted out to the King's subjects in Auvergne and Languedoc, or in Philip the Bold's Burgundy. While in the last analysis open conflict with France or England had been deflected by events beyond Fébus' ability to manipulate them, it was largely thanks to his pragmatic (some would even say cynical) dealings with the *routiers* that their threat was largely neutralized.

Moreover, in an era noted for the frequency and the severity of civil disorders, the Foix-Béarn domains remained remarkably free of internal convulsions. Early in his reign, Gaston III had not only witnessed the violent uprising that swept northern France, he had had occasion to confront the rampaging Jacques; he had seen the French monarchy threatened by rebellious Paris mobs manipulated at times by his brother-in-law the King of Navarre. Years later, the misrule of Louis d'Anjou would provoke a spate of ugly riots in neighbouring Languedoc, leading to the recall of the Duke – a development that, given his perennial ambition to obtain the lieutenancy of that royal province, Fébus certainly observed with great interest. But the brief tumult of Orthez in the summer of 1353, with which he had dealt decisively but without excessive severity, was the only notable instance of popular uprising recorded throughout his reign. This calm may have been due simply to the provincial remoteness of places like Foix, Orthez or Pamiers, far from the conspiratorial hysteria underlying the well-orchestrated mob actions that shook Paris. It may also be that, while veritable class conflicts were coming to the boiling point in the densely populated urban centres of trade and industry of Flanders and Tuscany, Pyrenean society remained stable and prosperous simply because of its semi-rustic character and its sparse distribution. But his subjects knew very well that it was Fébus' success in fending off foreign interference and minimizing the shock waves of distant conflicts that ensured stability and prosperity in the first place. And, while they had occasion to chafe under his increasingly authoritarian rule, they also had reasons to appreciate that rare phenomenon, a sovereign who attended to *their* day-to-day business.

Hᴵˢ apprenticeship under the regency of Aliénor de Comminges had taught Gaston the importance of the personal bond between the lord of Béarn and his subjects, a bond that needed to be constantly reaffirmed by his active involvement in their governance. The lessons of his youth were all the more memorable for having been learned, not in the comfort of a study, but on the road, while travelling in all seasons to exchange the mutual oaths of fealty with even the most far-flung communities of the Foix-Béarn inheritance. There are reasons, besides the absence of civil disorders, to believe that those lessons were remembered and applied throughout the long reign of Gaston Fébus. In the surviving records of his public acts, together with such anecdotal evidence as may be gleaned from Froissart's and other chronicles, it is possible to discern the profile of an uncommonly attentive ruler, and moreover one who was determined to exercise his personal control over all aspects of government.

From the first *tournées d'hommage* of 1344–5 at his mother's side, to his death in 1391, Gaston III was above all a visible, conspicuously present lord. His Baltic voyage of 1357, which earned him fame and justified his adoption of the Fébus persona and motto, had satisfied a youthful craving for knight errantry. Thereafter he rarely travelled out of his own domains, or very far from them – typically, for politically expedient visits to Toulouse. Unpleasant experiences may well have shaped those sedentary habits: Gaston's incarceration in the Paris Châtelet under the reign of Jean II had vividly demonstrated the risks of prolonged residence at a foreign court; his desultory campaign in the service of Aragon had been little more than a waste of time and a source of rancour between him and Peter IV – so much so that, when the time came to renew certain homages, Fébus dispatched his half-brother as a surrogate to Perpignan. Last but not least, when he had obeyed the Prince of Wales' summons in January 1364, he had again been in danger of arrest for defying an angry overlord: prudence had indeed prompted a quick departure from Agen after the ambiguous ceremony of homage. But it would be ungenerous to conclude that the fear of arrest or ambush alone explains Gaston's reluctance to venture far from his home base. Quite simply put, there was no need for him to look for distant enterprises: unlike his brother-in-law Charles of Navarre, he did not have vast domains to defend or claim in France; unlike such turbulent coevals as Louis d'Anjou and John of Gaunt, he was not driven by the chimerical craving for a royal crown; last but not least, the single most enduring challenge he had to face – the dynastic feud with Armagnac – was there, on his own borders.

But his deft handling of external challenges, his sang-froid in the face of calculated risks, balanced by a willingness to bide his time for action, suggest that Fébus also possessed a healthy sense of politics as the art of the possible. A degree of pragmatic flexibility does not seem to have deserted him when difficult issues arose between him and his subjects. Thus, when he chose to distance himself (at least temporarily) from the traditional pro-French policies of his predecessors, Gaston III, while reacting to perceived French affronts, was also mindful of the generally pro-English leanings of Béarn's nobles and commoners alike, and of the viscounty's economic ties to Anglo-Aquitaine. In the county of Foix, the Count's authority had long since been undermined by the interference of royal officers and by the Inquisition, intent on uprooting the last vestiges of Catharism in the high Pyrenean country. Those 'foreign' intrusions were the sequels of Roger-Bernard II's resistance to the Albigensian 'crusade' and of Roger-Bernard III's rebellion against Philip III. While they were much less severe now than they had been at the beginning of the century, it remained that in Foix and in other lands he held in fief, the authority of Fébus was limited by his status as vassal to a powerful suzerain. In a dispute with his subjects, the latter could appeal to the King of France – or, in the case of Donnezan, to Aragon, and in Marsan, to England. This right of appeal was the not-so-thin prying tool with which an enterprising overlord could at best browbeat his vassal in his own domain, at worst dispossess him: such had been the case leading to the proclaimed 'confiscation' of Aquitaine by the King of France – and so to the 'official' beginning of the Hundred Years War. Distances also made direct rule from Gaston's habitual seat of Orthez problematic. Hence his apparent readiness to concede as a grace what was more often than not the *fait accompli* of self-government by local élites. A case in point is his response to a conflict opposing the consuls of Foix and the lord of Mirepoix, in the course of which the municipal militia had attacked his castle of L'Herm, nominally under the Count's protection. Gaston III's ordinance of 31 August 1357, issued soon after the affray, not only contains no word of reprimand, let alone any suggestion of punishment, but clearly reinforces the authority of the consuls, decreeing, for instance, that no man could be arrested or tried without their agreement. They were also given the discretionary power to call the militia whenever it was deemed necessary to defend the community, its property and franchises 'in the city of Foix, on its territory and wherever you have wood-cutting and grazing rights'.[1] To be sure, the young Fébus was then about to embark on his Baltic adventure, and probably anxious to forestall any cause of discontent while he was away, but whatever his reasons, the autonomy granted to the elected consuls of Foix went some distance beyond the immediate need to close the books on a minor incident.

## The reins of power

WHILE geographical dispersion and the constraints of vassalage required a somewhat liberal approach to the governance of the fiefs Gaston III held from royal overlords, Béarn was quite another thing. There, in a land he held 'from no man on earth', he reigned as sovereign lord (*senhor senhoreyant*; literally: 'lord lording'), and thus none of his decrees or judgements could be appealed to Paris or Bordeaux. Béarn had clearly been, since the Moncade succession, the most prized possession of the counts of Foix, a fact eloquently underscored by their adoption of the dynastic forename of Gaston, and the establishment of their principal residence at Orthez. And in this Béarn that was his by the grace of God alone, Fébus was determined to be as absolute a master as the least of his subject was in his own *ostau*, however humble.

The powers young Gaston III inherited as Viscount of Béarn had been somewhat eroded since the beginning of the century. During the minority of Gaston II the rivalry between his mother Jeanne d'Artois and her mother-in-law Marguerite de Moncade had driven both regents to seek popular support by extending the most favourable franchises – such as the *For of Morlaàs* – to many other townships, and permitting the *Cour des communautés* – a very occasional assembly of commoners, hitherto summoned only in exceptional circumstances – to be called henceforth concurrently with every mustering of the nobles in their *Cour Majour*. While the two bodies did not sit together, and while their sessions remained occasional, nevertheless a framework was now in place, within which the conjoined *Cours* might one day constitute an embryonic Parliament capable, with support from nobility and bourgeoisie alike, of imposing new limitations to the Viscount's authority. That moment might have come at the death of Gaston II, when government finances were in some disarray and the Castelbon party challenged the regency. But Aliénor de Comminges had gone directly to the local communities to renew the mutual bonds of fealty between lord and vassals, and thus by-passed the *Cours* and

---

[1] *Ibid.*, 79.

short-circuited their ambitions, however inchoate. Gaston III followed his mother's lead, if a policy of omission can be said to 'follow' anything: there is no document indicating that either body had been summoned at any time during his reign. Conversely, the record of his acts shows that Fébus as sovereign judge adjudicated in his own seigniorial court (the *audienci*) most of the suits that would otherwise have been heard by the *Cour Majour* and the *Cour des communautés*. Thus, while they were not exactly abolished, these two bodies were simply made irrelevant.

At the local level, the head men of villages and town *jurats* (literally: 'sworn men') served as representatives of their respective communities, appointed by the Viscount and answerable to him for a variety of administrative tasks – law and order, military levies, and of course tax collection. Over time a weakened central government had allowed their office to become elective, and the *For général* of Béarn had been amended in that sense. This was the same kind of evolution whereby their counterparts the consuls of Foix, for instance, were constituted in a veritable municipal council, whose authority Fébus not only acknowledged but extended rather liberally. In Béarn, however, he succeeded in reversing the trend towards elective office by resorting to the same inertia whereby he kept the *Cours* dormant: no order were issued for the elections of new *jurats*, and those retiring were simply replaced by the Viscount's appointees. Chosen among the richest and most influential men in their town or village, these municipal magistrates were therefore less its representatives than officers of the central power, and not infrequently its 'administrative hostages' answerable for their communities' compliance with its decrees.[2] According to Tucoo-Chala, the control thus installed by Fébus were so inescapably efficient that in the district of Navarrenx, 'when a community was delinquent in its tax payment, the *jurats* came of their own accord to be jailed in Orthez'.[3] Nor was this autocratic severity limited to Béarn proper, but it extended apparently to all the lands Fébus could conveniently control directly: thus, in 1376 he ordered all the *jurats* in the adjacent viscounties of Marsan and Gavardan jailed until their communities had delivered to his household the required provisions in kind.[4]

Gaston III's despotism appeared to be somewhat balanced by the restrictions he imposed on the powers of the *bailes* (bailiffs) overseeing the administration of the nineteen *baylies* (bailiwicks) of Béarn. These officers, serving at the pleasure of the Viscount, had often become capricious in their dealings with the communities. One frequent complaint was about the practice of calling village assemblies without previous notice, in order not to discuss local problems, but to hear the *baile*'s own decrees. Fébus ruled that henceforth such assemblies

---

[2] *Vicomté*, 117 and n. 7.

[3] *Prince*, 260.

[4] *Vicomté*, 411.

– which *jurats* and other magistrates were obligated to attend, under penalty of fines – would be held only on scheduled dates. But this, as well as other measures regulating the powers of the *bailes*, was also part of Fébus' strategy to forestall the emergence of a permanent body of professional – and eventually hereditary – office holders (ironically, the very process whereby counts and viscounts had become, from royal officers, hereditary lords in their own right). To further curtail their independence, Fébus often appointed *bailes* from districts other than their assigned *baylies*, and only for very limited terms. If one effect of these measures was to protect the communities from abuses of local power, the primary intent was nevertheless to concentrate all authority in the hands of the Viscount – or rather, as he now styled himself, the Lord of Béarn.

The same principle guided the form of Fébus' central administration. Traditionally, the Viscount was served and advised by a number of 'grand officers', such as the Seneschal, the Chancellor and the Treasurer. The baron of Andoins had been Seneschal throughout the reign of Gaston II, but under Fébus that office – from times immemorial held by a member of the upper nobility – appears to have become purely honorific, if not virtual. Upon his accession the young Gaston III conferred it first on a knight from Comminges, and eventually – and significantly – on his bastard uncle Bernard de Béarn 'l'Aspois'. Moreover, while there are recorded lists of the Seneschals of Marsan and of Foix, no mention is found of a Seneschal of Béarn after 1360. Likewise, little is known of the chancellery of Béarn under Fébus. As one of the chief functions of the Chancellor was to verify and ratify the acts of the *Cour majour*, this is not surprising, given what became of that body during the reign of Gaston III. While it had been traditionally made up of an indefinite number of Béarn's nobles, Fébus restricted its membership to ten barons and two bishops, and effectively confined the Cour to a honorific rôle by hearing most of its potential cases in his own seigniorial court. With the evident intention of marginalizing the barons and prelates of Béarn, Fébus governed with the help of his private cabinet. Sometimes called 'the Count's council' (*lo cosselh deu comte*), sometimes 'the lord's court' (*la cort deu senhor*), this was a rather informal group without a fixed membership, made up of trusted familiars. Typically these included first of all members of the Count's family, such as his half-brothers Arnaud-Guilhem and Pierre de Béarn, and later his bastard sons Yvain and Gratien; among the few noblemen, the knight Espan de Lion, lay abbot of Orthez and present in the *Chroniques* as the travelling companion and chief informant of Froissart during his journey to Orthez, seems to have been one of Fébus' most constant attendants. Professional jurists – sometimes given the title of 'learned and discreet master' appear to have been the most numerous of the Count's technical advisers, but it was his camarilla of illegitimate kinsmen and hand-picked familiars that maintained around the autocrat the desired aura of secrecy and self-sufficient power.

This 'government' functioned as informally as it was constituted: the Count's familiars were entrusted, on an *ad hoc* basis, with many of the tasks that would have traditionally devolved to permanent office-holders. Commissioned as *procuradors* or *messadgers deu senhor* (a title curiously reminiscent of the Carolingian *missi dominici*), and armed with broad but temporary police or judicial powers, they were delegated to deal in their master's name with specific problems. Despite (or perhaps because of) the absence of a fixed, organized structure, and the appearance of perpetual improvisation, this system was in fact the flexible instrument of a single will, that of Fébus, and as such it functioned efficiently throughout his reign. Likewise, in the absence or dormancy of the traditional chancellery, the Count's ordinances and other official acts were recorded by his own staff of notaries and secretaries. Their minutes, collected in a number of surviving registers, constitute a veritable profile of Fébus' official activities, allowing limited but well documented insights into some of his preoccupations and his methods of government. Here again, the informality of the recording process, whereby private (not to say trivial) transactions are memorialized next to, and in the same ink as momentous affairs of state, illustrates the range of the counts' interests, and the extent of his direct control of all aspects of his administration. The diversity of the acts recorded from January to March 1374 might be taken as typical of this eclecticism: there we see that on 6 January Fébus received at Pau the homage of the lord of Audaux; back at Orthez on 7 January he granted an annuity to Hannequin, his hunting valet; on 22 January another homage is received at Pau; on 23 January, at Lacq, the Count appoints guardians for the children of a deceased gentleman; on 13 February, at Pau, he sentences a former treasurer of Orthez accused of corruption; on 6 March he grants his freedom (subject to payment) to a serf and to the land he holds; on 19 March, at Dax, he signs a treaty with the Duke of Lancaster; etc.[5]

While it opens only a very small window on his working days, this random sample of official acts suggests that, in order to address day after day such disparate tasks, Fébus had to be endowed with remarkable mental agility. From a comprehensive overview of surviving registers, however, there emerges a hierarchy of problems that were clearly in the forefront of his preoccupations. Leaving aside the issues relating to external relations, Gaston III – like other rulers of realms small and large, would have seen control of his country's resources and maintenance of internal peace as the primary goals of his administration.

## Ruling the land

In an era when capital (and consequently power) was predominantly territorial, one of Gaston III's most urgent tasks was to reclaim his seigniorial property rights that had been allowed to lapse, chiefly during the troubled regency of his grandmother Jeanne d'Artois. These long-established

5 *Ibid.*, 403.

rights, formally acknowledged in the *For général*, in effect made the Viscount the supreme landlord of all Béarn, and sole proprietor of all uncultivated lands, moors, forests and waters.[6] But for several decades the communities had enjoyed, with or without the formal permission, free access to, and rent-free use of the seigniorial properties. Gradually Fébus reasserted his prerogatives, first by imposing tolls on livestock passing through his lands during the seasonal transhumance, then by demanding substantial user fees in payment for more extended grazing rights.

The direct benefit of this stiffened policy was of course financial, in the form of a regular income accruing to the Count's treasury. It also served notice that, as an interested party, he would not tolerate the transgressions that had hitherto gone unchecked and unpunished. The most endemic of such offences were the all too frequent trespasses of the mountain folk through the cultivated lands of the piedmont. Those invasions had long been the causes of sometimes violent confrontations that successive viscounts had not been able to prevent. Gaston III seized a particular instance as his opportunity to tackle the issue. In 1344 Aliénor de Comminges had achieved partial success in restraining the men of Ossau, guilty of particularly gross usurpations in the lowlands near Pau, by having their community assessed the huge fine of 15,000 *sous*. The Ossalois' depredations had ceased, but ten years later it was her son who collected the yet unpaid fine, thus serving notice that henceforth the law had teeth and would use them. Although Fébus could no more than his predecessors achieve complete control of the quasi-autonomous communities in the remote high valleys of Aspe, Ossau and Barétous, he was eventually able to impose the framework for negotiated right-of-way agreements between pastoral highlanders and lowland farmers.

Another particular case, that of a dispute between two communities, was the pretext of rulings that grew into a full-blown forestry code. Here again, the Viscount's right of eminent domain was invoked to justify the imposition of access and user fees, but beyond these lucrative measures, precise limits were set for the exploitation of forest resources. Cutting timber was subject to preliminary authorization and of course payment of a tax of 6 deniers per tree. Oak, chestnut and ash trees could be cut down only exceptionally, to be used only in building houses or in the manufacture of agricultural implements. Charcoal-making was allowed only in amounts not exceeding household needs; swineherds were forbidden to knock down acorns, and must let their pigs be content with what already lay on the ground; cutting down beech trees was prohibited in some regions where they had been over-exploited. Beginning in 1354, forest rangers were appointed to collect taxes and fines and enforce the new regulation. Subordinated at first to the Viscount's bailiffs, they eventually were constituted into a distinct administration, capped towards the end of Fébus'

[6] *Ibid.*, 127, n. 44.

reign by the appointment of a veritable superintendent of natural resources, the *Maître des Eaux et Forêts*. Although these were remarkable innovations, to equate them with the environmental concerns awakened in the twentieth century would be a gross anachronism. On the other hand, to see only in Fébus' motives a huntsman's concern for the preservation of game habitat, and the opportunity to collect yet another kind of rent, would be too cynical a reduction: the regulations regarding particular species, the off-limits status of those endangered by excessive use, suggest a broader and longer view.

## Fébus and his florins

IF we are to take at face value Froissart's account of his journey to Orthez, it was on the road, between Montréjeau and Tournay, that he put to Espan de Lion the question that the knight answered thus: 'You asked me to what purpose [the Count of Foix] keeps so much money. I will tell you that he is always concerned about the feud he has with the Count of Armagnac, and about his envious neighbours, the King of England and the King of France, neither of whom he would want to provoke. He has managed until now to avoid war with both of them [...] As for his other neighbours, the King of Aragon and the King of Navarre, he does not take them into account, for he has acquired so many friend with his gifts, and could have so many more with his money, that he would field more men-at-arms than those two kings could do.'[7]

Espan's explanation is all the more convincing as it echoes the official justification of his master's fiscal innovations. Chief among these was the imposition in 1367 of an annual hearth tax, the *fouage* that had hitherto been levied only in exceptional circumstances and, as it were, as an emergency measure. For once apparently accurate, Froissart's account clearly links the creation of the new tax to the preparation of defences: 'The Count, who greatly feared the Prince [of Wales ...] began to assemble a great treasure to help him defend himself in case of an attack. Thus he created taxes in his lands and his towns, which are still in place and will be so as long as he lives.'[8] The new annual tax of 2 francs per hearth, which indeed remained invariable until 1391, was not an improvisation: in December 1365 Fébus had ordered the compilation of a census and a detailed inventory of all the feudal dues in cash and in kind owed him by his subjects, and there is little doubt that, beyond its immediate purpose as a ledger of disparate and sometimes purely symbolic obligations, the census of 1365–6 was meant to help establish the rolls of the permanent tax.

The Count of Foix was not the only ruler who resorted to the generally hated *fouage* in order to finance a war effort. In fact, he was only following the lead of Charles V, who had been the first to make the occasional hearth tax

---

[7] *Voyage*, 31.

[8] Cited in *Vicomté*, 136.

an annual levy earmarked for the defence of his beleaguered kingdom. In this endeavour, Fébus was on the whole more successful than his other neighbour the Prince of Wales, whose attempt to levy a *fouage* in Aquitaine provoked many of his Gascon vassals to 'turn French'. Froissart's assertion that 'people were so eager to pay the tax that it is a wonder' can perhaps be taken as an exaggeration, for there were incidents of resistance to the collection of the levy. But these seem to have been isolated cases, and in the long run Fébus' subjects must have acknowledged that, as the chronicler reports, 'neither French, nor English, nor any marauders caused them even a penny's worth of damage'.

Like the incipient forestry service, the financial administration is an exception to the apparently improvisational style of Fébus' government, and conspicuous enough to attract the attention of a chronicler usually uninterested in such mundane matters: according to Froissart, the Count appointed 'to receive his dues twelve notable men', who served as his collectors for rotating two-month terms, reporting and giving their accounts to 'the most special', *i.e.* the traditional comptroller, or *thesaurer generau*.[9] The collection of revenues, which had hitherto been the task of the *bailes* reporting directly to the central treasury, was progressively shifted to a more formal network of 'receivers', 'proveditors', etc., with distinct responsibilities for the hearth tax, feudal rents and dues in kind, judicial fines, tolls and other fees, until by the end of Fébus' reign, a whole new administration was in place. In one respect, however, the system remained profoundly feudal, in that the 'treasure' was not a public fund, but the sole property of the lord of Béarn who kept it literally within his reach, in the strong rooms of his castle at Orthez. Unfortunately, the 'book of the treasure' in which were recorded the receipts and disbursements of funds, has been lost (as have been the ledgers pertaining to the county of Foix), but at the Count's death the inventory of Moncade Tower reported a hoard of 737,500 florins.

While far from the 3 millions cited by Froissart, some estimates conclude that this amount exceeded Fébus 'normal income' by about 600,000 florins, corresponding roughly to the total of the ransoms exacted after the Launac victory of December 1362. That spectacular windfall was by no means the only 'exceptional' sweetening of the Count's revenues: under the historian's chaste heading of 'diplomatic and military successes', various other ransoms, treaties, peace settlements, and outright bribes and extortions may have added up to 1,400,000 florins.[10] In addition to the annual *fouage* and other cash levies, Fébus collected substantial non-monetary dues, such as 'provisions' for the seigniorial household, fodder for the lord's livestock, billeting rights for the Count's troops, stipulated periods of unpaid labour for the maintenance of roads, fortifications, etc. It is, of course, impossible to evaluate the sum total of these in-kind contributions, some of which were progressively replaced by cash payments, but

---

9   *Voyage*, 67; cf *Vicomté*, 137–8.

10   *Vicomté*, 146–7 and n. 112.

from what is known of the opulent style of Fébus' hospitality, the provisioning
of his table must have made considerable demands on the farmers of Foix and
Béarn. Also extensive but not precisely known were revenues from the tolls
and rents paid by communities for access to, and use of moorlands, forests and
streams, and fees for the use of seigniorial mills and ovens. Fébus is known to
have acquired urban real estate, probably on speculation or as rental property.
He was also an active money lender, his frequent loans being secured by liens
on the borrower's properties. Thus the faithful Espan de Lion was required in
1383 to pledge 'his own worldly goods and those of three knights' as security
for the loan of 100 *écus*: clearly, no friendship was allowed to interfere with the
strict application of business procedures. The same sources chronicle the swift
ruination of the baron of Castelnau-Tursan, from the initial loan of 2,000 *écus*
on 25 June 1367 to the sequestration of his property on 14 April 1374. Nor did
its insignificance shield the most meagre estate from confiscation: a number
of instances are recorded of orders to seize and sell at auction the houses and
other goods of peasants who had fled without paying the hearth tax.[11]

The least that can be said of Fébus' approach to financial gain is that he
was not hampered by any affectation of aristocratic contempt for money, or
even by the religious prohibition of usury. He was not, of course, the first or
last feudal prince to shed such scruples, but he was perhaps the one who did
so the most candidly, by simply legalizing interest-bearing loans, in defiance
of Church prohibitions.[12] Some of Gaston III's most profitable transactions
come very near to the definition of extortion – as in the case of the baron of
Castelnau – or swindle, as in that of the Count of Denia's ransom. Taken at the
battle of Najera (1367), this Aragonese prince – a nephew of Peter IV – was
assessed by his captors, the Prince of Wales together with Sir John Chandos
and other English knights, the huge ransom of 150,000 gold doubles, one of
the highest demanded of a noble prisoner at that time. Ransoms were then
one of the commonly traded commodities, as mortgages and other debentures
still are. Fébus seems always to have been alert to opportunities in that area.
Thus in 1380 he dispatched two of his closest advisers to negotiate the release
of the Seneschal of Bordeaux, Thomas Felton, recently taken by the French in
Périgord: since the Count of Foix was interested neither as a belligerent nor as
the prisoner's overlord, his officious intervention may well only be construed
as a medieval form of ambulance-chasing. In the case of the Count of Denia,
Fébus undertook to go surety for one-half of the prisoner's debt, and began by
collecting from him 30,000 florins in cash and a promissory note for 60,000
more. The Count of Denia was set free, but only after twenty years of tortuous,
dilatory manœuvres too complex to unravel here. For a simplified version of
that tangled scenario, it is roughly correct to say that, counting for impunity

[11] *Ibid.*, 395–403, 393, 425, 428, 434–5.
[12] *Prince*, 201.

on the disarray of English power in the South West, the Count of Foix simply ignored the letters and envoys demanding payment of the 75,000 doubles of which he was the guarantor. His evasion paid off handsomely: in 1390 Richard II, in an effort to gain Gaston III's alliance, released him of his debt. In no such forgiving vein, Fébus collected the 60,000 florins still owed him by the Count of Denia. This was not the end of litigation that dragged well into the next century; but for the time being, Fébus was the sole party to profit – by about 90,000 florins – from the transaction.[13]

The Count of Foix also enjoyed the profits of the mint of Béarn. For generations, the silver *sous* struck at Morlaàs since the eleventh century had enjoyed wide circulation in the entire Pyrenean region, as well as in Languedoc and the Iberian peninsula, but it seemed to have suffered from successive devaluations in the second half of the fourteenth century. It was Fébus, however, who took the initiative of coining gold florins, modelled after the florins of Aragon, whose obverse, with the Florentine lily and sword, bears the inscriptions *DNS Bearni* or *Febus comes*.[14] There is no documentary evidence of the profits he may have personally derived from this operation, but it may have been primarily intended to bring Béarnais coinage to parity with other regional currencies, and thus an advantage to Béarnais merchants. Another, perhaps more directly lucrative measure, was the offer made by Fébus to free the serfs, many of whom were surprisingly able and willing to pay for their freedom. There had been isolated instances of such transactions – twenty-four instances of of serfs being freed, sometimes together with their land, are recorded between 1371 and 1376, – but in 1387 the Count decided on a wholesale approach and ordered a survey of all serfs and of the amounts they might offer for their freedoms. In the bailiwick of Sauveterre alone, they are known to have offered collectively 1,000 florins. While it serves as yet another instance of Fébus' financial opportunism, this particular operation suggests a degree of social mobility in Béarn, as actual wealth and productivity displaced the hitherto rigid boundaries of feudal castes.

## Defences and armaments

THE obsessive pursuit of money was undoubtedly one of Fébus' chief preoccupations: of 229 official acts recorded in a five-year period, fifty-three pertain to the collection of rents, ransoms, and debts.[15] His avarice invites comparison with another formidable predator, his contemporary and sometimes rival Jean de Berry, but whereas at his death the estate of the Duke could not cover his debts, the Count of Foix not only left to his heirs the vast hoard of

---

[13] *Vicomté*, 284–5.

[14] Respectively 'Lord ( *dominus*) of Béarn' and 'Fébus, Count.'

[15] Tucoo-Chala and Staes, *Notaire de Prince, passim*.

the Moncade Tower, but he also bequeathed to his subjects a much improved defence establishment.

At Gaston III's accession Béarn was only partially protected from foreign attacks. Most villages were shielded by a moat and stockade, with some more important centres designated as refuge for their immediate neighbourhoods. The town of Oloron, key to the Somport pass, had a stone wall, and the viscounts controlled only a few castles at Orthez, Bellocq, Sauveterre and Sault-Navailles, all at the western extremity of Béarn, bordering on English Aquitaine. On the viscounty's eastern frontier, the castle of Pau was still surrounded by its eponymous wooden stockade (in Béarnais a *pau*). In the county of Foix, only the Upper Ariège valley, south of the Plantaurel range, boasted an impressive number of castles: Foix proper and ten more, including the former Cathar strongholds of Montségur and Roquefixade, guarded the roads and passes to Andorra and Catalonia. The lowlands of the northern county had very few defences apart from a few walled towns, such as Pamiers and Mazères. None of Fébus' predecessors had had the means, nor had felt the same urgency, to fortify their domains. Under his reign, however, such energetic neighbours as the Prince of Wales and the Duke of Anjou – not to mention the unpredictable King of Navarre and the marauding Companies – were all clear and present threats to the lands of Foix-Béarn. And now the windfall of the Launac ransoms provided a starting capital that allowed Fébus to embark on the most ambitious programme of military construction undertaken by a vassal of Charles V.

This upgrading of territorial defences began modestly but systematically with repairs and improvements of existing fortifications: in Béarn's open country, the communities were required to reinforce – or as the case may be to rebuild – the wooden *reculhides* around villages. More durable stonework was added to the castles of Bellocq and Sauveterre; Fébus half-brother Arnaud-Guilhem saw to the rebuilding of the walls of Oloron; at Orthez the bridge over the Gave was fortified (and of course given a toll-house) and the castle heightened. After 1370 a new series of construction was entrusted to a specialist brought from Foix. Under the supervision of the appointed castellan of Orthez, Sicard de Lordat, the northern and eastern frontiers of Béarn were now given new defences. Athwart the direct road from Orthez to Tarbes, Pau was transformed by the addition of the several towers and the square keep, whose medieval silhouette is still clearly visible despite the transformation of the fortress into the Renaissance palace of the kings of Navarre. To cover the approach to Orthez from the north, a new castle was erected at Morlanne for Arnaud-Guilhem. The old Viscount's castle at Morlaàs was enlarged, a project that required the purchase by Fébus of thirteen townsmen's houses and their gardens; the masonry, however, was at least partly paid for by a fine levied on a 'rebellious' burgher. But the most remarkable of that series of works was the raising of Montaner Castle, on the north-eastern edge of Béarn. This was no mere defence of an access route, since none traverses its relatively remote district: Montaner, with its keep rising 40 metres above the motte crowning a natural hill, would be in fact the watchtower controlling the nearby plain of Bigorre and the western frontier of Armagnac, as well as the roads linking Tarbes to Auch and the Garonne valley. Behind walls 3 metres thick, it would serve also as the secure base for a garrison ready for immediate deployment. On the two keeps at Pau and Montaner, the heraldic stones bearing the proud inscription *Febus me fe* ('Fébus made me') are still visible, but Sicard's signature is his distinctive use of the brick as his basic material. Given the number and magnitude of the projects, the choice of brick over the more expensive ashlar stone was probably made with an eye on the budget, as well as the more ready supply. To this end, skilled workers were brought to Béarn from Foix, to teach the locals brickmaking techniques. Thus the new fortifications, notably the square keeps of Pau and Montaner, exhibit surfaces reminiscent of the monuments of Languedoc and Roussillon. In Béarn, however, the ubiquitous red brick was often layered with the native river pebbles, the well-polished *galets du Gave* later used for decorative dressing on the walls of the Renaissance castle of Pau.

Beyond the viscounty, Gaston III eventually controlled, either directly or through his allies, a veritable chain of castles and fortified towns along the routes linking Béarn and Foix. In Bigorre, the most notable was Mauvezin, to which Fébus gave its definitive shape, while Lourdes, nominally English, was manned by a garrison commanded by his kinsman Pierre-Arnaud de Béarn; farther east, the Count's own castles of Saint-Gaudens and Montpezat, together with Montespan – fief of another kinsman, Roger d'Espagne – and the walled town of Cazères, controlled the upper valley of the Garonne. Saint-Girons, Rieux and the castles of Montesquieu and Carlac (now Carlat-Bayle) guarded the last stages between the Garonne and Ariège valleys. Last but not least, the castle Fébus added to the older bastide of Mazères, within a leisurely day's ride of Toulouse, was his favourite residence in the county of Foix.

To garrison castles and walled towns, or to field armies capable of responding quickly to any external threat, the viscounts of Béarn had been hampered by the traditional liberties they were sworn to preserve. The *fors* stipulated, among other restrictions, that nobles owed the Viscount military service only in the case of invasion. Commoners may be called to serve outside the borders of the viscounty for only three annual periods, each of no more than nine days; moreover, they may not be led across the Garonne. However, since these limitations pertained to the feudal, unpaid *service d'ost*, Fébus was able to ignore them by resorting to the simple if costly expedient of paying his troops. In a remarkably egalitarian manner every Béarnais called to serve, regardless of social or military rank, was to receive a monthly pay of 25 florins, while men brought from Foix, Lautrec, or other fiefs of Gaston III, were paid 30 florins (this may be an indication that the system was extended to all of the Count's domains).[16] Given that those called to serve had to procure and maintain their own equipment, this munificence was probably not excessive. Strict guidelines were laid down for the recruitment of conscripts. The rule for the nobles was the simplest: all were to serve in the cavalry, and, of course, provide their own mounts, remounts and armour; commoners were to send and equip one man for each group of twenty-five households. The villagers were also to bear the cost of much of the army's equipment: each *sinquoantaine* (a group of fifty households) was required to provide one horse, one suit of armour and the equipment, offensive and defensive, of two foot soldiers or archers; in addition to this collective imposition, each member of the *sinquoantaine* was assessed an individual contribution pegged to his own wealth, ranging from two horses for an annual income of 400 florins, to a single piece of armour for an income below 200 florins. Nor did the clergy escape the obligation to support the Count's armament: cloistered monks excepted, every priest with an annual income of 200 florins or more was required to provide a fully equipped horse. The particular emphasis on procuring remounts reflects the fact that horses were the most notable casualties of medieval warfare: in one (perhaps extreme) instance, the rolls of the army during the war of Comminges show that in a four-month period a kinsman of Fébus lost eleven out of the fourteen horses with which he had begun the campaign.[17]

Given Gaston III's readiness to innovate, it is not surprising that he should have availed himself of contemporary advances in military technology, particularly with regard to ordnance. A special corps assigned to siege warfare and transports was equipped not only with the catapults known since Antiquity, but also with cannons. These were of regional manufacture – from foundries in Morlaàs and Saint-Jean Pied-de-Port – a sign of the lively interest taken by the rulers of Béarn and Navarre in the development of firearms. Since several of the ingredients necessary for the production of gunpowder (notably sulphur and mercury) were imported by way of Barcelona, where Béarnais merchants enjoyed a privileged status, commercial enterprise contributed also to the needs of national defence.[18] To verify the readiness of the troops and the good condition of their mounts and equipment, periodic musters were held, thanks to which it is possible to evaluate the numbers of Fébus' armies. Thus for the campaign of 1376, the muster for the viscounties of Béarn, Marsan and Gavardan counted 1,200 foot and archers, 750 mounted men-at-arms with their remounts, and the 700 men of the ordnance and train commanded by Sicard de Lordat – a total of 2,500 men, probably matched in the county of Foix by

---

[16] To compare with other monthly rates of military pay: the King of England paid a mounted knight 20 florins, a mounted esquire 10 fl., and a mounted archer 5 fl.; in the French royal army, the rates were respectively 32 fl., 16 fl. and 13 fl. See Fowler, 308.

[17] *Vicomté*, 160, n. 138.

[18] *Ibid.*, 159 and n. 134.

equivalent numbers. Hence Fébus could field a force of 5,000, or even more in an emergency: when Louis d'Anjou threatened the viscounty in 1372, a mass mobilization mustered 6,000 men in Béarn alone. But this seems to have been the only instance of a *levée en masse*: the existence of a new kind of standing army, half-way between the traditional feudal levy and the mercenary company, clearly obviated the need for such hasty improvisations. Moreover, it is worth noting that in the armies of Foix-Béarn duties and responsibilities were more often than not assigned without regard to social rank, but rather on the basis of military ability: not all who served in its considerable cavalry were nobles, and even such an élite unit as Fébus' household troop – a personal escort that would have been traditionally an aristocratic preserve – includes only one of the twelve barons of Béarn, together with a few knights and a greater number of 'adventurers'.[19] And as might be expected, key commands were entrusted to his most habitual associates, such as his bastard Yvain, his half-brothers Arnaud-Guilhem de Morlanne and Pierre de Béarn, and Espan de Lion. All told, Fébus disposed of ready forces second only to the armies available to France and England, and superior to those of most feudal magnates.[20] The mere existence of that army proved an effective deterrent to invasion, and even in the context of the hereditary feud with Armagnac, the campaigns waged during Fébus' reign were relatively few and brief, with only one major battle – Launac – fought in those forty years.

A strong standing army was also an asset in safeguarding the lands of Foix and Béarn from the unpredictable ravages of the *routiers*, the mercenary companies idled by lengthy truces and now practicing their trade – pillage and extortion – impartially on any and all former belligerents. But unlike Jean II of France, whose army had been routed in April 1362 by the well-trained Companies, Fébus did not fall into the error of applying force alone. Here again, the readiness of his defences was a partial deterrent, but he was also open to arrangements that guaranteed the safety of his lands without interfering with the *routiers'* industry. The connection with the *compagnons* of Lourdes had been especially helpful to Gaston III in securing his hold on the southern half of Bigorre (see p. 74 above); at first informal, it was eventually sanctioned by a contract signed on 12 November 1379 – i.e. several years after Fébus had acquired control of the castle from the Duke of Lancaster. In this carefully drawn document, Gaston's cousin Jean de Béarn 'and all the *compagnons* of Lourdes' agree to give the Count half of the money, grain and wine, they shall collect in *patis* or 'protection' payments from the towns and villages of Bigorre. Moreover, each party was to respect the safe-conducts issued by the other:

[19] *Ibid.*, 158, n. 132.

[20] A comparison of troops to population ratios places the Foix-Béarn of Gaston III on par with the Prussia of Frederick II. See Philippe Contamine, *War in the Middle Ages* (Oxford, 1984), 307.

to that extent Fébus' subjects would have benefited from his rather ignoble alliance.

Froissart's account of his journey to Béarn indicates that this agreement between Fébus and a brigand chieftain was not the first and only one of its kind. While relaying the story of the castle of 'Ortingas', taken in some indeterminate past by one Pierre d'Anchin (or d'Antin), perhaps an earlier 'captain' of Lourdes, the chronicler notes that in a period of five years the *routiers* reaped a profit of '30,000 francs from the merchandise they found [*sic*] and in [ransomed] French prisoners; but all those who came from the county of Foix or from Béarn they let go free, together with their goods, without hurting them.'[21] The fact that 'Ortingas' (now Artigat) lies between two of Fébus' castles, on the road linking the Ariège and the Garonne valleys, and that it had been taken from a French garrison, may suggest that he was complicit in the operation from its start, especially if the events coincide with a period, under the reign of Jean II, when young Gaston III's relations with the French court were less than cordial. Another document, drawn on 12 May 1375 at Orthez, records the oath taken before Fébus' notary by a group of 'captains' seeking safe-conduct through Béarn. These men (including that forerunner of Shakespeare's Othello, the Nègre de Valence) undertake 'upon their honour' not to tarry or cause damage while travelling through the Count's domain, and not to stray from the route that his appointed guides will show them. Failing any of which they will be regarded everywhere as 'false, bad men and traitors to the said Count', and they will make full reparation for any damage or rapine committed by their people – all this sworn 'on the Holy Gospels of God, touching them with their right hand.'[22] The implication being clearly that Fébus had the means to punish any transgression, the agreement illustrates what seems to have been a routinely applied policy of conditional tolerance: apparently ignoring the repeated condemnations fulminated by several popes against the *routiers*, the Count of Foix was willing to let them live and prosper – and occasionally share in their profits – so long as they kept their hands off his own lands and subjects.

While it is now impossible to evaluate the profits accruing to Fébus from his compacts – explicit or implicit – with the *routiers*, they were of such an occasional nature that they probably could not be counted as a reliable source of the revenues needed to offset military expenditures. In addition to an ambitious building program and the maintenance of a standing army for periods far exceeding the feudal obligations of old, Fébus also used his economic power to secure the feudal allegiances of lords and castellans beyond the borders of his own domains. Gaston III did not invent the concept of the *fief-rente* – King John is known to have granted money fiefs as early as 1200 – but he appears

[21]  *Voyage*, 5.

[22]  *Vicomté*, 355.

to have made a more systematic and inventive use of it.[23] In its simplest terms, the transaction consisted in the exchange of a pledge of service for a grant of money – lump sum or annuity – rather than of land. There was no single model for those contracts between Fébus and his 'money-vassals': some were hardly distinguishable from conventional loans, some just stopped short of a formal homage. Some grants were in lump sums: thus, in exchange for 1,000 gold francs, one Bidau de Bazillac in Bigorre pledged him his service 'against all, save the King of France'; a first instalment of 6,500 francs to a group of lords in Comminges, as well as similar transactions in Soule, all appeared to be phases of Fébus' systematic infiltration of lands bordering on Béarn. The true *fief-rente*, typically, an annuity of 100 francs, was sometimes baited with a bonus – up to 2,000 francs – or a 'free gift' of horses. In all cases Gaston III wielded money as a diplomatic weapon not only to purchase the military services of the grant-ees, but to some extent undermine their feudal obligations to other overlords – neighbours or potential adversaries of Foix-Béarn.[24] Some grantees would have been hard put to reconcile this pledge to Fébus with duty to their 'natural' suzerain, as for instance in the case of the lord of La Mothe in Périgord, who promised to serve the Count of Foix with '[his] person, [his] power, and [his] whole domain' (*de tote ma terre*): with the engagement of his land, he became in effect a vassal without any mention of homage. In another instance, the lord of Curton pledged his services to Fébus against all adversaries, with the usual exception of his 'natural' lord of Albret, but an additional clause restricted the exception in such as way that Curton – and his own vassals – could be called upon to serve the Count of Foix even against the lord of Albret. With such imaginative use of *fiefs-rentes*, Fébus was not only waging a new kind of warfare, using money as an invasion force, he was also subverting the very foundation of the feudal 'system', the man-to-lord personal relationship, and replacing it with what was in effect a mercenary transaction.

## Despotism, tempered

ALL was quiet in Foix and Béarn for most of the reign of Gaston III, but this is not to say that everyone was happy with his rule. His methodical exploitation of every available source of revenue – taxation, rents, usury and judicial fines – was bound to generate discontent in all social classes. Surviving records of the seizure and sale of the houses and goods of defaulting villagers suggest that desperate flights of peasants unable to pay the *fouage* increased in frequency towards the end of the reign. Heavy penalties in cash or in kind were often levied against other delinquents: thus, among other examples, the case of the burgher of Morlaàs condemned to defray the cost of masonry work on

---

[23]  W. L. Warren, *King John* (Berkeley, 1961), 147.

[24]  *Vicomté*, 289–92.

the Viscount's castle, and that of Guilhem-Arnaud, the Count's farrier and his wife Marianne, compelled not only to give him their vineyard and other land bordering the castle park of Orthez, but to till their erstwhile possession for life. Although taxes may have been less of a burden for the nobles, they fell often enough victims to their lord's merciless usury. Some may well have been set up to fail, as the already mentioned baron of Castelnau-Tursan and his neighbour Pierre d'Ornessan, co-owners of the fief of Ognoas in Marsan: their combined bankruptcies netted Fébus control of that estate and of its revenues. Through similar operations, the Count acquired several more domains in Marsan and Béarn, as well as seigniorial rights in the town of Ax in the county of Foix. Among the lands confiscated were those of the lord of Méritein in Béarn, one of the three knights whose estates had been given as securities for a loan of 100 *écus* to Espan de Lion: evidently there was no forgiving of debts, even to the closest familiars.

Nor was residence outside the Count of Foix' jurisdiction an effective protection against his legal and sometimes military might. Two examples from different epochs of his reign show that the ruthless efficiency of his youth did not mellow with age. In 1362 the Count of l'Isle-Jourdain, taken prisoner at Launac and unable to pay his ransom, mortgaged his domains to Fébus for a loan of 3,000 francs. Over the years, this loan was renewed, increased and extended several times, until the vassal of Armagnac owed the Count of Foix 10,000 florins. The cession of the forest of Mondonville near Toulouse only bought him a further extension, and at his death in 1374, the new Count of l'Isle-Jourdain still had to promise to honour his father's remaining debt of 7,000 florins. More than twenty years after Launac another 'foreign' debtor, Roger Bernard de Lévis, was brought to his knees: having initially borrowed 400 francs in 1378, by 1380 he owed Fébus 1,300 francs, plus 100 francs in penalties and interests. When he failed to pay, the Count seized his castle of Mirepoix; soon afterwards, Lévis stormed and recaptured his own castle, killing a number of Fébus' soldiers. By January 1382, however, he was forced to come to Mazères, and promised to accept the demands of his creditor. Two more years passed before he was summoned to Orthez to hear the terms: to the outstanding debt were now added a fine of 2,000 francs for damage done to the Count of Foix; 1,900 francs for masses on behalf of the men killed in the attack on Mirepoix; and 1,900 francs to the heirs of the dead soldiers. Moreover, the lord of Mirepoix was henceforth forbidden to sell or mortgage any of his properties without his creditor' s permission; last but not least, he swore 'on the body of Christ' to serve the Count of Foix 'against all other lords in the world, except the King of France'.[25] This political clause is not only notable because it is an example of the means Gaston III employed to extend his sphere of influence, but also because the lord of Mirepoix, a vassal of the French Crown, came nominally under the jurisdiction of the seneschal

[25] *Ibid.*, 288.

of Carcassonne and the King's Lieutenant in Languedoc – neither of whom seems to have intervened or even interceded on his behalf. If Fébus was thus able to reach beyond his borders with impunity and force the submission of men who were not his subjects, it is easy to understand how *a fortiori* he could make himself obeyed in his own lands.

There was indeed little resistance to the Count's decrees, and very few instances of civil disorders are recorded throughout his reign. Conversely, the repression of those known incidents was relatively mild by the standards of the period. The instigators of the Orthez tumult of October 1353, together with those magistrates found derelict in their duties, suffered several months of imprisonment; the city, its franchises provisionally suspended, was assessed a collective fine of 10,000 silver marks (see p. 34 above). This is a far cry from the atrocities devised by Peter IV of Aragon for the punishment of the rebellious burghers of Valencia, made to 'drink' the molten bronze of the bells that had signalled the uprising; or even from the threat of mass executions (most of which were remitted, however) that followed the Montpellier riots of 1379. Those events must of course be viewed from rather different perspectives: in Aragon, the participation of Valencia to a widespread revolt had seriously threatened the integrity of the Crown, and in Languedoc the good folk of Montpellier, however provoked by the misrule of Louis d'Anjou, had massacred perhaps as many as eighty-five of his officers. But then it must also be noted that Fébus' subjects were never driven to the anger that moved others to such desperate defiance of royal armies. While Froissart's casual report that they were eager to pay the newly instituted taxes can be read as a verbal flourish, the Count's fiscal innovations were received by and large with resignation. The timing of the *fouage* of 1367, for instance, was not a mere psychological manœuvre, taking advantage of the threat posed by the Black Prince's army: fiscal measures could plainly be seen to coincide with effective military preparations for the defence of Béarn, which would again prove their worth six years later, by discouraging a threatened French invasion. Nor was Fébus' active concern for the welfare of his subjects limited to military defences. Thus in 1374, in order to relieve a famine in Béarn, he initiated and underwrote the import of corn from Brittany. Fraught with the risks of seizure at sea by one or other belligerent, the enterprise could only succeed with the diplomatic as well as the financial support of Gaston III.[26] This is in sharp contrast with the scandalous situation in Languedoc, where the revenue from a crushing tax burden seemed earmarked for the financing of Louis d'Anjou's personal ventures in pursuit of a crown, rather than on stopping the depredations of marauding *routiers*.

It is also worth noting that Fébus seems to have sensed the limits beyond which he dare not squeeze his subjects. Thus, while he may have been inspired

---

[26] Safe-conducts notwithstanding, the two ships were in fact detained, one off the Breton coast, the other in La Rochelle. See *Vicomté*, 252–3, and *Prince*, 197.

to levy the annual hearth tax by a similar measure in France, he refrained from imitating the imposition by Charles V of a salt tax – the hated *gabelle* that would provoke many a rebellion through the centuries and make folk-heroes of salt-smugglers. Moreover, once instituted, the burden seems to have remained constant: the 2 francs cited by Froissart in 1388 was the same rate levied since 1370, and probably from the inception of the *fouage*. When faced with resistance, Fébus also appears to have preferred a low-keyed response to the deployment of armed force: when in April 1367 the townspeople of Morlaàs rebelled against the hearth tax, only one burgher was taken from each neighbourhood, to be kept not in irons in the castle, but under house arrest in the *baile's* own home. Meanwhile, local magistrates went 'from street to street' and presumably from door to door, to collect the *taille*.[27] This quelling of a 'rebellion' with a minimum of force and, more importantly perhaps, by delegation to the local authorities, was repeated elsewhere, and may well have been a habitual pattern of Gaston III's use of power in internal affairs. On another occasion a new tax on capital gains, levied across all social classes, raised such a general outcry that it does not seem to have been collected again.

This is not to say that Gaston III's exercise of his seigniorial prerogatives as chief justiciar was not often harsh and arbitrary: the record of his official acts is punctuated through and through with instances of arrests, individual or collective, of *jurats* and other magistrates held responsible for the offences or omissions of their communities. But in none of the recorded cases did an arrest lead to an execution. Here, however, it would be naïve to trust entirely the official records. Like any other feudal magnate, the Count of Foix and lord of Béarn would have had no need to make public, or account for, his exercise of high justice. There would be indeed a tragic episode ending with at least fifteen unnamed persons being put to death, without a scrap of record corroborating the mention by Froissart of their torture and execution (see p. 152 below): if their story could be so thoroughly suppressed that only a truncated and patently distorted version of it survives in the *Chroniques*, it not impossible that other unheralded executions of Gaston III's enemies may have taken place and been as efficiently hushed up. From both fact and legend, one can indeed infer a pervasive control of information and opinion. As noted earlier, every one of Fébus' subjects was bound by his oath of fealty to safeguard 'with his own life, property and honour' any state secret with which he might have been entrusted. Sworn to take no part in any secret meeting or league against his lord, he was also required, if he was made aware of such goings-on, to make them fail, or to warn the Count as quickly as possible (see p. 23 above). If this provision was enforced as conscientiously as was the collection of the most trivial fee or toll, it must have gone a long way to inhibit the dissemination of unfavourable news or comments. Nor should the power of superstition be discounted: the

[27] *Prince*, 136–7.

rumours about the familiar spirits that kept Fébus instantly informed of events happening may well have a similar effect. At any rate, the tight control exercised by the Count over police and administrative matters ensured a swift and measured response before an incident – such as the Morlaàs 'rebellion' – could get out of hand.

Scale was, of course, one of the factors that made Fébus' domains a relative oasis of peace and security in a Western Europe rent by war, civil strife and brigandage. Proximity – he was never more than a day's ride away from any part of Béarn, and he could certainly be in Pamiers or Mazères in much less than the ten days of Froissart's journey – made it possible for Gaston III to act quickly wherever his personal intervention might be needed, a luxury that was available neither to Charles V in ruling distant Languedoc, or to Edward III with regard to Gascony. But more profoundly perhaps, Fébus' presence within reach of any and all of his subjects, in a era when the feudal relationship was above all seen as a personal bond symbolized by the physical ceremony of homage, gave him far more than a mere tactical advantage. However burdened they may have justly felt by their lord's taxes, tolls, fees, rents, etc., his people could not but acknowledge that he was also protecting and promoting their interests as vigorously as he did his own.

As early as 1354 one of Gaston III' s earliest claims of sovereign rights in Béarn was made on behalf of Pélegrin de Fosse, the merchant from Sauveterre who had been detained and despoiled by the magistrates of Montpellier as a presumed Gascon – and therefore an enemy alien.[28] It is significant that the young Count chose an issue regarding free trade as an occasion to proclaim his princely prerogative as lord of Béarn 'by the grace of God'. A few years later, despite his poor showing as an ally and vassal of Peter IV, he obtained from that irascible monarch the confirmation of rights granted to the merchants of Oloron throughout the Crown of Aragon.[29] In both instances Fébus was clearly conscious of his domains' potential as the commercial intermediary between belligerents, linking French Toulouse and Montpellier with English-held Bordeaux and Bayonne, thus saving both end-regions from economic asphyxiation. With free access to Barcelona and other Catalan ports, the merchants of Foix and Béarn were indeed connecting the entire Mediterranean market with the Atlantic seaboard. Whether by coincidence or by conscious design, Fébus' policies just met the conditions of neutrality and security required for this commerce to exist, let alone flourish. Since his quiet withdrawal from French service after 1353, he had managed to avoid aligning himself with either party in the Anglo-French conflict; and while the subjects of the Count of Foix – a vassal of France – could be regarded in Aquitaine as enemy aliens, it was now generally accepted that those of the sovereign lord of Béarn had no other suzerain.

[28] *Ibid.*, 61–3. See also p. 38 above.

[29] *Vicomté*, 74.

As for security, the chain of castles held by Fébus and his allies between Mauléon in the Basque country to the edges of Roussillon and Languedoc safeguarded the roads so efficiently that one of his agents could boast that 'From Orthez to Albi, no one dares steal as much as a chicken.'[30] Moreover, Fébus had more than one way of maintaining effective control over diverse bands of brigands. The fear of his military might was sometimes enough to keep them from stealing that proverbial chicken – this seems to have been the case of the several companies granted conditional safe passage through Béarn in 1379; but when the *routiers* were unlikely to be cowed – as were the Compagnons in quasi-impregnable Lourdes – the Count was not above negotiating with them a cynical contract combining profit-sharing and protection. Whatever the form of a particular, more or less formal 'insurance' pact, Fébus' subjects reaped double profit from it, for as the protection did not extend to their competitors from other nations, the merchants of Foix and Béarn enjoyed a virtual monopoly, so long as they travelled under its umbrella. Lastly, the decision to mint gold florins – a decision that could only have been made by Fébus – is yet another instance of his active interest in promoting economic growth.

More locally, the Count's foreign and domestic policies also benefited mere villagers. Thanks to his diplomacy and his military might, they enjoyed the rare luxury of several decades without an invasion by either regular armies or bands of marauders, a privilege they could appreciate when hearing tales from such neighbouring lands as Quercy, Gascony, or Languedoc. However much the annual *fouage* and *taille* weighed on the peasantry, those charges were a bargain compared to the devastation of war. Equally important to social and economic stability was Fébus' adjudication of the immemorial feud between highlanders and lowlanders. If the compromises he imposed on disputed rights-of-way and grazing privileges sometimes seemed to confirm the usurpations of piedmont pastures by the cattlemen and shepherds of the high valleys, they at least spelled out much-needed limitations and compensations. Above all, the threat of effective sanctions, and the Count's ability to apply them, brought an end to the seasonal battles between the contending communities.

Besides those major issues of interest to the public at large, the notarial registers of his acts show a Fébus always ready and willing to dispense his seigniorial justice in private disputes between his subjects, however humble. Even while on the march with his army, he would find the time to witness a contract of debenture between two soldiers. Such frequent personal contact with people of all classes would have only encouraged a tendency to think of government in practical terms, and if need be to depart from traditional models. If we had nothing but the evidence of his own writing, Gaston III was clearly capable of reflecting on the long-term effects of his actions. In freeing the serfs, for instance, he must have looked beyond the immediate gain of collecting the

---

[30] *Prince*, 236.

substantial sums offered for their redemption. While his decision here can hardly be termed social engineering, it would have the effect in practically all of Béarn of abolishing an entire class and integrating its former members into the mainstream community of free men. Likewise, Fébus appears to have been not averse to elevating some freeholders to gentle rank, by the simple act of promoting their house – the *ostau* – and lands to the status of *domenjadure*, or noble domain – which in Béarn conferred nobility to its owner. Whether the Count agreed to such promotions in exchange for a 'free offering' is not known, but even if a one-time fee accrued to the treasury, it is unlikely to have offset in perpetuity the loss of revenue from a henceforth tax-exempt estate. However, while the lord of Béarn gave up a fraction of his revenue, another member was added to the ranks of the lesser nobility, the class in which he recruited most of his personal followers.

Froissart sums up Fébus' administration of his disparate domains with the simple phrase: 'he governed wisely'. And yet elsewhere the same chronicler hints at the Count's avarice, his short – not to say violent – temper, and a particularly disturbing, vindictive inflexibility: 'One is careful not to make him angry, for in his anger there is no forgiveness.'[31] In short, this is the temperament of an autocrat, brooking no opposition. And while it cannot be denied that his rule brought peace to his lands and a degree of prosperity to his subjects, this is not now and was not then a perfect world. In time one devastating event would show that under the surface of obedience, discontent was simmering among the most dangerous elements of Béarnais society. But the brief violence they incited could not disturb the works and days of one of the safest lands in all Christendom.

[31] *Voyage*, 49.

# 7

# Fébus at Home

Like many feudal rulers, Gaston III had no fixed capital in the modern sense of a central seat of government located in or near his principal residence. The coterie of familiars that formed the rudimentary governing council of Foix-Béarn under Fébus normally followed him wherever he chose to be at any given time. What remains of the several castles where he dwelt in various parts of his domains suggests that they were primarily fortresses, accommodating rather cramped living quarters. The oldest may have been the castle of Foix, on a site inhabited since prehistoric times and fortified since the tenth century. Perched on a crag 200 feet above the town and the bridge on the Ariège, its aspect had discouraged a potential attack by Simon de Montfort during the Albigensian 'crusade', and it remained an important military base for Gaston III, especially in the months leading to the Launac victory in December 1362. Thereafter, he made little use of the ancestral seat, and, when in the county of Foix, made Mazères his habitual residence. His choice was probably due in large part to the proximity of Toulouse. Fébus does not appear to have owned an *ostel* in the capital of Languedoc, but Mazères, only a day's ride away, and at about equal distance from Carcassonne, was ideally situated for keeping an eye on the affairs of that French province, as well as those of neighbouring Catalonia. Jointly founded in the thirteenth century by an earlier count and the Cistercian abbot of Boulbonne, Mazères was a *bastide* – a new city built according to a strict gridiron plan – and a prosperous market town, with a tributary of the Garonne providing good fishing and water power for several mills. Nearby woods also offered ample opportunity for Fébus to hunt regularly. The castle he ordered rebuilt was razed in the seventeenth century, together with the adjacent city walls, but it is known to have had six strong towers. It was still unfinished when Jean de Berry came to Mazères in the summer of 1381, and the Count, leaving the castle to his guest, moved to the abbey of Boulbonne for the duration of Duke's visit. The complaints voiced after the death of Gaston III by the Mazérois suggest that even under ordinary circumstances – let alone the extraordinary ones of royal visits – the living quarters were inadequate to lodge Fébus, his retinue and the garrison, and that the townspeople were expected to accommodate the overflow of retainers.

In Béarn, Fébus is known to have repaired and enlarged the viscounts' castle at the old capital of Morlaàs, but the dating of his official acts in notarial registers shows that he stopped for longer periods at nearby Pau, where he had the earlier castle rebuilt on a larger scale. On a rocky spur commanding the crossing of the Gave, as well as spectacular views of the Jurançon vineyards and the perennial snows of the Pyrenees, the castle of Pau was destined to be the capital of Béarn, and eventually a royal residence. At the western end of the viscounty, Fébus occasionally stayed at Sauveterre-de-Béarn, hard by the border with Navarre, but Orthez was by all accounts his most habitual residence. Situated on the road to Compostela where it crosses the Gave de Pau, and at the intersection of the Toulouse–Bayonne and the Bordeaux–Pamplona trade routes, Orthez had become the seat of the viscounts when Gaston VII Moncade had built his castle on the steep hill north of a town of little more than 500 hearths. The most complete remnant of the castle is the keep erected between 1250 and 1270; with its sharp prow turned eastward, the four-storey pentagonal tower probably housed the garrison and the Count's treasure. Of the attached residence, only the rectangular foundations remain: they suggest a rather small dwelling, surely too small to accommodate more than the Count's immediate family and servants. Some of Fébus' huntsmen, and even his ward Jeanne de Boulogne, were lodged in the surrounding suburb, the 'Bourg Moncade', in effect the castle's outbuildings. Travellers have mentioned the existence of a (necessarily small) deer park within the walls, and the notarial registers record instances of Gaston III hearing pleaders in the castle vineyard. The dimensions, as well as the semi-rural aspect of the setting, conjure up the image of a modest seigniorial seat rather than a princely court, but its repute was enough to attract the attention of the busiest chronicler of that age, and start him on a long journey from his northern home.

I N 1388 Jean Froissart made up his mind to visit the court of the famed Count of Foix, there to collect for his chronicles many stories of the gallant deeds and dramatic events that had occurred during the recent wars in Spain, Portugal and other southern lands. Twenty years before, as a guest of the Prince of Wales and Aquitaine, Froissart had observed an earlier round of Peninsular campaigns. From the safe vantage point of the court of Bordeaux, he had reported on the army's arduous crossing of the Pyrenees, on the victory of Najera, and on the melancholy return of the Prince, now sick and bankrupt. Since then, the sons of Edward III had again intervened in Iberian conflicts, hoping to overthrow or at least undermine the Trastamara dynasty of Castile. Both the Duke of Lancaster and the Earl of Cambridge had failed in their efforts, and in the end John of Gaunt had agreed to a reconciliation of sorts, sealed by the marriage of his daughter Catalina to the heir of the Trastamara usurpers. But several years of campaigning had yielded a crop of war stories rich enough to send a reporter of chivalry on a long, long journey.

Thanks to its proximity to both Spain and Aquitaine, and to Gaston III's *de facto* neutrality in the conflicts that ravaged neighbouring countries, the court of Orthez had been throughout that period an ideal listening post for news – and rumours – from beyond the Pyrenees. Memories of Lancaster's disastrous

Orthez: the Moncade Tower, north and east walls

Orthez: the west wall of the Moncade Tower, with visible outline of a former building

venture of 1386–7 were still fresh, and so was the grief over the many Béarnais knights who, heedless of Gaston's entreaties, had enlisted in 1385 for an
ill-advised Castilian invasion of Portugal, and been slaughtered at Aljubarrota.
Echoes of those events had reached Froissart in his native Hainault, where
he enjoyed a comfortable sinecure as a canon of Chimay. But, while another
chronicler might have been satisfied with second- or third-hand reports, he
was intent on telling the entire history of feats of arms in his time, and to glean
as many details as he could from the participants and other eyewitnesses. And
so, he writes,

> to ascertain the truth of far-away and unknown deeds without sending
> anyone in my place, I took the wise course and occasion to go myself and
> visit that mighty and redoubtable prince, my lord Gaston, Count of Foix
> and Béarn. And well I knew that if I was granted the good fortune of
> coming safely to his house and biding there at leisure for a while, I could
> find no better place in the world where I would be truly informed of all
> news, for a great many foreign knights and squires abide there and gladly
> return for the sake of his noble welcome.[1]

Jean Froissart was 'granted the good fortune of coming safely' to Orthez, but
only at the end of a very long road. He had probably left Chimay or Valenci-
ennes in the spring or very early summer, perhaps with a halt in Paris, and then
gone on to the Loire valley residence of his current patron, Guy, Count of Blois
and lord of Hainault, in whose *mesnie* Froissart held the at least nominal post
of chaplain. On the road to Blois he had met two knights, one of whom was
returning, as it were, from Orthez, where he had received from the Count of
Foix a parting gift of a horse and 200 florins. This chance encounter must have
surely strengthened the chronicler's resolve to visit a host of such munificent
disposition.

Guy de Blois seized the opportunity to entrust his chaplain with the con-
veyance of a courtly gift to Gaston Fébus. One of Froissart's light-hearted rustic poems – a *pastourelle* – relates how, at an unnamed abbey 'between Lunel
and Montpellier', he was to take charge of four greyhounds and deliver them
safely to the Count of Foix. A present of hounds was a not infrequent token
of loyal friendship between great lords, and particularly suitable for the author
of the *Book of the Hunt*. If Froissart's verse is to be believed, the noble beasts
were named Tristan, Hector, Brun and Roland – after three heroes of legend
and the bear of animal romances.[2] The arrangements for this offering may
have been partly to blame for delaying Froissart's departure: correspondence
between Blois and the monastic kennel in Languedoc, the redaction of letters

---

[1] *Chroniques*, XI, 2–3.

[2] Jean Froissart, *Poésies*, 3 vols. (Brussels, 1870–2), II, 321–3.

of introduction, perhaps some requests for safe-conducts, would have taken some time. The chronicler may then have left Blois in mid-October, travelling probably down the Rhône valley to Avignon. The route would have been familiar: years before, he had journeyed to the papal court in order to solicit an ecclesiastical living, and the search for patronage had even taken him as far as Narbonne. But while we can only attempt to reconstruct the early stages of Froissart's 1388 voyage to Béarn, the last ten days of his itinerary are well documented in his account, from his departure from Carcassonne in mid-November to his arrival at Orthez ten days later. on the feast of Saint Catherine.

The narrative becomes especially rich in anecdotes after a halt at Pamiers, 'a most pleasing city, for it is situated in the midst of good and bountiful vineyards on the bank of a beautiful, clear and wide river named La Liège [l'Ariège]' where 'there chanced to come, on his way back from Avignon, a knight of the household of the Count of Foix, named Messire Espan de Lion, valiant, wise and handsome, who may have been then about fifty years of age …'[3] Writing several years after the fact, Froissart exhibits occasional lapses of memory, and it is possible that their meeting had been pre-arranged in Avignon. This would account for an otherwise unexplained three days' halt at Pamiers, where the chronicler might have been awaiting the arrival of Espan and his armed retinue. Although travel was then much safer than it had been for decades, banditry was far from being eradicated, especially in the mountainous regions Froissart still had to cross on his way to Béarn. But more than an escort, Messire Espan was to be a knowledgeable, and mostly co-operative, informant about the ways of the court of Orthez. He is also the source of many of the stories and digressions in Froissart's recollections. One would look in vain in these for the visual spice of aesthetic appreciation, or even for the dramatic details of unforeseen hazards: a dangerous ferry crossing, made necessary by the broken bridge over the Garonne, is dispatched in a few annoyed lines; as for cities and castles, they are evaluated only in terms of their prosperity and their strategic value. But even where it is clear that he has not kept them in very good order, the chronicler had taken copious notes, and the stories gleaned while riding alongside Messire Espan, or drinking with the castellan of Mauvezin, and later with the Bascot de Mauléon, make up the bulk of his 'travelogue'.

In 1388 Jean Froissart was in his mid-fifties, and a seasoned traveller. As a young writer he had gone to England to seek the patronage of his compatriot Philippa de Hainault, Edward III's queen. Kindly received, he had also visited Scotland and Wales. He had been at Bordeaux in 1367, on the day of Epiphany, to report the birth of the future Richard II. The following year he had attended the wedding in Milan of Lionel, Duke of Clarence, with Violante Visconti. There he might have met Geoffrey Chaucer and been presented to Petrarch, but there is no hint of such meetings having taken place, and one

---

[3] *Voyage*, 1.

can only wish they had. After the Milan festivities Froissart had followed the progress of King Peter of Cyprus through northern Italy, and then pushed on to decaying Rome, where Pope Urban V had recently returned from Avignon. One of his most generous patrons had been Duke Wenceslas of Brabant – a son of John of Bohemia, the blind hero of Crécy – whose court was famed for the magnificence of its tourneys and other feasts. Froissart then was no naïve bumpkin: not only had he been the guest of some of the grandest princes of Europe, he was an aficionado of chivalric prowess and courtly entertainments. By comparison with the splendours of Milan and Brussels, among others, Fébus' court at Orthez was a relatively modest establishment. But the chronicler was clearly fascinated by its opulence, its peculiar routine, and especially by the prince whose tastes it reflected. Given his career in the shadow of the great, it is tempting to dismiss Froissart's praise of Fébus as mere flattery, or at least to take it as grossly inflated currency. But a closer reading will show that the relationship between the 'reporter' and his subject was not so simple. Writing – probably in Chimay – several years after Gaston's death, Froissart could expect no further largesse from him, nor fear his displeasure. When he says that, had the Count lived, he would have gladly visited his court again, his regret can certainly be taken at face value. Moreover, courtier and snob though he was, Froissart did not shirk the risks involved in reporting the misdeeds of the great or unflattering opinions of them: thus, for having quoted the dying Charles V's reservations about his brother, he incurred the wrath of Louis d'Anjou. Nor, despite his admiration, did he gloss over the darker aspects of Fébus' personality. It may be Froissart's flair for the dramatic scene that ensures the inclusion of anecdotes illustrative of the Count's violent temper, and of his vindictive cruelty. But it is the thinly veiled sarcasm of the chronicler of chivalry that we hear when the Count of Foix, instead of following the Black Prince's banner to Castile, chooses the inglorious alternative of staying at Orthez 'close to his florins'.

That Jean Froissart was a poet as much as a 'reporter', can be deduced from the *Chroniques* alone. The firmly proprietary tone in which he often refers to *ma matière* ('my subject') distinguishes his enterprise from the majority of contemporary chronicles. Those are more often than not anonymous, or else the efforts of scholars have yielded little more than the name and the bare social placement of a conjectural author, usually the cloistered recipient of what news were brought to him from the outside world. But Froissart's constant presence in his text as interviewer – questioning, exclaiming, sometimes on the point of challenging his informant – is an extension of his active gathering of 'facts' in the field, at the same time revealing the author's will to shape his *reportage* into a literary construct, a creative act amounting to a kind of participation in the events reported. In lyric and epic verse, he was free to identify even more intimately with his chivalrous *matière*, and reinvent the fantasy world of Arthurian knighthood in a work that has deserved the accolade of 'purest example of chivalric revival'.[4] In a narrative of epic proportions – upward of 3,000 lines – the verse romance of *Méliador* relates the ritualized quest of a knight of Arthur's court who seeks the hand of a Scottish princess. In the narrative, Froissart inserted 'all the chansons' once composed by his late patron, Duke Wenceslas of Brabant, a literary move less bizarre then than it would appear now, and one sure to please an aristocratic audience. Whether by design or by coincidence, this and other aspects of *Méliador* made it a particularly appropriate offering to bring to Orthez. Would not the grand seigneur who chose to style himself Fébus see his own reflection in a hero labelled 'the Knight of the Golden Sun'?

And it was indeed as a poet that Froissart was received at Orthez, with all the honour and respect due to his latest work:

> The rapport between him and me during that time was this: I had brought with me a book [...] called *Méliador* [...] that the Count of Foix was most eager to see, and every night after his supper I read him some of it. But while I read, no one dared speak even one word, for he wanted me to be clearly heard, and he took great pleasure from hearing me well.[5]

Clearly, the social tables were turned, and it was the prince who took the rôle of flatterer to the visiting chronicler. Upon arriving at Orthez at about sunset on 25 November, Froissart had stopped at the 'ostel de la Lune', where, he writes, 'Ernauton du Pin, a squire of the Count, was happy to receive me, on account of my being French.' (We may note in passing that the traveller is identified by his language rather than by his place of birth – which is not yet part of France; and that in Béarn a gentleman may also keep an inn.) The Count had then sent for him, for he was 'in the whole world the lord most eager to see strangers and hear their news.' Fébus turned on the charm and made the chronicler welcome

> with very good cheer, and said to me laughing, and *in good French*, that he knew me well, although he had never seen me, but he had often heard me spoken of [...] When I asked him about anything, he answered most willingly, and said to me that the history I was pursuing would be in times to come more praised than any other.[6]

Fébus kept Froissart as his guest for more than twelve weeks, during which the traveller notes that '[his] horses were also well fed and in every other way well cared for.' Like other guests who could not be accommodated in the castle (and with whom he would have lengthy conversations) Froissart was lodged in Orthez proper. The fact that his landlord of the 'ostel de la Lune' appears

---

[4] Peter F. Dembowski, *Jean Froissart and his Méliador* (Lexington, KY, 1983), 124.

[5] *Voyage*, 66.

[6] *Chroniques*, XI, 3. Emphasis mine.

to have been also a familiar of the Count, who sometimes entrusted him with diplomatic missions, suggests that the inn was often used as an annex of the Château Moncade, and that Ernauton may have been one of Froissart's most valuable informants. The house still stands at the edge of the 'Bourg Vieux', from which the company was summoned by the horn of the watchman, to the Count's midnight supper. The steep climb from the inn to the castle, the outlandish hour, and the season's weather, all elicit a mild complaint from the poet-chronicler in the *Dit dou florin*:

> ... I had much toil / For many days and many weeks / Getting up at mid-night / In the season when stags go a-belling. / Six weeks before Christ-mas / And four thereafter, from my hostel / At the mid-night I set out / And straight to the castle I went. / Whatever the weather, rain or wind,/ I had to go. Often, I tell you, / I was wet.[7]

But Froissart hastens to add that he was soon rewarded by the Count's gra-cious welcome, and the pleasure of reading seven pages ('un septier de feuilles') from his *Méliador* to a captive audience, in a hall so brightly illuminated that he could only compare it with 'the earthly paradise'. After the reading, and before bidding good night to the company, Fébus would have 'the remainder of his wine / That came from a fine gold vessel' poured for the poet, and saluted him as he drank.

The honour must be appreciated in the context of the host's table ceremonial and of what Froissart tells us of his bizarre daily routine. Sleeping by day, work-ing and eating at night, the Count appears to have kept hours at considerable variance with those of ordinary mortals, especially in 'a world lit by fire', where the cycle of natural daylight regulated most human activity. To be sure, there were exceptions, as on Christmas Day, when a banquet described as lasting 'until four hours after nones' must have been held in the middle of the day, and it is hard to reconcile Fébus' nocturnal habits with what is known of his pas-sion for the hunt. As described in his own book on the subject, the huntsman's day began well before sunrise. The chase then would last until at least midday, and sometimes longer: thus on the day of Fébus' death, he had hunted until 'basse none', *i.e.* approximately 3 o'clock after noon. The schedule observed by Froissart may perhaps be reconciled with the hunter's routine, if one allows that Fébus may have slept, after the hunt, the remainder of the day, and so put off his 'public' appearance until late at night. But it is at least equally plausible that the chronicler, rearranging as picturesque scenes the remembered high-lights (so flattering to his self-esteem) of his stay at Orthez, may have taken as ordinary a ceremonial that was the exceptional routine of a festive season – and incidentally the staging of that rare entertainment, the reading of his chivalric romance.

---

[7] Jean Froissart, *'Dits' et 'Débats'* (Geneva, 1979), 185.

Be that as it may, what Froissart reports as if it were the habitual practice, is that the Count would rise in mid-afternoon, dine 'at Vespers' (about 5 o'clock) and only at midnight come to supper into his dining-hall, 'which was full of knights and squires, and there were always plenty of tables set for whoever wanted to sup.' Unless there were high-ranking guests, Fébus sat alone, with twelve valets holding torches before his table, and no one spoke to him unless he spoke to them first. A somewhat picky eater, he consumed quantities of poultry, but mostly the wings and drumsticks. The chronicler adds that 'the next day, he ate and drank but little.'[8] The Count's aloofness, which to modern eyes may appear intolerably rude, does not necessarily signal an exceptional degree of arrogance. Contemporary iconography (*e.g.* Jean de Berri's *Très Riches Heures*) often depicts kings and princes dining in exalted isolation, surrounded by the apparatus – gold vessels, kneeling acolytes – of a quasi-religious ritual. A public meal was for the rich and mighty the occasion to show off their material wealth, not only in the form of gem-encrusted platters, ewers, goblets and other precious hardware, but also through the abundance and variety of expensive food, and the generosity of a table set for all comers. The prince presiding over this display, alone or flanked by a select few, was himself on display. Indeed, the spectacle of the king's dinner continued to be enacted at Versailles until the Revolution, with the general public filing past and staring at the monarch at the lonely altar of his table. As for the scant regard Fébus seems to have shown for the hardship imposed on others – guests trudging up to the castle in the wintry night, petitioners kept waiting until the small hours – such eccentricities were then the privilege of the great, as they are now of their modern caricatures, the 'celebrities', and they were expected as the idiosyncratic corollaries of their singular magnificence. Froissart evidently took them in his stride, and on the whole the experience seems to have been a high point of his career as a courtier.

T HE portrait he penned of Gaston Fébus is all the more valuable for being the only one that survives. Even when Froissart's objectivity is debatable, his is a first-hand account, conveying the impression Fébus made on an intelligent, articulate observer. Where the guest had been so honoured, it was only to be expected that the word-portrait of the host should run to superlatives. The Count of Foix, we are told, was then about fifty-nine years of age (in fact only fifty-seven),

> … and I tell you that I have in my days met many knights, kings, princes and others, but I have never seen anyone so handsome of limbs, form and stature, of such fair, fresh and gracious visage, with bright and kindly eyes.[9]

---

[8] *Voyage*, 68.

[9] *Chroniques*, XI, 3.

This is hardly a detailed *signalement*. Nor can the reader fill in the visual blank, for there are no known contemporary portraits of Fébus, such as the remarkably unflattering profiles of Jean II and the royal dukes of Berri and Anjou, or even – as is the case for Charles V and his queen – a credible *gisant*. As for the images purporting to represent the Count, none can be taken as a reliable representation, although some of the miniatures illustrating later copies of the *Book of the Hunt* may refer to lost portraits or sketches made in his lifetime. Those appear to corroborate Froissart's assertion that Fébus was a tall man, and that, contrary to contemporary usage, he went habitually bareheaded. Having rendered the physical features down to a few superlatives, Froissart then turns to an equally fulsome moral depiction, but now with emphases on specific aspects of Gaston's wisdom and largesse:

> In every way [the Count] was so perfect that one could never praise him too much. He loved what he ought to love, hated what he ought to hate. He was a wise knight, high-minded and full of good counsel.[...] He never kept company with Jews or miscreants. He governed wisely. He said many prayers every day, one of the night offices in the psalter, the hours of Our Lady, of the Holy Spirit, of the Cross, and the vigils of the dead. Every day, he had five francs in small coin given away at his door to all sorts of persons, as alms for the love of God. He was liberal and courteous in giving. [...] He was affable, and all manner of people could approach him; he spoke to them softly and amiably.[10]

This is, to be sure, what one might expect to read after the account of the chronicler's reception: an evaluation of the Count's wisdom, his piety and his generosity – the tripod of virtues particularly required of a ruler. Froissart cites no particular instance of wise government, but he quotes a specific amount to illustrate the regularity of Fébus' alms giving – apparently a well-organized 'social service'. Another detail of the Count's daily routine opens perhaps a small window on his spiritual life: to read all of the psalms and liturgy as diligently as Froissart reports, Fébus would have reserved a considerable amount of time for his personal devotions. Some of the more public observances he sponsored also served as reminders of his status as ruler 'by the grace of God'. Thus on the feast of Saint Nicholas, the court and the town celebrated together the anniversary of the Count's victory at Launac, for which he ordered

> ... a solemnity throughout his land, as great and even more than for Easter day. [...] The whole clergy of the town of Orthez and all the people, men, women, and children, went in procession to fetch the Count in his castle, and there he joined the procession and the clergy on foot. Then they came to the church of Saint Nicholas, singing the psalm of David that

[10] *Ibid.*

says: *Benedictus Dominus, Deus meus, qui docet manus meas ad prelium et digitos meos ad bellum ...* [11]

Unfortunately, Froissart fails to report the details of his host's work habits, except for a tantalizing vignette of Fébus as the demanding boss of a permanent secretariat:

He had four secretaries for writing and rewriting letters, and they had better be ready for him when he came out of his chambers; nor did he call them Jehan or Gautier or Guillaume, but when they gave him letters and he had read them, he called them *Mau me sert*, either because of their writing, or for anything he ordered them. [12]

Whether the Count was in earnest, Froissart does not say: perhaps the epithet (literally: 'ill serves me') was only meant as mild teasing. Nor are we enlightened about the specific duties of the four, but from their number and habitual attendance, we can deduce a steady and substantial flow of correspondence. But it is to other sources that we need to turn for a glimpse of Fébus at the task of administering justice. While his notary's register (see Chapter 6 above) usually gives 'the Château Moncade' or more vaguely 'Orthez', as the location of recorded acts, it is sometimes specified as 'the chapel of the Château Moncade' or 'in the castle vineyard'. This is not just a mildly picturesque detail, but another reminder that, far from an anonymous institution, the government of Foix-Béarn was a part of the Count's daily routine, inseparable from his private habits, and that it was conducted from wherever he happened to be, perhaps concurrently with other pursuits: it is not too far fetched to imagine Fébus listening to petitioners while directing the pruning of his vines.

WHILE the lord of Béarn could be said to be a spectacle unto his assembled guests, he also enjoyed choice entertainments. As it was a stage for the display of wealth, a magnate's *tinel* – his dining-hall – also served as his private theatre and concert hall, and not infrequently his indoor circus. To some extent the show was on the table itself, with the presentation between the several courses of sculpted confections (the 'subtleties'), sometimes edible, sometimes even animated, representing castles, mythical beasts, or allegorical figures. Froissart relates that Fébus enjoyed those 'estranges entremés' and that, having viewed them, he would send them round to the guest tables. Whether he also regaled the company with jugglers, wrestling matches and dancing bears, can only be imagined. The only athletic entertainment mentioned by the chronicler is one recalled from a Christmas past by Espan de Lion, an impromptu

[11] Psalm 144, 'Blessed be the Lord my strength, which teacheth my hand to war, and my fingers to fight' in *Voyage*, 87.

[12] *Ibid.*, 67–8.

strongman act performed by a muscular castellan named Ernauton d'Espagne. On that occasion the Count had gone up after dinner to an upper 'gallery' overlooking the castle yard and the town of Orthez. Gazing at the fireplace, he remarked that the fire was 'small in regard to the cold'. Whereupon Ernauton, seeing in the yard some asses laden with firewood, ran down, 'most easily' hoisted on his shoulders the biggest of the animals, ran up again through the dining hall and then up the twenty-three steps to the gallery, and tipped his whole burden on to the andirons. Perhaps similar stunts and popular acts, mentioned in other accounts of feasts, appeared on occasions. On the 'ordinary' nights Froissart describes, the fare seems to have consisted of more sedate and refined entertainments. Of course, the storyteller is here part of the story, and it may be that the opportunity of having a famed author read his lengthy romance had determined the programme of that winter season.

As much as in the cadences of French verse, Fébus 'took great pleasure in minstrelsy, for he was well versed in it; he liked to have *chansons, rondels* and *virelais* sung before him.' This brief notice hardly does justice to the Count's informed patronage of the poetry and music that share the umbrella term of *ménestrandie*. From his enthusiastic reception of Froissart's *Méliador* – a poem looking back to twelfth-century models of courtly romances – we can deduce that his literary tastes were somewhat conservative, although he is also known to have appreciated the works of such 'moderns' as Guillaume de Machaut, the poet-composer who set the standards for the intricate rhymed forms of *ballade*, *rondel* and *virelai*, and in Gaston's youth a familiar of the Hotel de Navarre. Fébus' predilection for the older style is illustrated by his only known composition in verse, a formal Occitan *canso* that earned him a prize in the famed 'Floral Games' of Toulouse. But what is known of the musical establishment at Orthez yields a more complex map of the Count's interests in minstrelsy. The presence at his court of several musicians listed as *trobadors* indicates that the older genres were alive and well. In the twelfth century a 'troubadour' was a poet-composer (literally: a 'finder' – from the Occitan verb *trobar*, cf. French *trouver*) who may or may not have performed his own songs. In the fourteenth century, however, the term was used more loosely. The latter-day 'troubadours' at Gaston's court seem to have been performers of the traditional repertoire, with emphasis on the forms called *canso* and *dansa* – the latter enjoyed 'extraordinary vogue' in the fourteenth century, and the listing of a '*trobador de dansas de casa del comte de Foix*' suggests the existence of a resident dance band.[13] These musicians would presumably have been very much in demand for the lighter, more social entertainments such as balls and large banquets. But the court of Foix-Béarn was also one of privileged workshops of the fourteenth century musical avant-garde. Making up in part for the loss of Béarnais archives, accounts from other courts – especially Navarre and Aragon – record frequent

[13] Castéret, 32.

exchanges of visiting minstrels with Orthez. Those entries, whether they name the performer and his specialty, or simply note the passage of a 'minstrel of the Count of Foix', more than hint at the intensity of a sophisticated and cosmopolitan musical life. Moreover, the correspondence between Fébus and John I of Aragon not only bears witness to the regard in which his younger kinsman held the Count, it also gives a vivid image of the fashionable trends of the period and of the social importance of musical patronage.

Many, and perhaps a majority, of the minstrels in Fébus' employ were 'foreigners', most notably Flemish instrumentalists. Flanders, and particularly Bruges, was the locale of regular conventions of minstrels (the 'schools' of period documents) who gathered during Lent, when profane music was not performed. As modern fiddlers and other 'folk' musicians still do in more or less formal get-togethers, their medieval forerunners learned from each other new tunes and ornamentations, as well as new styles of playing often related to recent developments of constantly evolving instruments. That princely aficionados vied for the services of international virtuosos is made sometimes pathetically evident, as by the example of John of Aragon's efforts to secure in 1389 the return of an elusive shawm player, and his attempt to enlist the Avignon Pope and the King of France in that futile enterprise. The minstrel in question, who in the event was probably waylaid either by the brother of Charles VI, Louis de Touraine, or by the Duke's father-in-law, Galeazzo Visconti of Milan, had a history of slipping away from his employers: a little more than one year before disappearing on his way to 'the schools', he had left the service of the Duke of Austria to star at the Catalan court. On that occasion, John I ('lo rei music') had sent him to Orthez, to seek the opinion of the Count of Foix as 'a person who knows how to judge the skills and proficiency of good minstrels'.[14] This, and the frequent exchanges of performers and instruments eagerly sought by John I, indicate that even a prince much more absorbed than Fébus with every aspect of music held him in high esteem as an enlightened connoisseur.

The Foix musical establishment was probably much smaller than the upward of twenty resident musicians at the court of Aragon, but Froissart's account of the feast of Saint Nicholas that Fébus celebrated as the anniversary of his victory at Launac 'as solemnly as they would do on the day of Christmas or Easter in the chapel of the Pope or of the King of France', suggests that reinforcements were brought in for that and other special occasions, 'for he had *at that time* a great many good singers.'[15] During that service, the chronicler adds, 'I heard play the organ as melodiously as I ever did anywhere I went', a significant detail, since an organ was then an expensive luxury, possibly in this case

[14] *Ibid.*, 113; also in M. C. Gomez Muntané, *La música en la casa real catalano-aragonesa durante los años 1336–1442* (Barcelona, 1979), I, 158, no.97.

[15] *Voyage*, 87. Emphasis mine.

a gift from the Count to the church. More directly, Froissart also reports that the Christmas banquet was entertained by 'a great many minstrels, with the ones belonging to the Count, as well as the foreign ones'.[16] As for the make-up of minstrel 'bands', the correspondence with John I of Aragon correspondence and other accounts suggest that the *haut mestier* or 'loud' instruments – especially shawms and bagpipes were then at the height of their vogue, at least in the households of fashionable secular princes. However, Fébus' predilection for the *bas mestier* or 'soft' variety (viols, dulcian, harps and lutes) is also recorded by Froissart on the occasion of the Count's meeting with Charles VI at Toulouse in 1389: 'The tables were taken away and then the King and all the lords remained standing [...] for almost two hours to hear the *bas mestier* minstrels, for the Count of Foix took great pleasure in them.'[17] Nor did it hurt his social standing to distribute 200 gold florins to the diverse musicians, when on the next day he returned the King's hospitality.

But a more lasting tribute to Gaston III's patronage is found in a number of vocal compositions in his praise. Together with other examples of sacred and profane music, they survive in a few collections, most notably the 'Ivrea manuscript', probably originating from Avignon, and the Chantilly Codex, a sumptuous book probably compiled, only a few years after the death of Fébus, for his successor Matthieu de Castelbon. A dozen pieces either in honour of Fébus, or celebrating an occasion under his auspices – such as the wedding of the Duke of Berry – indicate probable connections between these manuscripts and the court of Orthez. Two *ballades* from the Chantilly manuscript 564, 'Se July Cesar' and 'Se Galaas', quote the war cry 'Fébus avant' in their refrain; in other pieces, such as 'Phiton, Phiton, beste tres venimeuse', or 'Le mont Aön de Trace', the educated listener would have been expected to recognize Fébus, the huntsman and patron of *ménestrandie*, under the guise of Phébus-Apollo, slayer of dragons and leader of the Muses. In addition to these compositions on French texts, three Latin motets also celebrate Fébus, but through much more recondite allusions to mythology and contemporary politics, and further obscured by a complex polyphony and the simultaneous singing of up to three different texts by the various voices. The motets 'Febus mundo oriens' and 'Altissonis aptatis viribus' from the Ivrea manuscript have been interpreted as 'veritable pro-French manifestos' dating probably from a period when Gaston III was anxious to effect a rapprochement with France.[18] The anonymous 'Inter densas', in which one catches a glimpse of Fébus' 'blond curls' (see p. 50 above) offers also a poetic description of Béarn as a new Garden of Hesperus, protected by the heraldic emblem of the viscounty, the 'mother cow'. Yet another richly illuminated collection, the 'Vogüé manuscript', may be none other than

[16] *Ibid.*, 113.

[17] *Chroniques*, XIV, 76.

[18] Castéret, 98.

the 'most beautiful and good book of Guillaume de Machaut' that Fébus is known to have owned and loaned to Queen Violante of Aragon. Together, the three manuscripts constitute a representative anthology of the 'manners' – the styles of composition and of performance that evolved during the reign of Gaston III. At the mid-century Machaut had been the most prolific composer and poet, and the greatest innovator in both secular and church music. His *Messe de Notre Dame* is the first known example of a complete setting of the mass written by a single composer; equally at ease in four-part polyphony and in simpler, more dancelike forms, his vast output represents the culmination of the *Ars nova*, a movement that, beginning around 1320, sought to perfect the theory and practice of music with particular regard to the notation of complex rhythms. After the death of Machaut, the last decades of the century 'witnessed one of the strangest developments in the entire history of music.'[19] The newest music, dubbed 'mannerist', or *Ars subtilior*, was characterized by ever more intricate rhythms – necessitating ever more 'subtle' notation – and a predilection for a polyphony 'in which the individual lines achieved a maximum of rhythmic independence.'[20] Inevitably, this in turn often resulted in startling syncopation and harmonic dissonances. Although it paved the way for Renaissance composers, the *Ars subtilior* would soon fall into disrepute, victim of its own extreme refinements, and such bold effects would not be heard again until the twentieth century.

A layman's untrained ear does not always find it easy to discern the differences between the two styles, as one evolves into the other, and both are closely related to contemporary developments in thought and rhetorics. The musicians patronized by the Count of Foix were clearly of both persuasions: while 'Magister Franciscus', composer of 'Phiton, Phiton', was probably a follower of Machaut, the likes of Jehan (or Jacquemart?) Cuvelier and Trebor (or Borlet, Robert, etc.) were in the avant-garde of the *Ars subtilior*. The enigmatic Solage even belonged to 'a group of marginal rhetoricians, the *fumeurs*', and the bizarre, wobbly harmonies of his three-voice rondeau 'Fumeux fume' raise the tantalizing question of what it was that they smoked.[21] There is, however, no doubt that Fébus was capable not only of appreciating the recondite art of his minstrels, but of making it serve his public relations needs. The motets extolling his fidelity to the French allegiance were almost certainly commissioned pieces, and some particularly pointed passages may even suggest at least his partial authorship of the text, a hypothesis made plausible by Fébus' more than adequate command of Latin (see p. 68 above).

---

[19] Richard H. Hoppin, *Medieval Music* (New York, 1978), 472.

[20] *Ibid.*, 475.

[21] The reference to fumeurs is made in programme notes for the Huelgas Ensemble CD *Fébus Avant!* (Vivarte, 1991).

THE patronage of a musical avant-garde, the almost ostentatious consideration shown to Froissart, generous gifts to performers and parting guests, all contributed to inspire the very image that the poet-chronicler did not fail to draw. That this was the intended effect should have been quite clear to the chronicler from a conversation with Espan de Lion, as they were riding to Béarn. When Froissart, perhaps a little taken aback by the knight's assertion that Fébus gave away 60,000 florins every year, asked who were the recipients of this (no doubt inflated) expenditure, Espan readily answered: 'Strangers, knights, squires, who travel through his lands; heralds, minstrels, all people who spoke to him. No one leaves without gifts from him, and he would be angry if they were refused.'[22] Froissart had the opportunity to witness the Count's munificence at the Christmas feast, when 'on that day the Count gave to both the minstrels and the heralds the sum of 500 francs, and he clothed the minstrels of the Duke of Touraine, who were there, in fur-trimmed cloth of gold, valued at 200 francs.'[23]

But – and therein lies one of the many ambiguities of the Count's character – this generosity, and the sensibility of an enlightened devotee of music and poetry, seem to have coexisted with less engaging traits. Contrasting with the largesses, his well-established reputation of avarice is supported by anecdotal evidence and by the fact that at his death, huge outlays for construction, armament and lavish entertainments, seem to have made almost no dent in the treasure of the Moncade Tower. It has also been noted that Espan himself – a stalwart retainer if there ever was one – had to mortgage all of his estate to the Count, against a loan of 60 florins, and that 'after three months of loyal service', Froissart himself was given only 80 florins.[24] And yet, not only did Espan not complain, but he continued to extol his master's liberality. As for Froissart, he appeared to be quite satisfied, as he had cause to be, for in addition to the intangible but priceless reward of an audience for his poem, and every mark of the Count's high esteem, he had been lodged, fed, and toasted at his expense. What we see then is not so much the pointless greed of a robber dragon crouching on his hoard, but rather a policy balancing parsimony with the manipulation of opinion – especially that of the 'strangers … who travel through his land' and will eventually broadcast through Christendom the lauds of the mighty and magnificent Count of Foix.

Other dark shadows can be perceived in the background to Froissart's portrait. Two episodes of vindictive violence are casually – almost complacently – recalled by Espan de Lion, as he and the chronicler ride towards Tarbes. In both instances, the victims are blood relations of Fébus, who have somehow crossed his political aims. The first involves Fébus' cousin Pierre-Arnaud de

[22] *Voyage*, 30.

[23] *Ibid.*, 113.

[24] *Vicomté*, 270, n. 26.

Béarn, who held the formidable castle of Lourdes for Edward III (see p. 73 above). In Froissart's tale, Pierre-Arnaud obeys a summons to Orthez, but with such misgivings that he first makes his brother Jean swear never to give up the castle, save to his 'natural lord the King of England'. His suspicions are confirmed when, after dinner, Fébus demands that he surrender Lourdes to him. Pierre-Arnaud refuses politely, invoking the fealty he has sworn to the King, whereupon the Count flies into a rage:

> ... his blood turned in anger and he said, drawing his dagger: 'Ho! Traitor, do you say no to me? By my head, I'll pay you for it!' Then he struck him with his dagger in such a way that he wounded him most severely in five places, and no baron or knight dared come forward. The knight [Pierre-Arnaud] said: 'Ha! My lord, this is not nobly done. You summoned me, and now you kill me.' But all he got was five dagger wounds. Then the Count ordered him put into the pit, and so he was, and there he died, for he was poorly treated for his wounds.[25]

The other example, much more briefly cited by Espan, is that of Fébus' first cousin, the Viscount of Castelbon, held 'eight months jailed in the tower of Orthez' and then 'ransomed for 60,000 francs'.

Froissart's second-hand narrative is truncated in one case, and badly garbled in the other. As noted earlier, while the castle of Lourdes was nominally held from the King of England, its captain was – and acted as – the agent of Fébus; moreover, Pierre-Arnaud was healthy enough in October 1378 to be appointed the Count's lieutenant in Marsan, and again in June 1381, sent as his surrogate to perform the homage to the King of Aragon.[26] Last but not least, he reappears under Froissart's pen as one of the notables attending the funeral of Gaston III. As for the Viscount of Castelbon, the enmity between the two branches of the Foix-Béarn family went back to his father's attempt to challenge the regency of Aliénor de Comminges. His son Roger-Bernard II had been the only nobleman in Bigorre to remain 'English' when the tide turned after 1368, but nothing more precise is known of the circumstances of his incarceration. Neither Espan nor Froissart venture to pass moral judgement on Gaston III's cruelty – Espan only remarks that 'people are careful not to anger [the Count], for in his anger there is no pardon', and seems to shrug off both episodes with a curt 'Anyway, that was how it happened!' It is to Froissart's credit that he does not try to gloss over or whitewash the viciousness of the supposed outrages, but that may be simply because to him and his contemporaries, they would not have appeared as sinister as they do to modern sensibilities. Most rulers were the law in their own lands; their moods determined the degree of the offence; and punishment

---

[25] *Voyage*, 48–9.

[26] *Vicomté*, 413, 420.

was routinely cruel and unusual. The chronicler is shocked enough to report the two instances, but what prompts him is not so much the severity – or even the injustice – of the pains inflicted, as the fact that they were visited upon noblemen, one of whom was the Count's lawful heir. And in the story of Pierre-Arnaud's alleged stabbing, it is perhaps less the nature of the crime that gives the canon of Chimay such a shudder, than the spectacle of a great nobleman behaving like a low-born thug – his fall, as it were, from the grace of chivalry.

Set against the account of the gracious welcome extended to foreign guests, of splendid banquets and refined entertainments, these stories serve as useful reminders of the contradictions of a culture in which legalistic punctilio coexisted with arbitrary violence, and irrational impulses together with intellectual sophistication. While Froissart may not have perceived them, these contradictions are reflected in his tableau of Fébus and his court. On the one hand, there is order, good sense and decorum in the Count's management of his finances, in his secretariat, and in the staging of his table ceremonial – all in all, an establishment that functions smoothly and reflects the tastes and 'good counsel' of a master who 'loved what he ought to love, hated what he ought to hate, etc.' On the other hand, Orthez is full of rumours and speculations about the supernatural goings-on at the castle up the hill, and the 'ostel de la Lune' was surely as good a place as any for picking them up. Without either vouching for them or denying their veracity, Froissart relates two pieces of fantastic gossip. The first has as its protagonist one of Fébus' half-brothers, Pierre de Béarn, a sleep-walker whose affliction comes from being haunted by a bear he had killed in Biscay. The story is notable for its literary connection, for the poet-chronicler would make indirect use of it by introducing a sleep-walking character in the final version of his *Méliador*. But, more directly relevant to an impression of Fébus' entourage, it tells of a curious parallel to the Count's marital situation, as the wife of Pierre de Béarn, frightened by his sleep-walking, has fled to her native Spain. Whether intended or not, the anecdote serves as an oblique reminder that, for all of its musical and literary sophistication, the court of Orthez appears very much as a predominantly masculine club. This does not necessarily imply a deliberate exclusion of women from the Château Moncade, but can be explained simply as a consequence of the estrangement of Fébus' consort: in the absence of the Countess – and her female attendants – unspoken protocols of medieval modesty would have discouraged women from attending a court without a hostess.

The other tale borders on the comic: it begins when a Catalan cleric, having lost a suit against a baron of Béarn, sends a little demon named Orton or Harton to torment him; the baron, Raimon de Coarraze, turns the tables and persuades the imp to serve him. A loyal friend to his lord, Raimon then reports to Fébus the information delivered to him by Orton, about what has just occurred 'in England or in Scotland or in Germany or in Flanders or in Brittany or other countries'. Not being privy to the inner workings of Gaston

III's extensive intelligence network, Froissart's informants would have been unable to explain how the Count could receive news of the death of an emperor in Prague, or of a battle in Portugal, weeks before it was brought to Béarn by slow-moving merchants and pilgrims. In and age when kings routinely consulted their astrologers, and where the common belief was that this world is permeable to the invisible beyond, it was only natural for people to assume that Fébus disposed of some kind of supernatural assistance. A less benign version, published in the sixteenth century, makes him a forerunner of Peter Schlemihl: the Count, says the *Historia Fuxensium Comitum*, had no shadow, having sold it to a demon from Toledo, who in return was his universal spy.[27]

From Froissart's account of his visit to the court of Orthez, supplemented and sometimes corrected by such documentary evidence as the Count's correspondence with other princes and the records of his administrative and judicial acts, we can try and piece together a composite sketch of Gaston Fébus. It will not be a full portrait, or a still picture, but a fragmentary, changing image, showing now one bright facet, now a dark patch, for the affable (albeit aloof) host will also fly into murderous rages, and the generous patron of minstrels is also a merciless usurer. Contemporary chronicles being rather short on psychological observations, they yield only the most superficial assessments: thus the sophistication of the amateur troubadour and connoisseur of subtle music only hints at the Count's aesthetic sensibility, whereas the explanation for the repudiation of the Count's wife is taken at face value. As for the suspicions of necromancy, they commonly attached to men regarded as too clever, or too inquisitive – but far from detracting from their charisma, they could only add to what appears as a deliberately nurtured aura of mystery. And so, in his own lifetime, began the legend of Fébus.

[27] *Ibid.*, 269, n. 25.

✦   ✦

✦

# ✦ 8 ✦
## Fébus, the Author

IN the account of his visit to Orthez, Froissart sketches an unusually vivid picture of the Count of Foix and of his life style, a recollection in which are thrown together dramatic instances of Fébus' dangerous temper (the 'stabbing' of Pierre-Arnaud) and mundane details of his eating habits (his large consumption of chicken wings), as well as the number of torches lighting the Count's supper table, the amount of his daily alms distributed at his door, and his appreciation of minstrelsy. From other sources – such as the inventory of his library – it can be inferred that Fébus was an omnivorous reader: he is known to have possessed French paraphrases of works by Ovid, Pliny, Livy, and Valerius Maximus. There is reason to believe that one of the 'textbooks' procured for his education was the *Elucidari de las proprietats de totas res naturals*, a richly illustrated Béarnais version of that most famous of medieval encyclopedias, the *De proprietatibus rerum* ('On the nature of things') of Bartholomeus Anglicus. Other encyclopedic works in the Château Moncade library included the *Livre des merveilles* of Marco Polo and the *Speculum major* of Vincent de Beauvais, which encompassed not only natural history, but also universal history, psychology, poetics, laws, and diverse crafts and occupations. Fébus himself commissioned translations of Arabic treatises on medicine, mathematics and philosophy by the tenth-century Andalusian Abul Kasim and the Persian Ibn Sina (Avicenna). While some of his books must have been inherited, Gaston III was evidently keen to add to an already respectable collection.

From Froissart's account, it is evident that Fébus had not merely collected fine books as a perquisite of his social rank. Nor was he a passive consumer of literature. The chronicler gives us a vivid image of his host engaging him in discussion of his work: while the poet read from *Méliador*, 'when it came to something on which he wanted to debate or argue, he was wont to speak to me, not in his Gascon language, but in good and fine French.'[1] To do so, the Count must have been well read in the literature of chivalry, particularly so in the Arthurian romances that Froissart sought to continue, 'cult' objects that one would not venture to comment upon, or 'debate', without a thorough knowledge of their most recondite details. But for all his praise of Gaston as an active patron of poets, the visitor makes not even an oblique allusion to his literary accomplishments. Of course, Froissart cannot be faulted for an omission that

[1] *Voyage*, 66.

stems in part from the very nature of authorship in the pre-Gutenberg era, when the labour-intensive production of manuscripts precluded a wide dissemination. There was, strictly speaking, no publishing, in the modern sense of a commercial distribution of books to the public. Each medieval volume, more or less luxuriously penned and illustrated, was a uniquely produced copy, commissioned by a patron, of a text by an author whose identity would often remain vague. Even those who made an open bid for posthumous fame and who, like Froissart and Machaut, cast themselves as the heroes or at least the interlocutors of their tales, could not expect their reputation to spread beyond a restricted circle of connoisseurs.

It was therefore in the normal order of things for Fébus, as a patron, to be cognizant of Froissart's works, and for the chronicler to remain in ignorance of writings that the Count would have shared only with members of his own social caste. In this he was hardly innovating: a form or other of literary pastime had been part of aristocratic culture since at least the end of the eleventh century, when great feudal lords – particularly in the regions of the *langues d'oc* – had begun to amuse themselves by composing profane songs. Duke Guilhem IX of Aquitaine, whose granddaughter Aliénor would become the matriarch of the Plantagenets, is often dubbed 'the first troubadour'. Later, in the period called the 'golden age of troubadours', many of the known poets, from Limousin to Provence and Catalonia, were noble men and women, who so thoroughly infused the art of *trobar* with aristocratic values that all songwriters, regardless of their social status, paid tribute in their verse to the subtle ethos of *cortesia*. Much has been written about the 'invention' of romantic love by twelfth-century poets.[2] Perhaps equally epoch-making, another innovation of Occitan troubadours and their counterparts in other linguistic domains (French *trouvères*, German *Minnesänger*, etc.) was the attention paid to the formal aspect of lyric verse, an aesthetic concern for intricate rhyme schemes and varied meters, hitherto unknown to the clerical – and mostly anonymous – authors of epic narratives and *Lives* of saints. Long after Guiraut Riquier – the 'last troubadour', sometimes patronized by Count Roger Bernard II of Foix —had gone to his grave, that courtly tradition endured, as aesthetic traditions do, under the guise of a strict formulary, watched over by such forerunners of Renaissance 'academies' as the *Consistori de la gaia sciencia* of Toulouse. It is under the auspices of that predominantly bourgeois body that Fébus is known to have entered in the poetic tournaments known as the *Jocs florals* ('Floral games') a strophic poem for which he was awarded a prize, the *joya* (literally: a 'jewel', but also punning on 'joy', the quasi-ecstatic emotional prize of the troubadour's quest).

[2] *E.g.* Denis de Rougemont, *Love in the Western World* (New York, 1940), and more recently Linda M. Paterson, *The World of the Troubadours* (Cambridge, 1993).

This *canso* harks back to a form already well established in the twelfth century: a variable number of stanzas, each comprised of the same number of lines, with a repeated rhyme scheme, and a shorter, concluding strophe, the *envoi*. Fébus' composition is of the simpler variety: five stanzas of eight eleven syllable lines each, and a three-line *envoi*, all on a single rhyme. As with prosody, so with rhetoric: the poem adheres strictly to the traditional development of a familiar courtly theme, that of the Lover as a Pilgrim who, obedient to the dictates of Love and tormented by his Lady's absence, seeks solace in the contemplation of her merit. The ornamental motifs, such as the mandatory evocation of springtime ('Now when I see the woods in leaf again …'), the 'deadly arrow' of Love, the 'wind and rain and mists' that cannot hinder the Lover's pilgrimage, also come from the same twelfth-century store of accessories, as do the convention of addressing the Lady with the masculine 'my lord' (*mi dons*) and giving her a secret code name – the *senhal* – in order to safeguard her good repute. Here, for reasons perhaps known only to himself and his lover, Fébus refers to her as *Mos Xapayros*, 'My Hat'. To the modern reader, it all seems rather like a collection of shop-worn clichés, but one must remember that the fundamentally insular *gaia sciencia* of the erudite Toulousains aimed not at originality, but at the preservation of an art that had been the glory of their language. All in all, Fébus' performance of that antiquarian exercise is competent, but not dazzling: anticipating Castiglione's Renaissance *cortegiano*, or even Molière's *honnête homme*, the Count seems to understand that a gentleman owes it to himself to be good at such games, but that virtuosity, let alone innovation, should be left to the low-born professional.

This surviving piece, and the mere fact that it was entered in a contest, hint at the well practiced skill of an 'advanced amateur'. Although no other lyric compositions has been attributed to Fébus, he could plausibly have authored the Latin motets of the Ivrea manuscript, in which the political allusions are so punctual that they must have been at least prompted by the Count himself. It has even been suggested that he might have composed the music of those motets. The fact that Fébus corresponded frequently on musical matters with his kinsman John I of Aragon, himself a composer, together with what is known of the Count's predilection for certain contemporary styles, makes the hypothesis attractive, but there is so far no documentary evidence to support it.[3]

[3] *Prince*, 290–7. See also *Castéret*, 100–6.

W HEREAS his participation in poetic games appears to have been the
occasional condescension of a *grand seigneur* to a social pastime, as well
as a tribute to the historic glories of the *langues d'oc*, it is with a truly professional pride that the Count of Foix presents himself as the author of the French
*Livre de chasse*:

> I Gaston, by the Grace of God, also named Fébus, Count of Foix Lord
> of Béarn who in all my days have taken especial delight in three things,
> war, love and also the chase, since in the first two there have been better
> masters than myself, for many have been better knights than I am, and
> many have had finer love adventures than I had, it would be foolish of
> me to speak of those. [...] But I want to speak of the third art, in which
> I doubt that I have had any master, even though this be vanity, that is of
> the chase [...][4]

Forty-four manuscripts of Fébus' *Book of the Hunt* have survived, most of them
dating from the fifteenth century, with a few from the early sixteenth century.
This vogue over several generations, and the translation of large excerpts made
before 1415 by Edward Duke of York, under the title of *The Master of Game*,
suggest that the author's bold claim of preeminent expertise was not so vain
after all. Naturally, the subject itself would have ensured the success of the
book, for while the hunt is regarded in modern industrial society as a mere
sport, and is, moreover, restricted in the interest of conservation, it was one
of the principal, habitual and quasi-necessary occupations of the medieval
nobility. At the most practical level, abundant game supplied much of the meat
consumed at the seigniorial table. The chase also provided a strenuous, almost
daily exercise whereby knights and squires maintained their riding skills and
fighting stamina. Last but not least, in a natural environment where a rural
economy existed in close proximity to, and sometimes even hemmed in by the
wilderness, the nobleman's favourite pastime could be seen to coincide with
his feudal obligation to protect his tenants' livestock from wolves and foxes,
his crops from grazing deer and rooting boar, and stocked fishponds from the
ravages of the otter.

While the *Book of the Hunt* is essentially a practical manual, Fébus is
true to the medieval tradition of seeking the highest moral justification
for what moderns might regard variously as archaic amusement or wanton
slaughter. This intent is clear from the Prologue, where the author states
that he began writing his book on 1 May 1387, 'to this end, namely that all
those who shall read or hear it, will know that from the chase much good
can come.' The delivery alternatives ('read or hear it') are worth noting, as a
reminder that Fébus' book did not exist solely as the sumptuous manuscripts
offered to usually literate nobles, but also as a text to be read aloud for the

---

[4] Gaston Phébus, *Le Livre de chasse*, ed. Gunnar Tilander (Stockholm, 1971), 51.

Cõment on doit huer et corner
pres li vueill a
prendre tous
lengaiges da
peler chiens de
menascier les
de reslaudir les

Et brief tous lengaiges que on
parole a chiens. les quieulx ie ne
pourroie dire. quar trop de legues
sont et trop de lengaiges et selon
le pais dont len sera. et aussi dun

meisme lengaige parole len en chasi
se duisement selon les bestes que len
chasse. quar on ne pole nue a ses chi
enz quant chassent le sanglir. einsi
cõme on fer quant on chasse le cerf
ne quant on chasse chevreul ou he
vre ou autres bestes. len ne pole
nue a ses chiens einsi cõme feroit
on chasse le cerf ou le sanglir. Aust
si li vueill aprẽdre toutes manieres
de corner. Premierement corner:
quant on vuelt que les cõpaini

Fébus teaches boys how to call and sound the horn,
from the Livre de chasse, Bibliothèque nationale de France, ms. fr. 619

instruction of unlettered apprentices. The beneficial effects of the chase are then summarized:

> First, it makes one avoid all of the seven deadly sins; secondly, it makes one a better and faster rider, more intelligent and more skilled, more at ease and more daring and more familiar with all kinds of lands and situations.

Fébus then demonstrates how hunting acts as spiritual as well as mental and physical hygiene, chiefly developing the theme of idleness as source of all vices. Consistent with his own confession, in the *Book of Orisons*, of a lustful temperament, he explains that he who is without an occupation is prey to 'imagination of the pleasure of the flesh' – and incidentally to thoughts of pride, avarice, anger or gluttony, etc. (The extended indictment of 'imagination' may indeed tell us more than the author intended about his own particular susceptibility.) Fortunately, the huntsman is so busy that from dawn to dusk he has no time to indulge in daydreams conducive to sin and foolishness, and at the end of the day can desire only a good night's sleep. The point is illustrated with a sketchy but vivid evocation of a professional hunter's duties, from the care of hounds and horses, to the last episode of the chase – the ritualistic *curée* at which the quarry is cut and the hounds are given their spoils. Avoidance of sin is of course not the only benefit, and Fébus sets out to 'prove' that hunters live happier lives than anyone else. The motif of a 'day-in-the-life' is taken up again and developed with great gusto, but this time the accent is on the delights that await the hunter, from the moment he beholds the dewdrops of a sparkling dawn, to that of his evening bath and last stroll in the evening air, before going to his bed of 'fine clean sheets and linen'. The page is almost lyrical, with the drama of a sprightly action sequence ushered in by the cry from the whole company: 'Look at that great stag!' Lastly, the author wishes to show that, thanks to strenuous exercise and a sober diet – for they 'eat little and sweat the whole day long', hunters live longer than other men.

As announced in the Prologue, the treatise begins with descriptions of diverse animals and of their ways of life, first the *beste douces*, the (literally: 'gentle') grazing beasts, 'for they are the most noble ones', then those who prey or slay. Pride of place goes to the favourites quarries of the chase, the broad family of the cervids. First, the hart or stag, a 'strong, fast and cunning beast', is deemed too well known of huntsmen to require a detailed description. Fébus therefore discusses only the aspects of its 'nature' that should be of concern to the huntsman, as for instance the fact that during the mating season, which begins in September and lasts about two months, the deer is most irritable and dangerous, thus justifying the saying: 'After the boar, the doctor; after the hart, the bier.' The second chapter, in which Fébus draws with undimmed wonder on the recollections of the Scandinavian stage of his Baltic adventure, is devoted to the reindeer (O.F. *rangier*), 'the strangest beast, and therefore I shall tell you how it looks.' A brief technical discussion of the differences between the antlers of the hart and of the reindeer leads to that of the defensive stance of the Nordic species:

> When the reindeer is hunted, he does not run much, because of the great weight he carries on his head, but he backs up against a tree, so that nothing can approach him except from the front, and he lowers his head to the ground. And there is neither deerhound nor greyhound in the world who dares enter [his defences] or who can get hold of him, because of the antlers that shield his whole body, unless one comes upon him from behind. While stags strike with their lower prongs, reindeer strike with the upper tines; they do not strike such great blows as the stag, but they frighten the hounds by the sight of their strange and wonderful heads. They are no taller than the buck, but thicker and fatter [...] I have seen them in Norway and Sweden, and there are some beyond the sea, but in Latin country I have seen but few [...] And since they are not hunted very much, I shall say no more of its nature, for I have said enough.[5]

With the same systematic emphasis on details relevant to the hunt, Fébus then treats of the fallow deer, the wild goat, the roebuck, the hare and even the humble rabbit. Of the latter, he notes that although it is not hunted *à force* (with the full apparatus of the chase), its pursuit still requires a certain mastery. But of the chapters on herbivores, the longest is devoted to the two kinds of wild goats found in the Pyrenees.

Here again Fébus speaks from first-hand observation, a clear indication that he must have been, not only an experienced huntsman in lowland fields and forests, but also a capable mountaineer. It is perhaps more as a naturalist than a hunter that he describes these elusive animals, even though they do not provide very good sport, for 'there is no great mastery to taking them'. Fébus names the two species *bouc sauvage* and *bouc ysarus* – respectively the ibex (*Ibex capra*) and a Pyrenean subspecies of chamois, called isard (*Rupicapra rupicapra*) – and remarks that they are not 'common beasts, that everyone knows'. He describes the large, heavily ringed horns of the ibex, and how it uses them to break a potentially fatal fall:

> It is a wonder to see the great leaps they make to save their lives, from one rock to another, and I have seen a *bouc* jump from a height of ten *toises* [approximately 60 feet], and not die, for they stand as firmly on a rock as a horse on sandy soil. However, it happens sometimes that they fall from such heights, and they are so heavy, that they cannot brake with their legs. To do this, they use their heads against the rock, and so save

---

[5] *Ibid.*, 66–7.

and right themselves. Still, they fail sometimes and break their necks, but it is rare.[6]

The much lighter isard, however, can be the victim of its own short, sharp horns:

> Sometimes the *boucs ysarus* want to scratch their hind thighs with their horns, and they push so hard that they get their horns into their backside [*par les fesses*] and cannot pull them out, because [the horns] are curved and barbed, and so they fall and break their necks.[7]

Whether Fébus himself witnessed such bizarre accidents, or only retells a bit of local (and perhaps facetious) folklore, is open to conjecture. But some comments are characteristic of his attention to the everyday lives of his most remote subjects, as he notes that the pelt of wild goats is much sought 'in my mountains', where 'People are clothed in it more than in scarlet'. And, if goat venison is 'not very wholesome, as it brings about fevers', it is, however, good once salted, 'for people who cannot have better fresh meat when they want'. This chapter also offers strong evidence that Gaston must have directly supervised the illustration of his book, as he refers the readers to specific images ('as is figured here') on the same page as his verbal description of both kinds of wild goat.

Fébus' personal experience of the dangers the hunter may face is sometimes vividly recalled, as in his recollection of encounters with the wild boar. While not a carnivore, this cousin of the pig is nevertheless described as more dangerous than lions and leopards, for the boar does not kill, like the great cats, by clawing and biting, but in a single blow, 'as with a knife':

> I have seen [the boar] strike a man, slitting him open from knee to breast, and kill him with one blow, dead before he could speak to anyone, and I have myself often been thrown to the ground, together with my horse, and my horse killed.[8]

Other exceptions to Gaston's programme of treating only those beasts commonly hunted, are the chapters devoted to the bear and to the a kind of wild cat, 'as large as a leopard'.

Almost legendary, the Pyrenean bear (whose skull adorns one of the restored upper rooms of Mauvezin Castle) is not entirely extinct today, and a few specimen still roam the precarious sanctuaries of French and Spanish nature reserves. Fébus acknowledges that although it is 'common enough beast',

[6] *Ibid.*, 71.

[7] *Ibid.*, 72.

[8] *Ibid.*, 88.

he needs to 'speak of its ways, for there are few people who have had a good look at it.' But where direct observation ceases to be possible, he subscribes to the conventional lore, according to which bear cubs are born dead, then brought to life by the mother's licking and breathing on them. In the same vein, the bear is credited, like the American groundhog, with the ability to forecast the change of seasons: when he wakes from forty days of hibernation, if the weather is then clear, he concludes that there will be forty more days of winter, and so returns to his cave. But the bulk of Gaston's remarks are evidently drawn from his own hunting experience. He makes a clear distinction between two sub-species of different sizes; notes that the bear standing menacingly on his hind legs is bluffing, whereas the one that remains on all four means to fight; and he judges bear meat neither tasty nor wholesome – but, if one must eat bear at all, the paws are the best part, and the fat, mixed with other ointment, is good against gout.

As for the wild cat, the species (or subspecies) described is somewhat controversial. However, Fébus cautions that although 'some call them *loups cerviers*, and others call them *chaz loux*', both terms referring to the lynx, 'they are neither [...] One could better name them *chaz liéparz* than anything else, for they resemble the leopard more than any other beast.'[9] Whether the Count of Foix is solely responsible for future migrations of the word, the name he proposes translates exactly into the Italian *gattopardo*, which eventually returns to the French language as *guépard*. The most widely known illuminations, in the manuscript listed as 'Français 616' of the Bibliothèque nationale de France, indeed show a long-tailed, spotted cat lacking the characteristic tufted ears of the lynx. While some modern commentaries contradict Fébus and identify his wild cat as a lynx, one may choose to assume that the artist of Ms. 616 was sufficiently faithful to an earlier model supervised by the Count, and the possibility remains that the questionable (and now extinct) feline was a kind of European leopard.[10]

Fébus' overview of the game beasts ends with a description of the otter, such a voracious consumer that 'Only one pair [of them] can destroy most of the fish stocked in a large pond, and that is why they are hunted.' The naturalist then yields to the huntsman, with ten chapters (ch. 15–24, ff. 37v–53 in Ms. 616) devoted to the hounds. The sequence begins with fervent praise of 'the most noble, most reasonable and most intelligent beast that God ever made'. The legendary examples (one of which is famous enough to be 'found painted in France in many places') of two loyal greyhounds who managed to bring to justice the murderers of their respective masters, are cited in full. The chapter culminates in a lyrical cadence: 'Dog is loyal to his lord and well and truly loves

---

[9] *Ibid.*, 104.

[10] For a contrary opinion, see W. Schlag's remarks in *The Hunting Book of Gaston Phébus* (London, 1998), 30.

him. Dog is very intelligent and knowing and very clever. Dog is strong and good. Dog is wise and trustworthy. Dog has great memory. Dog has great sentiment ... etc.'[11] Fébus concludes that 'the worst that can be said of dogs is that they do not live long.' He follows then with chapters on the ailments of dogs and their cures, and on specific breeds: alaunts – good at hunting bears, wolves and wild boars; greyhounds – the noblest of them all, and heraldic emblems of loyalty; 'running hounds', hunting in pack, by scent; bird dogs or 'espaignolz' (spaniels); mastiffs, good as guard dogs and for cross-breeding with other kinds. Four more chapters treat of the building of salubrious kennels; exercising the hounds (who should be taken out to run and play twice a day); calling the hounds and sounding the horn; and leading the hounds while tracking game.

The most extensive part of the *Book of the Hunt* consists of sixty chapters (ch. 25–85, ff. 53v–120v) in which Fébus discusses various techniques for tracking, taking and killing game, as well as the proper cutting up and skinning of the hart, and the ritual *curée* for rewarding the hounds. Even to the layman, this is easy reading, as the author clearly explains technical terms and even allows himself a few touches of humour. For instance, the reader is cautioned against approaching a wounded bear, not as one should a wild boar, *i.e.* on foot with sword in hand, but mounted and with lance or throwing spear: otherwise, the bear would 'embrace and kiss [the hunter] none too graciously'. But one of the main reasons for the book's enduring success, both in its own right and as a source for other works, may lie in its broad treatment of the subject. For, while one might expect the Count of Foix to write only about the more aristocratic aspects of cynegetics, in fact he does not exclude from his treatise any effective method. Although he clearly favours the hunt 'à force' (*i.e.* the sporting chase), he nevertheless examines all means to take and kill game 'par maistrise' (by cunning, or craft): various kinds of traps and snares, carts camouflaged for a stealthy approach, and even the killing of wolves with 'aiguilles' or needle traps – sharp tension devices hidden in chunks of meat, causing a cruel death by internal lacerations. While 'no one is a good huntsman, if he does not know how to take beasts both by strength and by ruses', Fébus does not hide his reluctance to discuss the latter kind, of which he disposes quickly with such comments as: 'I wish to say no more about it, for it is a nasty sort of hunt.' He concedes, however, that those who use traps and other 'ignoble' devices may – as competent huntsmen – gain admittance to Heaven, not 'in the centre', but in 'some suburb or barnyard' thereof. Aside from ethical considerations, Fébus fears that the use of relatively easy devices, good for those who are too old and feeble, or too lazy, for the chase, may bring about a depletion of the game. On the other hand, he had noted the need to control by any means the rabbit population, a threat to garden crops, and the otter, a couple of which can quickly devastate a fishpond.

---

[11] *Le Livre de chasse*, 109–10.

With such remarks, it is tempting to see Fébus as an early environmentalist. One does not need, however, to venture on such an anachronistic limb, to recognize in the *Livre de chasse* the product of a well organized, rational mind, capable of embracing not only details of an art, but also the larger issues of rapport between man and nature.

The breadth and depth of Count Gaston's command of his matter would be remarkable even if his book were only a work of erudition. To be sure, he was conversant with earlier treatments of the subject but, in an era when – absent the arrogant concept of 'intellectual property' – literary material was routinely recycled, with or without acknowledgment, he borrowed remarkably little. The chapters on the 'undoing' of the hart and of the wild boar are taken from the *Livres du roy Modus*, and the 'slight traces of Norman-Picard dialect' detected by Tilander in Fébus' 'good and fine French' may be reminiscences of the *Déduits de la chasse* of the Norman Gace de la Buigne.[12] But these are minor debts, and on the whole it is clearly the author's direct experience that his book conveys, keeping faith with his stated purpose of saying 'nothing that is not right and true'.

Thanks to its lively, conversational style, the text of the *Livre de chasse* remains a fresh source of enjoyment for the modern reader. There is no denying, however, that the surviving manuscripts are especially prized for their illuminations. These are justly admired for their aesthetic quality, but their value as adjunct documents to the text of the treatise remains open to question: while there is no doubt that the illustration of the original (or possibly several specimens thereof) were supervised by Fébus, none of these is known to exist today. Superb copies were produced in Avignon, Paris and elsewhere, for the most part in the fifteenth century, although a few may be dated from the end of the fourteenth century. How faithful they all are to the original illustrations depends on the ability of the copying artist to refer to those original models, as well as his familiarity with the subject matter. While we may give the later miniaturists the benefit of the doubt, and credit them with enough professional conscience to refrain from altering the 'nature' of the beasts 'figured' under the guidance of the author, their diverse representations of Fébus and his audience evidently reflect different historic perceptions. Thus in the already mentioned manuscript 'fr. 616', made in Paris, perhaps around 1407, the frontispiece (fol. 13) shows Count Gaston magnificently robed and enthroned under a marble canopy, with his huntsmen and hounds harmoniously distributed on either side of the throne, as well as below; the Count sports the forked beard sometimes fashionable in the last two decades of the century, and wears a black brimless hat. This miniature appears to be a more elaborate coloured version of the same scene, depicted in grisaille in the earlier 'fr. 619' made in Avignon, possibly in Fébus' lifetime. In this image (fol. 1), the Count is bareheaded, clean-

12 *Ibid.*, 44.

shaven, and seated on a marble bench without a canopy. Another image, that of Fébus instructing the hunters in the art of calling and sounding the horn, occurs in both 'fr. 619' (fol. 43) and in 'fr. 616' (fol. 54). Here the later manuscript shows the Count, albeit bareheaded and beardless, as a more majestic figure, seated on a gilded chair rather than the flat bench of the earlier image. This is not to say that the miniaturist of 'fr. 619' gives a realistic portrait, as he depicts Fébus as a youth rather than the mature man he was when he composed the *Livre de chasse*. But whereas the later artist of 'fr. 616' chose to emphasize the princely magnificence of the author, his predecessor, by representing him less as lord than schoolmaster, may have better illustrated Fébus' claim to professional status, strongly implied both in his Prologue and in his dedicatory Epilogue.

In 1394 – three years after the death of Gaston III – a *Trésor de Vénerie* named him, together with Philippe of Burgundy, Louis d'Orléans and Jean de Tancarville as the most famous huntsmen of their time. And it is to one of that select quartet that Fébus presents the *Livre de chasse* – to 'most high, honoured and mighty lord, Philippe de France, by the grace of God Duke of Burgundy, etc.', whom he acknowledges as 'master of us all who make the hunt our occupation.'[13] The honour could have been bestowed on any one of the noble champions of the chase, or even on that royal kinsman of Fébus, John I of Aragon – called 'el Cazador' – with whom he also shared a taste for avant-garde music. Diplomatic expediency, which often directed such gifts, may be the reason why this youngest son of Charles V was singled out. The dedication is couched in humble terms, sometimes contrasting sharply with the claim of mastery made in the Prologue. Fébus apologizes not only for his French – not, he explains, his own language – but also for the shortcomings of his book for 'I am not such a good hunter, even though it is my *droit mestier*, that one could not find much to amend and correct in it.' Here and elsewhere, the Count refers to the hunt as his *mestier*, not merely meaning a skill, but – especially in the expression 'mon droit mestier' – a professional occupation. Addressing the Duke, Fébus speaks of himself as 'of his mestier, and his servant'. It is as if, for all their responsibilities and ambitions, these great territorial lords regarded the chase as their true calling.

In his dedicatory letter to the Duke of Burgundy, the Count of Foix also refers to the attached gift of 'some orisons I made long ago when Our Lord was angry with me'. This collection of prayers – comprised of three in Latin and thirty-four in French – is included in six of the forty-four extant manuscripts of the *Book of the Hunt*. The *Book of Orisons* has generally been attributed to Fébus as its sole author; likewise, historians have read the allusion to the wrath of God as a veiled reference to the violent death of the Count's only

---

[13] *Ibid.*, 290–1.

legitimate son in August 1380. Both assumption have been lately challenged. Since the interpretation of several of the orisons is closely tied to speculations about the root causes of that tragic event, it will be addressed in that context (see p. 147 below). As for the issue of original authorship, a contribution to a recently held colloquium revealed that the thirty-four French pieces are either literal translations, paraphrases or patched-up excerpts of much earlier Latin texts, *viz.* the *Meditationes* of Anselm of Canterbury (1033–1109) and the *Soliloquia* and *Manuale* of Jean de Fécamp (*c.* 990–1078), two authors whose work had enjoyed renewed interest and widespread readership since the thirteenth century. Likewise, monastic prayer collections from the twelfth and thirteenth centuries provided the framework of the three Latin texts constituting Fébus' personal 'confession'.[14] Moreover, the library of the counts of Foix is known to have held a French translation of Saint Anselm's *Méditations* – perhaps one commissioned by Fébus.[15] These discoveries do not necessarily cast doubts on the Count's sincerity, or on his claim of authorship: in the medieval perspective on intellectual production, originality was a very minor virtue, whereas imitation was viewed as a laudable aspect of *translatio studii* – the transmission of knowledge from one era or one generation to another. The texts of the orisons, borrowed as they were from devotional sources intended for the guidance of a community, had to be adapted and adjusted to the spiritual needs of a private person, to such an extent that passages wrenched out of their original context take on a quite different tone – the voice of Fébus, and none other. Even if his personal contribution was limited to choosing and arranging the patchwork of borrowings, the resulting rhetorical construction must be of his own design, and in a broader sense he could truthfully say that he had 'made' the *Book of Orisons*.

The prayers form a sequence of variations on the theme of God's necessary grace, a peculiarly argumentative approach whereby the sinner in effect admonishes his Maker and demonstrates that, since He is ultimately responsible for His creature's fall, His glory will not be complete unless the sinner is redeemed by His mercy. Nor should we expect the Count of Foix to bare his soul very explicitly. To be sure, he performs a remarkably candid *examen de conscience*, but of a general nature, and somewhat shielded by its Latin from the gaze of the less educated, casual reader. In the first orison where, in a possibly unconscious display of ingrained vanity, he refers to himself not by his baptismal name of Gaston – surely more appropriate in this context – but by the self-bestowed Fébus, he sounds the theme that resonates through the entire book: having granted him so many favours and even miracles, God owes it to Himself to show mercy and guide the Count so that he will rule his people

---

[14] Geneviève Hasenohr, 'Le *Livre des oraisons* et ses sources', paper given at the colloquium 'Froissart à la cour de Béarn,' 21 October 2006. Cited in Pailhès, 199.

[15] Pailhès, 200.

in accordance to the Lord's divine will. The second Latin orison then recalls past examples of the supplicant's rescue, by God's grace, from impending perdition. Fébus confesses that as a child, he was so depraved and frivolous (*multum parvus et frivolis*) that his parents were ashamed of him and that everybody said: 'This one will be worthless, and woe is to the land of which he will be lord!' Having prayed to God to give him wisdom and judgement (*sensum et discretionem*) enough to govern his land and his subjects according to the Lord's pleasure, this was granted to the young Count, but then the common murmur was that 'It is a great misfortune (*perditio*) for such a strong and wise man to be worthless in arms (*nil valet in armis*)!' But again, Gaston's prayers were heard, and God allowed him to reap honour on the field of battle, so that his name was known 'among the Saracens, the Jews, and the Christians of Spain, France, England, Germany and Lombardy, on this side of the sea and beyond.'[16] Under the pen of Fébus, this attribution of military success to God's favour was no mere figure of speech: as we have seen (see p. 117 above), he never failed to commemorate the anniversary of his victory at Launac with a solemn procession and the singing of Psalm 144. There follows a general and fulsome thanksgiving for 'all the delights and solaces and all the bounty that a man can possibly enjoy in this life.' God, says Fébus in a startling summary, has indeed given him everything he asked for, 'whether it was just or not' (*esset justum vel non*). The orison then turns upon the expected *ergo*: therefore, since the Almighty has already amply demonstrated His benevolence, how can He now withhold His mercy from the repentant sinner?

This appeal to the deity may seem tainted with self-serving sophistry, and the acknowledgment by Fébus of his youthful imperfections could be taken as self-congratulation as much as repentance. In a similar vein, the third orison may be seen as a rhetorical attempt to deflect God's wrath. There is, to be sure, a renewed plea for divine mercy, and another reminder of past favours. But then, shifting from the particular to the general, the penitent confesses that if God is showing an angry visage to mankind, it is 'not without cause', for the Devil truly seems to rule on earth, and 'people are less than beasts, as they see the wrath of God and do not want to see it, but instead do worse things every day.' Lamenting the depravity of the age, Fébus then singles out the clergy: 'Monks, prelates and others in virtuous vestments are worse than other people.' This diatribe echoes a familiar theme, the repeated indictment of the clergy by moralists, reformers and heresiarchs heard through the centuries of medieval Christendom. In Fébus' own lifetime, the old charges of corruption, immorality and sloth had been voiced with unprecedented vehemence since Petrarch's denunciation of the Avignon papacy – the 'Babylonian captivity'. Whether in the jocular mode of Boccaccio, or in the apocalyptic *Vision* of the Catalan Bernat de Sò, the sins of clerics high and low were seen as the worst

---

[16] Gaston Fébus, *Livre des oraisons*, 28.

manifestation of evil in this world.[17] And even as Fébus was composing his prayer book, Christendom was rent by the scandal of the Great Schism – but on that politically delicate issue, the Count of Foix maintained his diplomatic silence.

On the whole the orisons appear as a more conventional exercise than the *Book of the Hunt*. But while they are essentially the expression of the aristocratic faith of a great feudatory making a bargain with his supreme Overlord, they still allow us a glimpse of the Count's understanding of his relation to God. In this, his private practice, it is intensely personal: the feudal rhetoric of the vassal arguing with his suzerain cannot mask the anguish of the sinner alone before the judgement of his Maker. It is also quite direct: in his dialogue with his Lord, Fébus rarely asks for the intercession of the saints. Even the Virgin Mary, so pre-eminent in medieval devotion, is only invoked in two places, once in the third Latin orison, and in a French one where Saint John the Baptist, Saint Peter and the Archangel Michael are also named.[18] This kind of private devotion is consonant with the contemporary shift of religious sentiment from the collective to the individual, and Fébus' outburst against the sins of the clergy is but a faint echo of a widespread disaffection of the faithful from the Church.

It would, however, be a mistake to read in that anti-clerical passage the signs of a serious estrangement on Fébus' part, or to interpret in the same sense his relative parsimony towards religious institutions. Because of his failure to make a will at all, we shall never know if he would have stipulated the usual bequests for masses and chantries, whereby great men sought to buy prayers for the salvation of their own souls. But during his lifetime, and in the context of his well-known 'closeness' to his florins, Fébus nevertheless made significant contributions to several religious establishments. Together with his mother he built and endowed the new women's abbey of Salenques – where Aliénor de Comminges was eventually buried; he provided for repairs and maintenance of the abbey of Boulbonne, near Mazères, as the traditional burying place of the counts of Foix. In Béarn, Fébus endowed a Carmelite priory at Sauveterre, and extended various privileges and gratuities to Dominican and Franciscan communities. On the whole, and despite occasional quarrels – about feudal issues – with individual prelates, the Count's behaviour towards the Church does not suggest a religious faith at variance with that of his contemporaries.

Against this background of normality, the contrition apparent in the *Book of Orisons* casts its tormented and enigmatic shadows. A sin for which the penitent Fébus can be eternally damned is confessed, but never laid bare. In several passages reminiscent of the penitential Psalms of David, an unnamed 'other'

---

[17] A chamberlain of Pere IV of Aragon, Bernat de Sò was also Fébus' vassal for his domains in the Donnezan. See Amédée Pagès, *La 'Vesio' de Bernat de Sò* (Toulouse, 1945)

[18] Gaston Fébus, *Livre des oraisons*, 49–50.

is associated to Fébus' confession. Are these references to his own Absalom? Was a privileged reader expected to decipher this riddle hinting at a sin too scandalous to be named – and if so, why was Philip of Burgundy singled out as the recipient of Fébus' coded confession? Far beyond the ken of any textual scrutiny of the Orisons, answers to these questions, if they are to be found at all, shall best be sought among the words and actions leading to the events of a time when it seemed that God 'was angry' with the Count of Foix, angry enough to render his entire achievement meaningless.

# PART III

# The Undoing

# ✦ 9 ✦

# The Orthez Mystery

IN the third of the thirty-seven penitential orisons Fébus composed 'when the Lord was angry with [him]', the pathos of personal anguish can be clearly heard through the protective layers of rhetoric and quasi-liturgical Latin, a pathos laced with mystery as the Count begs God's mercy not only for himself, but also for an unnamed, equally guilty other. The supplication is repeated five times: 'Lord, may it please Thee that we two (*nos duo*) not be among the damned'; 'Lord, look as us two Thy servants (*nos duo servos tuos*)'; 'Lord, save me and him (*salva me et illum*)'; 'Sweet Virgin Mary [...] pray for me and for him (*ora pro me et illo*)'; 'God Our Father [...] have mercy on me and on him (*mei et illius miserere*).'[1] Intimates of Fébus – those who had been by his side in the summer of 1380 – may well have known who was that 'other'. None could or would tell the tale, but it is almost impossible not to identify the unnamed one as young Gaston, bound together with his father in their mutual, mortal sin: the attempted parricide, the murder of a son.

## A troubled marriage

ALTHOUGH many links are missing from the chain of events leading to that double crime, the sequence can almost certainly be said to begin with the dismissal of Fébus' wife, Agnès de Navarre, only a few months after she had given birth to their only child, the boy whom tradition decreed must be named Gaston, as the legitimate heir born in and for Béarn. Twenty-five years later, Froissart's questions elicited only evasive answers from Espan de Lion and other familiars of the Count. Eventually, the chronicler would credit his account of Agnès' repudiation and of young Gaston's death to a single source, the unnamed squire – 'an ancient and most notable man' – who agreed to speak to him, on the implied condition that his identity be kept secret. This is not the only instance in which Froissart attributes to a conveniently anonymous informant the revelation of a tragic state secret: in his last rewriting (the 'Rome manuscript' of Book I of the *Chronicles*) of his visit to Berkeley Castle, he would recall hearing from another 'ancient esquire' the admission that the deposed Edward II had died an unnatural death, 'for they shortened his life'.[2] Given the sensitive nature of such stories, the recourse to unnamed

---

[1] *Ibid.* 29–30.

[2] See Michel Zink, *Froissart et le temps* (Paris, 1998), 105–6.

sources is not surprising, and it does not, in and of itself, invalidate the information.

However, in the case of the Orthez relation, there are enough inner contradictions in Froissart's narrative to suggest that, during his stay at the 'ostel de la Lune', he may have collected gossip and 'leaks' from more than one source. Be that as it may, he reports that the seeds of discord were sown between the Count and the Countess when Agnès' brother, the King of Navarre, agreed to post bail of 50,000 francs for one of most prominent lords taken at Launac, Arnaud-Amanieu d'Albret. Fébus, 'who felt that the King was devious and malicious', doubted his brother-in-law's good faith, and would not let the prisoner go. Upon hearing of this, the Countess spoke to him indignantly, saying: 'My lord, you do little honour to my brother, when you do not trust him with 50,000 francs. Even if you never get anything more from the Armagnacs and the Albrets, what you have already collected should be enough. Besides, you know that you owe me 50,000 francs for my dowry, which should be entrusted to my brother. And so, you cannot lose anything.' 'My lady', replied the Count, 'what you say is true. But if I thought that the King of Navarre was to default on paying his bail, the lord of Albret would never leave Orthez until I was paid the last denier. However, since you ask me, I shall set him free, *not for the love of you, but for the love of my son.*'[3]

While the speech is undoubtedly apocryphal, its attribution to Fébus may well reflect the common knowledge that he cared little for his wife. Then, according to the 'old squire', it was to retrieve the 50,000 francs bail that Agnès was dispatched to Pamplona, whereupon her brother, arguing that the money was owed her by Fébus, swore that it would 'never leave Navarre!' 'Ah!' cried the Countess, 'what you are doing will make great trouble between my lord and us, and if you do not change your mind I shall never dare return to the county of Foix, for my lord would kill me and he would say that I tricked him!' It is at this moment of the story that Agnès herself chooses not to return to Orthez, and it is only then that 'the Count of Foix, who saw the malice of the King of Navarre, began to hate his wife.'[4] However, the tenor and timing of the known facts do not support this version. It is true that the lord of Albret turned to Charles of Navarre in his hour of need, borrowing 60,000 florins (far in excess of the amount cited by the 'old squire'), but it was not until February 1365 that Arnaud-Amanieu travelled to Navarre to secure that loan, whereas Agnès was given her marching orders shortly after Christmas 1362, and was in Pamplona by March 1363. Froissart's informant is also confused as to who owed what portion of Agnès' dowry to whom. He understands correctly the nature of a dowry as property set aside by the husband to guarantee his wife an income in the event of his death; but the wherewithal was normally provided by the

---

[3] *Voyage*, 69–70. Italics mine.

[4] *Ibid.*, 70–1.

bride's family as part of the marriage settlement. Or at least it was promised, for a frequently recurring feature in the history of feudal marriages is the unpaid, or partially paid, dowry. Sometimes, it was simply held hostage. This seems to have been the case with part of Agnès de Navarre's marriage portion: in December 1349 the new Countess of Foix formally renounced her rights to the crown of Navarre, in exchange for the *promise* of payment of the balance of her dowry. It was presumably that sum – not 50,000, but 9,000 francs – still owed thirteen years later, that Fébus took as the pretext for sending Agnès back to her family.

Moreover, it would appear that, when she left Orthez, Agnès did not expect to return soon. In her deposition recorded in 1391, she states that her husband had sent word, relayed by his half-brother Arnaut-Guilhem, that 'she must go at once to the King of Navarre to demand the money that was still due to her […] and that she must not return without the said money, for [the Count] would not take her back nor would he give her anything for her living.'[5] The Countess also recalled that Arnaut-Guilhem 'ordered the pack animals to be unloaded, and he would let nothing out of the castle of Orthez.' The list of items – plate, tapestries, jewels, clothing, liturgical ornaments – she was thus forced to abandon suggest that she was prepared, if not for permanent exile, at least for an extended stay in Navarre. It is likely that if the object of Agnès' voyage was to retrieve the balance of her dowry – a delicate task that might have been more appropriately entrusted to one of the prelates serving the Count – she was not expected to succeed, and that the ostensible mission was a pretext for her *de facto* repudiation. The pretext (or so the Pope himself saw it) was rather thin: it was, and still is, hard to believe that the Count, whose victory at Launac had so recently made him one of the richest lords in Europe, would so abruptly make the future of his marriage conditional on the payment of a relatively small sum that, moreover, had been owed him for over thirteen years. But, while it is reasonable to suspect that the estrangement had a deeper cause than overdue monies, there is nothing in chronicles or documents that can point to it. Neither Fébus nor any of his intimates ever commented on the dismissal of Agnès de Navarre. During the inquiry conducted in 1391 on its circumstances, a witness recalled having asked the Count if he had any reason to doubt his wife's fidelity: whereas this was often enough the ground (true or not) for repudiation, Fébus answered that he had no such grievance against his wife. Lastly, a frequent political motive for royal divorces was absent from the equation: Gaston III never sought the formal annulment which would have allowed him to enter another matrimonial alliance. But, despite the entreaties of his mother – who had arranged the Navarre match – and the admonitions of Pope Urban V, he never allowed his wife to return to Orthez.

5 *Vicomté*, III, nn. 18, 19.

At that political juncture the dismissal of Agnès de Navarre was not the most prudent of moves: it was an affront generally to her French royal blood, and more immediately to her brother Charles 'the Bad', only too famous already for his vindictiveness and his capacity for murderous treachery. Fébus had nothing to gain by making an overt enemy of such a dangerous next-door neighbour, and the hypothesis that he repudiated the sister as a signal of his intention to break with the brother makes little sense. There remains the strong likelihood of a non-political scenario, a private estrangement between a husband and his wife, and a sudden impulse to end a situation that had become intolerable. The abruptness of his decision must have taken everyone by surprise – it certainly did Agnès, and perhaps Gaston III himself, caught up in the trap of his own emotions. The timing of his action is significant: with the elation of his triumph over the Armagnacs, he may have felt himself vested with a new-found power, and a sense of freedom bordering on impunity.

Inevitably, there have been attempts at psychological (even 'psychoanalytical') explanations of Gaston III's motives. Inconclusive at best, these interrogations of a subject who cannot be interviewed can be wildly misleading, but they can also be useful, insofar as they compel a second look at circumstantial evidence. Thus Tucoo-Chala construed the repudiation of Agnès as a gesture of rebellion, the declaration of Fébus' independence from the moral domination of a mother's 'crushing presence', and by extension from any female interference.[6] More recently, Claudine Pailhès carried this hypothesis to an extreme conclusion, by asserting that the sin cryptically 'confessed' in the *Book of Orisons* was not the killing of young Gaston, but '*une affaire de mœurs*' – the French police-blotter euphemism equivalent to the English 'gross indecency' – in short: sodomy.[7] This startling deduction rests chiefly on the interpretation of an ambiguous turn of phrase in the third Latin orison, from which it may inferred that the unnamed 'other sinner' bound to Fébus by the same guilt was not his dead son, but a person still alive. This is, however, a highly debatable reading of what may be nothing more than a borderline solecism in the Count's awkward Latin.

There are no compelling reasons to believe in an estrangement between Fébus and his mother. His part in the foundation of the abbey of Salenques suggests on the contrary a desire to honour the Dowager Countess, and the fact that where all other negotiators had failed, she nearly succeeded in brokering a reconciliation between Fébus and his wife, implies that even in her retirement Aliénor remained her son's most persuasive adviser. Likewise, no documentary evidence has been cited to suggest that Fébus was involved in a homosexual liaison. It is true, of course, that his private life was defended by a formidable apparatus of censorship – witness the clause of their oath of fealty requiring his

---

[6] *Prince*, 112–14.

[7] Pailhès, 252–6.

subjects to report all 'subversive' conversations. But Froissart demonstrates that, despite all precautions, a patient investigator would always find the anonymous 'old squire' ready to speak of forbidden matters. The chronicler did not shy away from instances of the Count's cruelty and violence: it is hard to believe that he would have ignored any gossip he might have heard about a scandalous 'favourite'. It is also true that, as described by Froissart, the court of Orthez appears to be *une cour sans femmes*.[8] But, as we have already noted (see p. 125 above), the absence of the Countess would explain that of women guests. Moreover, in the *Dit dou florin*, the travelling poet clearly identifies the Count's household (*son estat grand et fier*) with an establishment primarily devoted to falcony and the chase (*tant de voler com de chacier*). Thus the retinue of Fébus – who saw the hunt as his *droit mestier* – could be likened to a sporting club, a brotherhood of sorts, devoted to male prowess – and to the hounds. Typically, the motets and ballades composed for the court of Orthez reflect its masculine rituals: eschewing the familiar themes of courtly love, they mostly sing praises of Fébus – the Apollonian master of the hunt. But the ambient misogyny inherent to such a fellowship is, so to speak, an institutional given that can hardly be stretched to imply a homosexual culture.

On the other hand, the heavy emphasis the *Book of Orisons* puts on sins of the flesh may be the confession of a heterosexual lust somewhat out of control. However, dynastic marriages seldom, if ever, failed because of the husband's philandering, no matter how egregious. In the end, the only clear window we have into Fébus' private world is his manifest attachment to the two 'fine young bastard knights' named by Froissart. Sired and acknowledged since his marriage to Agnès, the fact that they are often referred to as a pair suggests that they may have been full brothers. Fébus' affection for Yvain and Gratien was openly displayed: both were brought up at his court; they would be by his side until the last hour, and he is clearly reported as having had very high hopes for their future establishment. It is possible to imagine that he held the mother of those cherished sons to be more a wife to him than his legitimate consort. The existence of such a ménage might explain why the Count was not keen on seeking an annulment, which in turn would have brought upon him some pressure to contract another, more advantageous union. But here again there is a void where documentary evidence might be expected. Whereas the mothers of bastards fathered by Gaston I and Gaston II are known, largely from bequests in their favour, Fébus' failure to make a will consigned his lover(s) to perpetual anonymity. It is possible, then, that the Count had already become quite attached to his bastards when, by producing a legitimate heir, Agnès had at long last (there had been at least one still birth) fulfilled her dynastic function. Fébus may have then regarded her as expendable, or even resented the birth of young Gaston, now bound to take precedence over his other sons. At the

[8] *Ibid.*, 248.

same time the spoils of Launac freed him from the need to coddle his devious brother-in-law. On impulse perhaps, and yet not daring to face the woman he was about to shame for no fault of her own, he dispatched his bastard brother, a soldier who would not be moved by the tears and lamentations of women. And because Gaston III knew that his action had been callous and dishonourable, he would never attempt to justify himself – hence the patently inadequate, transparent pretext of the unpaid dowry.

If, as it is only reasonable to assume, the King of Navarre took offence at the abrupt dismissal of his sister, he does not seem to have reacted with any overt, let alone forceful action. Honour in such a case might have required a public form of protest – a challenge, or some kind of retaliation – but there is no record of even a private remonstrance. In view of the dearth of documents pertaining to the entire episode, Charles' apparent silence is not surprising, but it can be also be because in 1363 he could ill afford to risk any move leading to war with his neighbour of Béarn. Enraged by the denial of his claim to the succession of Burgundy, he was already preparing to renew hostilities against France, an enterprise in which his chief adviser and military commander was Jean de Grailly, the same Captal de Buch who had, only a few years before, shared with his cousin Fébus the credit for saving the royal ladies at Meaux. Such overlapping relationships illustrate the delicate balance of loyalties that existed throughout Gascony, and how they would have been dangerously upset by an open conflict between the two great lords. Ancient territorial rivalries also gave Charles reasons to keep a wary eye on his Iberian neighbours, crafty Aragon and expansionist Castile, while north of the Pyrenees, the proximity of English power in Aquitaine was no unmitigated comfort to Charles: soon enough, Navarre would be the unwilling ally of the Prince of Wales for his intervention in the Castilian civil war. Last but not least, there remained for several years the hope that Fébus could be persuaded to recall his wife. Pope Urban V interceded with the Count in December 1364, and in 1368 Fébus' mother, Aliénor de Comminges, in concert with the Queen of Navarre, almost succeeded in removing the pretext of dismissal: Charles went so far as to earmark a special levy for the payment of the balance – plus accrued interest – of Agnès' dowry. The death of Aliénor took the momentum out of that initiative. Agnès seems to have lived for a while in France, with her sister Blanche, widow of Philippe VI, and only returned to Pamplona in 1373, after the death of the Queen Dowager. It was not until then that Charles provided a regular income for her, and that her household at the court of Navarre was formally organized.[9]

Not only was there no open break, but there was undeniably a degree of co-operation between Charles and Fébus in the years immediately following the expulsion of Agnès from Orthez. There exists a curious letter addressed to an unnamed familiar of the Prince of Wales, in which an equally anonymous

[9] *Prince*, 207–9.

'English agent' reports having eavesdropped on a conversation between the Count of Foix and the King of Navarre, 'at Saint Palais in the Basque country'. While much of what he claims to have overheard appears to be absurd or at least garbled, such circumstantial details as the date – 'Friday 21 June' – and the place – 'a lane by the riverside' lend the episode a ring of authenticity. Internal evidence, as well as that of the calendar, make it more than probable that the alleged meeting took place in 1364.[10] This was a critical year for Charles of Navarre: the defeat of his Normandy offensive at Cocherel had given even greater urgency to the preparation of the raid to be led by Louis de Navarre against Burgundy. As noted earlier (see p. 68 above), Fébus not only allowed the Navarrese free passage through his land, but he had also facilitated the hiring of mercenaries by Charles. These arrangements alone would have required a certain amount of diplomatic traffic between Orthez and Pamplona, and the issues were serious enough to require both princes to be directly involved in the negotiations. If Charles' strategy required at least the passive connivance of Fébus, the Count also needed, if not the active support, at least the neutrality of Navarre in his contest of wills with the Prince of Wales. Despite its bizarre flights of fancy, the report of the 'English agent' nevertheless suggests the possibility that, while he would not (or could not) stand in the way of his brother-in-law's attack on France, Fébus may have attempted to build a counterpoise to English power in the South West, by proposing a rapprochement between the King of Navarre and his Valois cousins.

Given the apparent reluctance of both parties to come to an open break, the dismissal of Agnès de Navarre can hardly qualify as 'a veritable declaration of war' to her brother.[11] This is not to say that the latter was not simply biding his time, waiting for an opportunity to avenge the affront to his royal house. Such at any rate is Froissart's fundamental assumption: not only was Charles, according to his version, responsible for the estrangement between the Count and the Countess of Foix, he was also the principal instigator of the events leading to the violent death of their only son. When the chronicler was conducting his discreet inquiry during his 1388 stay in Orthez, the reputation of the recently deceased King of Navarre as an habitual poisoner was solidly established. It seems to have been to some extent corroborated by his own steward, who testified with particular details how, in 1365, Charles had settled his debt to the mercenary captain Seguin de Badefol with a fatally spiced dessert. As the French saying goes, *on ne prête qu'aux riches*, and there was naturally a tendency to credit other, more or less premature deaths, to his undoubted vindictiveness: thus Froissart explains with clinical precision how Charles V fell victim to a slow poison administered twenty years before by his Navarrese brother-in-law. In any event, his accumulated record of violent crimes, treasons

---

[10] Delachenal, V, 551–4.

[11] *Prince*, 114.

and evasions, lends plausibility to at least parts of the narrative the chronicler puts in the mouth of his anonymous informant.

## The Old Squire's Tale

ACCORDING to Froissart's sources, the heir of Foix-Béarn had been brought up at Orthez together with his half-brother Yvain, for the two were 'of an age' and so habitual playmates. But then comes the fatal day when young Gaston visits his mother in Pamplona, and his uncle the King of Navarre, taking him aside, gives him a small bag filled with a white powder. This, Charles explains, is the potion that cannot fail to restore the love of Fébus for his wife, provided it is administered to him in secret. Naturally eager to bring about his parents' reconciliation, the boy returns to Orthez with the *boursette* concealed under his shirt, and waits for the right moment to sprinkle the contents on his father's food. As he sometimes shares a room with Yvain, there is friendly horseplay, then an exchange of garments, during which Yvain, having got hold of the bag and 'felt the powder in it', asks what it is. Gaston puts him off with evasive answers, but within three days, 'as if God had wanted to save the Count of Foix', the brothers quarrel at tennis, Gaston slaps Yvain, and Yvain goes straight to their father and tells him about the mysterious powder. 'I know not what it is for', he adds, 'nor what he wants to do with it, save that once or twice he said to me that his mother would soon be in better favour with you than she ever was.' His suspicions aroused, the Count nevertheless keeps them to himself until dinner time, when it is Gaston's regular duty to serve him and taste all his food. Closely watching his son, Fébus then sees the cords of the incriminating *boursette* showing under his doublet. Froissart's rendition of the scene deserves to be quoted verbatim:

> It made his blood boil, and he said: 'Gaston, come here, I want to say something in your ear.' The child came to the table. Then the Count unlaced and opened his doublet, took a knife and cut the cord holding the bag, which remained in his hand. He then said to his son: 'What is in this bag?' The child, who was much surprised and astonished, said not a word, but he turned quite pale and confused with fear, for he knew he was lost. The Count of Foix then opened the bag, took some of the powder and put it on a trencher of bread. He whistled for one of the greyhounds he had with him, and gave it the bread to eat. As soon as the dog had eaten the morsel, it fell with its feet up in the air, and died. When the Count saw how it was, he was angry, and with good reason. He got up from the table, took up his knife, and tried to lunge at his son. He would surely have killed him then and there, but some knights and squires rushed before him and said: 'My lord, have mercy in God's name, do not be hasty, but find out more about this business before you do your

son any harm.' And the first words the Count said were, in his Gascon language:'Zo, *Gaston, traitour*! It was for you, and to increase the inheritance that was to be yours, that I have had war and enmity with the King of France, the King of England, the King of Spain, the King of Navarre and the King of Aragon, and against them I held firm and steadfast, and now you want to murder me! It comes from your evil nature ...'[12]

Once again Fébus lunges at his son; once again his retainers, kneeling before him, entreat the Count not to kill Gaston, for he has 'no other children'. 'Perhaps', they suggest, 'the boy did not know what it was he carried, and is not guilty of this crime.' The Count reluctantly spares his son, and orders him taken to 'a room where there is very little light' – most probably the prison on the windowless ground floor of the Tour Moncade, where Fébus also kept his treasure.

The 'old squire' passes quickly over the ensuing investigation, saying only that not all members of the young prince's household were arrested, 'for many ran away', most notable among them the bishop of Lescar. Nevertheless, up to fifteen, whose only crime was that they had failed to bring the lethal bag to the Count's attention, 'died horribly' under torture. According to the same informant, Fébus then summoned an assembly of notables from both Foix and Béarn to debate the fate of his son. Again, his subjects begged for mercy, with the same argument voiced by the Count's attendant at the moment of discovery: 'Gaston is your heir, and you have none other.' Perhaps in response to their pressure, perhaps even sensing that a death sentence would alienate his people, Fébus relented: he would keep his son in prison for two or three months, and then send him 'on some voyage' (a pilgrimage, or a distant war?) for two or three years more, 'until he had forgotten his evil purpose' and gained, with age, a measure of wisdom. The delegates then disbanded, but not before the men of Foix had exacted the solemn assurance that Gaston's life would be spared. Meanwhile the Pope, who had heard the story, had also sent a cardinal to intercede for the boy. But the prelate was delayed and, by the time he had come as far as Béziers, word reached him that 'He had no more business in Béarn, for Gaston, son of the Count of Foix, was dead.'[13]

The squire's narrative now seeks to explain how this happened despite Fébus' solemn promise to spare his son's life. It appears that, after ten days in a dark cell, 'without any guard [...] or anyone to comfort and counsel him', the prisoner had sunk into a deep depression: he was still in the same clothes, never taking them off since his arrest; more ominously, he had not touched any of the food brought to him, so that 'it was a wonder he had lived so long'. When this was reported to Fébus, in terms that could have suggested a suicidal

[12] *Voyage*, 74–5.
[13] *Ibid.*, 77.

hunger strike ('he is starving himself'), the Count happened to be paring his fingernails with the point of a blade awkwardly described as a 'little long knife' (*un petit long coustelet*) – *i.e.* a kind of pen-knife. Still holding the knife in such a manner that only a fraction of an inch ('no more than the thickness of a groat'), protruded from his fist, he marched off angrily to the tower and confronted the boy. He only intended to discipline him, says the squire, but 'By mischance, when he hit his son's throat with that little knife-point, he struck I know not what vein, saying: "Ha! Traitor, why don't you eat?".' Fébus then left without another word and returned to his chamber, unaware that, as soon as he had gone, Gaston had 'turned the other way, and died then and there'.

The squire's relation leaves some ambiguity as to the immediate cause of death: the possibility of a punctured vein is mentioned in passing, but nothing is said about a fatal haemorrhage; instead, the narrator speculates that, weakened by his extended fast, the young prince may have died of shock and fright, either at the sight of his angry father, or from having felt the point of the knife at his throat. The Count was at first incredulous, but his dismay soon gave way to violent grief:

> Then the Count of Foix was aggrieved beyond measure, he mourned for his son very much and said: 'Ha! Gaston, what a sad mishap! It was for your doom and mine that you ever went to Navarre to see your mother! I shall never have joy as complete as I had before this.' He then sent for his barber, and had his head shaved, [...] and he put on black clothes, as did all those in his household.[14]

The old squire then closes with a last statement of the theme heard at the beginning of his tale: 'And so came to pass, as I tell you, the death of Gaston de Foix. It is true that his father killed him, but it was the King of Navarre that dealt him the death blow.'

O N the whole, and despite some unresolved ambiguities, this version of the events leads the reader, as it might have led a coroner's inquest, to conclude that the cause of Gaston's death was an unfortunate accident, the last act of a tragedy of errors, but that the fatal sequence had been set in motion by the treachery of Charles 'the Bad', in effect the one and only intentional murderer. However, closer examination reveals a number a inaccuracies and contradictions that may have at first passed unnoticed in the sweep of a story made up of a rapid succession of *coups de théâtre*. There is, for instance, the issue of young Gaston's age and status: throughout the tale of the 'old squire', he is referred to as a child (*l'enfes*), although at the time of his death, he was probably less than two months short of his eighteenth birthday. In an era when

---

[14] *Ibid.*, 79.

princes reached legal majority at fourteen, he was old enough to bear arms and to marry. He had, indeed, been a married man for over a year, and he had a separate household, with his own chaplains and a number of servants. Given the limited lodging space at the castle, it is likely that his *ostel* was in the town of Orthez, perhaps in the neighbouring Bourg Moncade, a suburb largely populated by the overflow of the Count's retainers and guests. In the event, he would have been past the age of sharing a room – if he ever did – with his half-brother. As for the two being 'of an age', there are indications that Yvain, who had fought by his father's side in 1376, during the 'war of Comminges', was by several years the older one. There is also reason to doubt that Gaston's court duties included tasting his father's food. If the function of the taster was to detect attempts to poison the Count, it would have been illogical to expose his heir to the same danger. Moreover, the taster would have needed uncommon dexterity to season a dish – and go undetected – after tasting it himself.

Then, after the high drama of Gaston's arrest, the narrative is curiously imprecise on the subject of a possible plot. Why so many of the young prince's retainers fled, if they were innocent, is easily explained: all were treated as suspects and faced torture. But those who were taken and 'died horribly' seem to have been chiefly victims of the Count's anger, and guilty of nothing more than their own lack of vigilance. Lastly, the admission that 'his father killed him' does not quite fit in with the fumbling about the immediate cause of Gaston's death. The suggestion of death-by-fright, the uncharacteristically precise measurement of the knife-point peering out of the father's fist, can be read as somewhat desperate attempts to disguise the fatal blow. But despite all the evasions, outright errors and muddled public-house gossip, three fundamental facts seem to emerge with some credibility: first, that an attempt was made on the life of Fébus; second, that there was, if not a full-blown trial, at least some sort of consultation with the notables of both Foix and Béarn; and third, that Fébus either killed his son, or had him killed.

Besides Froissart's 'old squire's tale', the only other contemporary account is a brief entry in the *Chronique des Quatre Premiers Valois* : 'in this year the sons [*sic*] of the Count of Foix tried to kill and poison their father. Their father learned of it, he had his sons arrested and confronted them with the fact, and then he had them put in jail. Some say that this was the doing of their uncle the King of Navarre.'[15] It is worth noting that, broadly inaccurate as this report is, it nevertheless concurs with Froissart regarding Charles' responsibility. Some fifty years later Juvénal des Ursins would narrate a more substantial variant of Froissart's tale. Writing even longer after the event, and subject to error in such matters of public record as the age of Fébus at his death, and the succession of Foix-Béarn, Juvénal is far from trustworthy. But he was also writing at a greater emotional remove from the events, and free of the virtual (albeit

---

[15] *Chronique des quatre premiers Valois*, 284.

self-imposed) censorship that seems to hamper Froissart. According to the fifteenth-century historian, young Gaston was not only a willing party to a plot against his father's life, but also the designated assassin. His grievance was that his household was not as grandly supported as it ought to be, although Fébus did 'his possible best' to maintain his son in a style appropriate to his rank. The motive put forward for Gaston's murderous intentions seems rather thin, but it can be viewed as the superficial aspect of the strained rapport between father and son, and of a deep disaffection on the latter's part. The syndrome of the impatient crown prince is common enough throughout history: the Planta-genets were famously plagued by it from the first; it was to bedevil the Valois until the end of the fifteenth century, and it would take a particularly virulent form in the Romanov dynasty, with Peter the Great's fatal flogging of his son. Besides the two relations of the Orthez tragedy, other documents suggest that, as is not uncommon in such situations, a party of malcontents had coalesced around the disgruntled heir apparent, who perhaps had reasons to feel some-what marginalized by his authoritarian father. In 1375, at a time when Fébus sought means to counter the threat posed by Louis d'Anjou, the young prince had been sent to Pamplona on a visit to his mother, a gesture that – together with the proposed Lancaster marriage – happened to serve his father's diplo-matic overtures towards Navarre and England. Whether he made other trips to Pamplona is not known, but this may have been the occasion of his entry into the conspiracy. Chief among the plotters – or at any rate the only one named in Froissart's account – Odon de Mendousse, bishop of Lescar, is known to have received money from the King of Navarre; as Gaston's tutor, he had accompa-nied him to Pamplona, and in June 1380, when the plot apparently ripened, he received a secret envoy from Charles. As Froissart's squire reports correctly, the prelate fled as soon as the failure of the coup was known. He was in Pamplona on 16 August, in the company of the baron of Andoins, and remained in exile until after the death of Fébus.[16]

Juvénal's much more succinct account of the attempted poisoning, while it lacks the theatrical flavour of Froissart's, has a somewhat more plausible ring: its tenor is that Gaston was simply caught, like a not very clever spy, when he made himself conspicuous in the wrong place, at the wrong time: 'Every day he looked for the moment when he could execute his uncle's advice […] and some-times he went to his father's kitchen, which was not his habitual way. By chance, the little box of poison fell to the floor, and one of the Count's servants picked it up.'[17] The contents of the box (not Froissart's *boursette*, worn like a magical charm) were then examined by the Count's physician and his apothecary, who declared it to be 'a very bad poison'. To put it to the test, a man already under sentence of death was brought in and given the poison with his, as it were,

[16] *Vicomté*, 319.

[17] Jean Juvénal des Ursins, *Histoire de Charles VI* (Paris, 1653), 78.

last meal. No scene at the Count's table, then, but a clumsy, hesitant approach
by the young conspirator snooping in the kitchen where he had no business.
The deliberate forensic procedure to determine the nature of an unknown substance suggests an orderly response, rather than panic. As for the cold-blooded
use of a condemned man as the conclusive guinea-pig, it is more believable
than the sacrifice of one of Fébus' precious greyhounds. Juvénal's relation winds
up briskly: he makes no mention of a trial, but nevertheless suggests at least a
rough but formal judicial process, followed by an execution, rather than any
kind of 'accident': 'The Count had his son interrogated and examined, who confessed the thing as I have written above. And because of this, he ordered his
head cut off.'

The more plausible elements of both Froissart's and Juvénal's versions,
together with established circumstantial facts – and a good deal of reading
between the lines – make it possible to attempt a hypothetical reconstruction
of the events leading to, and surrounding, the death of young Gaston. The
abrupt dismissal of Agnès de Navarre in 1363 had undoubtedly lit the slow
fuse that would, seventeen years later, set off the deadly explosion. It was probably at the root of the son's estrangement from his father, and compounded by
jealous resentment of the favour shown by the Count to his half-brothers, the
'two fine young bastard knights' that Fébus loved, according to Espan de Lion,
'as much as himself', and to Yvain in particular.[18] The foremost biographer of
Fébus suggests that the heir apparent may also have resented being used by
the Count as a pawn on the political chessboard: first betrothed to Philippa
of Lancaster, Gaston had then been married off to Béatrix d'Armagnac, 'a child
not yet nubile', within the framework of a peace settlement with the hereditary
foe of Foix-Béarn.[19] Such unions were common enough, and even a disaffected
Gaston must have known that they were part and parcel of a prince's dynastic duties. But something other than the age of the bride must have rankled:
groomed for a royal alliance, Gaston may well have felt the new match as a
kind of demotion, and himself manipulated to expedite the patching-up of an
old quarrel, the mere instrument of a dilatory manœuvre – as later events were
to show that neither adversary had sincerely buried the hatchet. The low-key
wedding ceremony, which neither the bride's nor the groom's father bothered
to attend, could also be construed as an added slight. In a society sensitive to
nuances of rank and visible marks of favour, the more enterprising of Fébus'
enemies lacked no opportunities and pretexts to seduce a disgruntled teenager,
especially as the boy's tutor, Odon de Mendousse, seems to have been one of
their busiest agents.

The participation of this presumably trusted bishop, and that of some of the
leading lords of Béarn, hints at the existence of a lively party of malcontents,

[18]  *Voyage*, 49.

[19]  *Prince*, 209.

nobles and prelates who had seen their prerogatives at home, and their influence at court, diminished under Fébus' centralizing government. This conflict
between a sovereign's 'absolutism', short-circuiting the traditional councils of
vassals, and the barons superseded by the hand-picked, often low-born advisers directly responsible to the prince, was not unique to Béarn: among other
instances of the same phenomenon, it would soon erupt at the court of France
when, after the death of Charles V, his brothers would gang up against his
staff of parvenus, collectively derided as his 'Marmousets'. The opposition to
Fébus may have been led by the baron d'Andoins, whose family had enjoyed a
privileged closeness to Gaston II, and by the Viscount of Castelbon. A measure
of the latter's disaffection is given by the fact that Roger-Bernard, head of this
junior branch of Foix-Béarn, and as such an heir presumptive, had bequeathed
his claim to the King of Navarre, in exchange for a pension and two Navarrese
fiefs.[20] The prospect of eventually adding to his own realm the territorial inheritance of Fébus, as well as the rumoured treasure in his coffers, would have been
motive enough for Charles to lend his expertise to the plot against his brother-
in-law: profit, furthermore, spiced with the satisfaction of avenging the affront
of his sister's dismissal.

It remains a matter of conjecture whether other foreign parties were
involved in the aborted coup. Certainly, the Armagnacs would have welcome
the removal of Fébus and his replacement by an heir now married into their
clan – and possibly under their control – but there is no indication of their
complicity. Nor is there any to support the notion that the French government, worried about the imminent consolidation of a 'Greater Foix-Béarn'
state, might also have favoured the plot.[21] Moreover, in the summer of 1380,
the Valois court had other, more pressing concerns: a new English *chevauchée*,
led by the Earl of Buckingham, was being launched from Calais; there were
new alarms from Brittany; lastly, the deaths of Bertrand du Guesclin and
of Charles V removed from the scene the two principal architects of the
French recovery in the preceding decade. It would appear then that Charles
of Navarre was the only active participant from abroad to the plot against
the Count of Foix. But he may well have made the decisive move of providing his nephew with the poison intended for Fébus: if so, Froissart's judgement, assigning to the King of Navarre the prime responsibility for the tragic
outcome, was broadly justified. It is, however, fair to note that no document
has emerged from the archives of Béarn or of Navarre, to support conclusively
that verdict and that of other French chroniclers generally hostile to Charles
'the Bad'.

---

[20] *Ibid.*, 211.

[21] *Vicomté*, 316–20.

## The aftermath

As with the extent of the conspiracy and its ramifications, very little is known about the repression that followed its discovery, other than the vague number cited by Froissart, of 'up to fifteen' of Gaston's retainers tortured to death. And yet, even in the absence of corroborating documents, it can be assumed that there was some sort of investigation, followed by some sort of open procedure. Froissart's account of the assembly summoned to Orthez, of 'all the nobles and prelates of Foix and Béarn, and all the notables of both countries', is too detailed, and too revealing of undercurrents, to be dismissed out of hand. Clearly, the delegates were not expected to give a verdict, only to acquiesce as Fébus probably announced his intention of having Gaston put to death. But that merely consultative body eventually asserted itself, to the extent that the men of Foix 'would not leave Orthez, unless the Count assured them that Gaston would not die, for they so loved the child.' In the retrospective light of subsequent manœuvres by Fébus to make his bastards Yvain and Gratien his heirs, his subjects' insistent argument that Gaston ought to be spared because Fébus 'had no other children', may well indicate that they were anxious to forestall any tampering with the normal order of succession. Why the Count's subjects 'so loved the child' is clearly explained in the passage where Espan first tells Froissart that Fébus once had a legitimate heir, 'a fine son who was the delight of his father and of the country, because through him the land of Béarn, which is in dispute, could remain in peace, for he had as his wife the sister of the Count of Armagnac.'[22]

As for the outcome of the consultation, different sources report different verdicts: the mere incarceration reported by the *Chronique des quatre premiers Valois* can be discounted, together with the pluralization of the culprit. This leaves the two accounts of Gaston's death, either Froissart's highly improbable 'accident', or a legally sanctioned execution. There are reasons to doubt the latter: first, the Count's solemn promise to spare his son's life, related by Froissart, would have been a matter of public knowledge, since it was made to the gathered notables. In all likelihood Fébus could not have reneged overtly on it by ordering an execution, without exposing himself to some protests, perhaps even more forceful opposition. He seems to have been in no position to reject the appeal of his subjects for clemency. Secondly, the virtual censorship clamped on the circumstances of Gaston's death would have been unnecessary in the event of a lawful execution pursuant to a judicial process. Thirdly, the death of the culprit would have resulted, not from a crime, but from the application of justice: in and of itself, due process of law would have at least mitigated, if not dismissed, any guilt on the part of Fébus. But the pathos that filters through the liturgical rhetoric of the *Book of Orisons* strongly suggests that, years after

---

[22] *Voyage*, 49.

the deed, Fébus was still tormented by the guilt of a perhaps unredeemable sin, crying out: 'Lord, Lord, […] I have committed a crime for which Thou canst damn me …'[23] It may be also that the dedication of the *Orisons* to the King's uncle Philip of Burgundy was intended as an indirect, oblique confession to the French Crown, to whose earthly justice he was in theory answerable.

On the other hand, Froissart's version of death by misadventure appears simply too finely crafted to be believed: a coincidence of selected facts, related with unusual precision, leads to a reasonable doubt of Fébus' guilt, with the hesitant conclusion that the boy may have died of fright, or from the chance puncture of a vein. This blurred account stands in sharp contrast with another tale of violent death, *viz.* the story, attributed to Espan de Lion, of the stabbing of Pierre-Arnaud de Béarn, for his refusal to surrender the castle of Lourdes to the Count. That this anecdote was patently untrue is easily demonstrated by the fact that the alleged victim not only did not incur the wrath of his cousin Fébus, but remained one of his favourite lieutenants and – by Froissart's own account – was present at the Count's funerals (see p. 124 above). It is not hard, however, to imagine the scene narrated by Espan transposed to the dungeon of the Tour Moncade, with the young heir of Foix-Béarn as its all too real victim; to imagine Fébus already overwrought, now faced with a sullen or defiant Gaston, flying into a rage and reaching for his ubiquitous knife – and this time, with no one quick enough to restrain him.[24]

To suggest that the chronicler may have deliberately scattered disguised (or 'coded') fragments of the truth among various episodes of his relation, would be a perilous leap into historical fiction. But, while Froissart's talent often lends verisimilitude to a demonstrably fictitious account, he is also notorious for frequently confusing the times and places of actual events. He had only come to Béarn eight years after the events, and there collected more or less clandestinely the fragments of a long-suppressed story, for we may infer from Espan's recurring evasions, and from the wish of the 'old squire' to remain anonymous, that on the topic of young Gaston's death, not only were the Count's familiars sworn to silence, but his subjects and his debtors, pledged to report any treasonable conversation, functioned effectively as a secret police for the enforcement of censorship. Froissart may have heard more than one whispered version of the tragedy, from more than one 'old squire'. How he chose to organize his narrative when rewriting it several years after his return from Béarn, may also reflect, more than a conscious and deliberate attempt to absolve Fébus, the version of events consonant with his admiration for a generous and civilized host, the 'truth' in which he wanted to believe.

[23] Gaston Fébus, *Livre des oraisons*, 55.

[24] On the theme of the knife in Froissart's narrative, and the possible connection between the two hypothetical stabbings, see Peter F. Ainsworth, *Jean Froissart and the Fabric of History* (Oxford, 1990), 160, n. 45.

The outbreak of the plot, its repression and the death of Gaston probably unfolded between mid-July and mid-August 1380. The first act signed by Fébus after that interval is dated 17 August, not from Orthez but from Pau, where the Count seems to have gone immediately after the tragic events. His hasty departure may have been prompted by the fear that his personal security at Orthez was compromised, either by ramifications of the conspiracy, or by some kind of disorder in the town when the death of the heir of Béarn became known. It has also been suggested that his 'flight' and subsequent absence from the Château Moncade, where he only returned in 1384, was primarily an emotional reaction, an escape from the scene of a double crime.[25] Although remorse and horror, plainly legible in the *Livre des oraisons*, may well explain why Fébus stayed so long away from Orthez, it will be seen presently that he had other reasons to take up residence for the next two years in the strategically sensitive vicinity of Toulouse.

The coup had failed in its principal object, but it had nevertheless struck hard at the mighty Count of Foix. The death of his only legitimate son made his dynastic enterprise meaningless. In this respect, the apostrophe to young Gaston that Froissart attributes to Fébus at the moment of discovering the attempted parricide (' It was for you, and to increase the inheritance that was to be yours, that I have had war and enmity with the King of France, the King of England, etc. ...') reflects a political reality: without an heir, the territorial edifice that Fébus had successfully expanded and preserved from foreign encroachments was in jeopardy. The extent of his dilemma, its impact on the country, and the solution he contemplated, can be inferred from the words of Espan de Lion, reportedly spoken as he and Froissart were riding between Tarbes and Morlaàs. In that episode of a ten-day long travelling conversation, the chronicler – hoping perhaps to discover the circumstances of Gaston's death – laments aloud the fact that 'to such a high and valiant prince [...] there remains not an heir born of lawful wedlock.' To which Espan can only concur, and this dialogue ensues:

– So help me God, but if he had one, [the Count] would be the happiest lord in the world, and so would be all the people of his land!

– And so, I said, will his land remain without an heir?

– No, said he, for the Viscount of Castelbon, his first cousin, is his heir.

– Is he a valiant man at arms? I said.

– So help me God, he said, he is not, and because of that the Count of Foix cannot love him. And if he can do it, he will make his two bastard sons, who are fine young knights, his heirs; he intends to marry them

---

[25] *Vicomté*, 321.

into high lineage, for he has plenty of gold and silver. And so he will find them wives who will help and comfort them.[26]

Froissart pretends to find obstacles to this unorthodox plan: 'Sir, I would like that, but it is neither proper nor reasonable to make bastards heirs to a country.' But his demur is only the cue for Espan to ask: 'Why not, if there are no suitable heirs?' and cite famous precedents: the recent ones of Enrique II of Castile and João I of Portugal, and the historic one of William the Conqueror, all examples of successful breach of the customary laws of royal inheritance.

Of the several remarkable aspects of this conversation, the first is that it took place at all, when very little was allowed to be said about the dead Gaston: clearly, Fébus' intention of making Yvain and Gratien his heirs was no secret. Moreover, it is introduced in Froissart's narrative of his journey to Béarn in such a way as to highlight the rationale put forward by Espan, perhaps intentionally: had the intended promotion of the bastards to heirs of Foix-Béarn, the *Chroniques* would have been the vehicle for the public justification of Fébus' actions. Nor was this idle talk, merely reflecting an abstract wish: Espan's allusion to the matrimonial future of the two 'fine young knights' suggests that Fébus had formed a plan for their irregular birth to be somehow varnished over by marriages into families of 'high lineage'. It is worth noting in passing that another 'bastard of Béarn', perhaps a son of the very young Gaston III, had married an heiress of royal blood, and acceded almost twenty years since to Castilian *grandeza* (see Appendix). It is also clear that the succession was a matter of direct concern to the Count's subjects: if Froissart, although only a foreign guest, is disturbed by the thought that the land 'will remain without an heir', and therefore an object of dispute, those who would be exposed to all the consequences – invasion or a breakdown of authority – have a vital stake in an orderly solution to the problem. The conversation, however, does not even touch on the eventual reaction of public opinion in general, and of the notables in particular, to an illegitimate succession. Neither of the men – nor presumably the Count himself – could have foreseen that the 'consultation' of the nobles and notables of Foix and Béarn after Gaston's arrest might serve in some yet undetermined future as a precedent for a similar assembly to assert their right to accept or reject an heir.

As for the unilateral exclusion of the Viscount of Castelbon, Fébus' cousin, and since the death of Gaston his next lawful heir, it appears to be a foregone conclusion. Froissart's question about the Viscount's worth 'at arms', and Espan's summary dismissal, point to a puzzling, but not surprising confusion – either in the chronicler's memory, or in the knight's – *viz.* the fact that at the time their conversation took place, Mathieu de Castelbon was only eleven years old, a child even by feudal reckoning, whose military virtues, or the lack

---

[26] *Voyage*, 60.

of them, could hardly be judged at all. Espan's reply could only have referred to Mathieu's father, Roger-Bernard II, who, however, had been dead since 1381. Such discrepancies are not rare in Froissart's *Chroniques*, but in this case, it does not greatly signify. The enmity between the two branches of the Foix-Béarn family probably dated back to the minority of Gaston III, when his uncle Roger-Bernard I de Castelbon had opposed the regency of Aliénor de Comminges. Years later Roger-Bernard II, as lord of Mauvezin, had wilfully obstructed Fébus' plan to control the county of Bigorre; perhaps for this or other perceived offence, the Count had him imprisoned, according to Froissart, 'eight months in the tower of Orthez', and only released him against a ransom of 40,000 francs. There is documentary evidence that in the spring of 1380 Roger-Bernard sold some of his lands in Catalonia in order to raise some of the cash required: revenge for this would have been as good a motive as any to push him into the plot against Fébus, and into his allegiance to Charles de Navarre. Whether Espan remembered in 1388 that the current viscount was a mere boy is immaterial: clearly, Fébus would not be reconciled with the Castelbons, and was determined to deny them at any cost the succession of Foix-Béarn. This resolve was perhaps the most steadfast motive of his policy during the next and final decade of his reign, and it would underlie some of his most bizarre – and perhaps his most desperate – political initiatives.

✦　✦
✦

# Endgame

THE dilemma about the dynastic succession was neither the only nor the most immediate concern raised by the death of young Gaston. By his marriage with Béatrix d'Armagnac, the heir of Foix-Béarn had been, as Espan de Lion put it, 'the delight of his father and of the country, because through him the land of Béarn […] could remain in peace.' But now, with its guarantor gone, the fragile peace mediated (not to say imposed) by the King of France and the Pope between the two greatest lords in the Midi was unlikely to hold – especially if the Count of Foix suspected the Armagnac clan of having had a hand in a plot to remove him. A series of recent and concurrent events in France could only aggravate this unstable situation. It had begun in the summer of 1380 with the recall of Louis d'Anjou from his lieutenancy of Languedoc; the Duke could perhaps find solace in the fact that he was needed elsewhere, but in fact his recall stemmed from the unrest provoked in Montpellier and other cities by his misgovernment. In mid-July the long overdue campaign to rid Auvergne and Languedoc of entrenched *routiers* was interrupted by the death of the Constable Bertrand du Guesclin; meanwhile, a new English *chevauchée* out of Calais – albeit of limited strategic importance – was adding to French woes, amid renewed fears that Buckingham's army would join forces with the rebellious Duke of Brittany. Then on 16 September Charles V died, leaving as his successor a twelve-year-old boy easily governed by the three 'fleur-de-lis princes', his uncles of Anjou, Berry and Burgundy.

A later chronicler of Foix affirms that after the death of Du Guesclin, the late King had appointed Gaston III his lieutenant in Languedoc. Unlikely as this was, especially in the wake of the violent events at Orthez, the rumour of that appointment seems to have been rife, at least in the western part of the province, to the extent that on 17 December 1380 the consuls of Albi sent emissaries to seek confirmation from their colleagues of Toulouse.[1] It may be that the rumour had been deliberately spread by agents of Fébus, as a means of making the French court face the embarrassment of having to disavow a popular appointment – for Fébus was well liked in Toulouse. If that was the case, the ploy had already failed, as in fact the royal council of regency had, one month earlier, given the government of Languedoc to the Duke of Berry. This was no more acceptable to Fébus than the appointment of the same prince had been in 1357: the eighteen-year-old Count of Poitiers had been then under the tutelage

---

[1] *Vicomté*, 323, n. 2.

of Jean I d'Armagnac, whose own tenure as King's Lieutenant had thus been prolonged by that of his godson – and soon to be son-in-law. It seemed that the honour and profit of governing Languedoc was a virtual apanage reserved for the hereditary rivals of the House of Foix and their closest ally among the royal Valois.

War had followed then – and Launac. Now, however, the obligations of fealty, and a realistic appreciation of the risk involved, simply forbade Fébus from taking arms against France as he had against the Armagnacs, but he was well versed in the art of having his way while giving every appearance of loyalty to the Crown, and the slow-moving Jean de Berry gave him such an opportunity. Appointed in November 1380, the Duke did not arrive in Languedoc until the end of June 1381. The seven-month delay left the province in effect without a royal governor, which would have been bearable – but also without a royal force to protect it from the still dangerous *routiers*. It was therefore not as a rebel, but as a vassal safeguarding his king's patrimony, that Fébus moved to occupy the vacant authority. And he moved fast: still in Béarn on 4 January, he was at Saint-Gaudens, on the upper Garonne, three days later; another week, and he had taken his quarters in the suburb of Saint-Cyprien, across the river from Toulouse. With the agreements of the consuls, he garrisoned the city with an army of about 1,000 men; from this it is reasonable to infer that he had also occupied key positions along the Garonne valley, south from Toulouse.

Having achieved military control of the roads from Orthez to Foix and to the capital of Languedoc, Fébus now attempted a direct diplomatic offensive. From Mazères, where he had settled after securing Toulouse, he wrote on 4 February to the King of France, protesting the appointment of Jean de Berry in terms that bordered on a declaration of open rebellion: 'Whoever counselled you to make [the Duke] your Lieutenant has not counselled you well [...] and as for myself, my liege, as long as I have life I shall not suffer in Languedoc any lord opposed to me.'[2] Such extraordinary provocation, together with the earlier rumour of his appointment by the dying Charles V, might well have been another move in a war of nerves waged by Fébus against the Regency Council. His commissioning of the best minstrels to proclaim his French loyalties (see p. 68), as well as his timely flattery of Froissart, show him to have been a master of public relations. But if he was bluffing to some extent, Gaston III was not laggard in extending his advantage on the ground: he underscored the meaning of his letter with another armed demonstration north of Toulouse, received the submissions of Albi and Montauban, installed his officers in key positions, and put down scattered opposition. Careful not to usurp the title of Lieutenant, he nevertheless assumed the authority to summon delegates from all the towns of Languedoc to meet at Mazères on 24 April – a clearly irregular convocation of the provincial Estates. It was only a partial success, as a number a key

---

[2] *Ibid.*, 324, n. 4.

delegations – among them Toulouse and Montpellier – decided to stay away rather than incur the royal displeasure. Nevertheless, the assembly in effect gave Fébus a free hand to consolidate his hold on the region, decreeing that for a flat fee of 4,000 francs a month, the Count would provide a protective garrison to any town or village that requested it.

The French government had no choice but to treat the Count of Foix as a rebel: on 3 April, the young King raised against him the *oriflamme* – the ritual war banner kept at the abbey of Saint-Denis. For the present, however, this could only be a symbolic gesture. While the situation in Brittany had become more stable after Duke Jean IV abandoned his English allies, other crises loomed at home and in the North. One of the last wishes of Charles V had been to abolish the hearth tax he had made an annual levy. It weighed on his conscience as unjust, and therefore a grave sin on the part of an anointed king. His deathbed promise could not be ignored, but how to substitute for the lost revenue was the question put to the Estates General summoned for 14 November, ten days after the coronation of Charles VI. It could not have been raised at a worst time, when a veritable epidemic of popular rebellion was spreading through Christendom. The first notable case had been in 1378 the revolt of the Ciompi – the urban proletariat of Florence; the next year saw the beginning of a protracted and many-sided struggle in Flanders, with the prosperous industrial cities now defying their Count, now at each other's throats, while at the same time torn by violent internal class conflicts. In England, discontent with the taxes consented by Parliament to finance the Duke of Lancaster's proposed war in Spain would soon erupt in the revolt of Wat Tyler. In France, the Jacquerie of 1358 may have been but a terrible memory, but its root causes had never been eliminated, and the fear of a savage rising of the villeins and urban poor was never far below the surface of the ruling classes' display of opulence. And indeed, when the Chancellor told the Estates of the need to raise new 'aids', the popular reaction was immediate and so ominous that on November 16 the government published an edict abolishing all taxes. This was by no means the end of unrest: the attempt to shift the responsibility for raising revenue on to the provincial Estates would provoke revolts in Normandy, Champagne, Picardy and Orléanais, with Paris rising once more in 1382 against the King, and everywhere the pogroms that were the usual by-products of urban uprisings.[3]

Still trying to recover in April 1381 from its 'stroke of fiscal suicide' (Tuchman), the Regency Council certainly could not have found the resources to field a royal army to quell the relatively peripheral nuisance of Fébus' rebellion. Moreover, two of the King's uncles, whose mutual jealousy had been on public display at their nephew's coronation, had more urgent preoccupations of their own. Louis d'Anjou was clearly bent on treating the regency as the

---

[3] On the various popular revolts in the fourteenth century, see Barbara W. Tuchman, *A Distant Mirror* (New York, 1978), 365–97.

springboard from which he would launch his conquest of his long-coveted kingdom of Naples and Sicily, while Philip of Burgundy, as son-in-law and heir to the Count of Flanders, was equally determined to use the royal army in an offensive against the rebellious Flemings. Between his two aggressive siblings, Jean de Berry had to await his turn before being given the means to assert his authority in Languedoc, where he arrived at the end of June. Better known as an art collector than a warrior, he then sought a peaceful exit, all the more eagerly as Fébus had dispatched his cousin Pierre-Arnaud de Béarn to negotiate with the King of Aragon an alliance against both Berry and Armagnac. By mid-July an offer brought to Pamiers by the Duke's envoy produced an agreement, pending a meeting of the two princes: for a financial consideration (65,000 francs cash, plus an annuity of 40,000 francs) Fébus would cease to oppose the Duke's lieutenancy; for his part, Berry promised to give 'no favour to the Count of Armagnac above that given to the Count of Foix'.

The Duke's willingness to distance himself from his brother-in-law was a substantial diplomatic victory for Fébus but, only a week before he was due to meet with the Duke, it was nearly derailed by an unexpected clash of arms. A clause of the Pamiers agreement stipulated that the *routiers* recruited by the Duke were not to be allowed to attack the Catalan county of Roussillon. They began instead to march north, towards the Rouergue country (present-day *département* of Aveyron), a possession of the Count of Armagnac. The fact that Jean de Berry did not order them to desist may suggest either that, even at the cost of letting Armagnac lands be ravaged, he was unwilling to jeopardize the tentative agreement with Fébus; but it is at least equally probable that the mercenaries were no longer under his control – or for that matter in his pay. At any rate, it was certainly not his wish that, a few days before he was to meet with Fébus, they should take a detour through some of his lands south of Albi. Perhaps unaware that they were trespassing on the lands of the redoubtable Count, some the men of the companies burned part of the corn harvest and killed five peasants in the vicinity of the River Tarn. Fébus, who had had them shadowed through their march, had an army ready to pounce out of Rabastens. On the morning of 21 July – a Sunday and the Feast of Mary Magdalene – the men of Foix and Béarn, some led by Yvain, made 'a great carnage' of the trespassers. The chronicler du Bernis cites the undoubtedly inflated numbers of 700 men at arms and 2,000 'looters' killed. More significantly, he refers to the slaughtered *routiers* as 'the Duke of Berry's people', adding that 'seven captains bearing his banner were taken.'[4]

While it is likely that Jean de Berry had not desired the provocation, it would seem that Fébus, well informed of the *routiers'* moves, was only waiting for an occasion not only to make an example of their massacre, but also to demonstrate his ability to defy the royal Valois. The seven captains (including

4 *Prince*, 240.

the Nègre de Valence and Bénazet de Chiperel, who had once sworn to respect the Count's domains) were brought to Mazères, and the Duke's banners presented as trophies. Two days later, Berry's protest of the affront, brought by the bishop of Langres, was curtly dismissed by Fébus: 'those people, who had killed five men and burned sheaves on the King's lands, should have been led out of Languedoc, as agreed earlier.'[5] Thus an incident that, strictly speaking, had not been a direct confrontation between Fébus and Jean de Berry, was widely perceived as one, as reflected in the chronicle of the Monk of Saint-Denis, and later in du Bernis. But in fact both antagonists wished to avoid a wider and more protracted conflict. Cautious negotiations resumed in early August, followed by a visit of the Duke to Mazères; a final agreement was reached in December. Although its precise terms are not known, it clearly left Fébus in control of the seneschalcy of Toulouse. With his lieutenantcy now unchallenged, and a free hand to squeeze the rest of Languedoc for his own profit, the Duke remained neutral when hostilities broke out again between his brother-in-law of Armagnac and the Count of Foix.

This new and not unexpected episode of the hereditary feud can scarcely be called a war: it had begun in the summer of 1381 with a few skirmishes, and continued with pillaging forays by both sides in the regions of Albi, raids by the compagnons of Lourdes against the Armagnac lands, and a bold Armagnac counter-raid against eastern Béarn. On that occasion – the only instance of a successful attack on the viscounty – the heir of Count Jean II struck far enough into the valley of the Gave to take and burn the town of Nay, half-way between Pau and Lourdes. A truce mediated by the Duke of Berry helped bring that confused bout to an end: after more than eighteen months away from Béarn, Fébus returned to Pau in the autumn of 1382. But the dating of his recorded acts shows that, except for a brief stay in the spring of 1383, he would not come back to Orthez until April 1384.

AFTER the tense four years that followed the tragic events of 1380, this homecoming respite may have given Gaston III the opportunity to take stock of his achievements and perhaps gauge the success of his 'grand design' – if indeed he had one. Even Tucoo-Chala, the foremost authority on Fébus, hesitates on this issue: in his 1959 thesis, the Béarnais historian identifies Gaston III's goal as the creation of 'un grand état pyrénéen homogène de Foix à Orthez', but thirty-four years later he refers more cautiously to 'un ensemble pyrénéen'.[6] The scaling back of a 'great homogeneous state' to a vague 'ensemble' reflects not only advances in scholarly research, but more importantly a matured understanding of the many nuances required to paint the political map of Europe in the fourteenth century.

[5] *Ibid.*

[6] *Vicomté*, 301; *Prince*, 175.

While the modern concept of the nation-state – diverse communities and provinces existing under the rule of a common law – would have been utterly alien to a medieval mentality, the notion of a unified Christendom, personified in epic legends by the outsize figure of Charlemagne, and institutionalized in the supposed pre-eminence of the Holy Roman Emperor, was one of the most constant postulates of political theory throughout the Middle Ages. In that imagined construct, authority stemmed from a single source – God himself, delegating his power to His earthly vicar – or vicars. Here of course, between the singular and the plural, sprang the perennial contention between the Church, claiming the overarching authority of the papacy over secular rulers, and the kings and emperors who maintained that they held their commission directly from God. But despite the many, often absurd complications gener-ated by that conflict, a hierarchy of theoretical powers was generally recognized, defining the prerogatives of various 'classes' or 'levels' of rulers. Because they were anointed, and thus made sacrosanct, kings – and the Emperor – stood apart from the crowd of dukes, marquesses, or princes they were empowered to create. In principle, only those anointed monarchs could be said to hold their land 'from no man on earth'. And yet a mere Viscount was able to make the same claim, and to obtain its recognition by the major powers – tacit recogni-tion, to be sure, but the reluctance of both France and England to invade Béarn signified more than any formal diploma.

The exact nature of Fébus' pretensions is almost as ambiguous as his diplo-macy. What is quite clear is the meaning of his shift in official styling: the sub-stitution, beginning in 1365, of *dominus Bearni* for *vicecomes Bearni*, proclaiming the status of Béarn as a freehold rather than a viscounty vassal to either the Prince of Aquitaine or the King of France. More specific, the minatory let-ter to the consuls of Montpellier in regard to the Pélegrin affair asserted that Gaston III held Béarn 'as any prince in the world holds his land' (*sicut aliquis mundi princeps terram suam tenet*) and that over this land at its subjects he had 'eminent jurisdiction and imperial power' (*tante eminentie et juridictionis seu imperium*).[7] These punctual formulae, together with the habitual qualifier *gratia Dei* appended to the Count's titles, and the regalian prerogative – long enjoyed by the viscounts of Béarn – of minting their own coinage, can only mean that in Fébus' view, his authority was of the same nature as the *imperium* contemporary political theory attributed to anointed kings. But those piecemeal claims were usually put forward in response to certain well-defined pressures from would-be overlords of Béarn. The best example of this successful tactic was Gaston III's evasion of homage to the Prince of Wales at their meeting of January 1364: the effect of surprise, the dilatory reference to past precedents that it would take lawyers many months to document, had the desired effect of gaining time for the Count of Foix, who then used the delay to multiply

---

7 *Prince*, 63.

the affirmations, symbolic and real, of his *imperium*. Eventually, the danger of foreign intervention passed, but by then no one disputed the sovereign status of Béarn.

Was then the assumption of a power comparable to that of 'any prince in the world' merely a tactical weapon that Fébus used to ward off potential oppressors, or was it part of a long-range strategy, its object being that ultimate prize of feudal ambition – a royal crown? Gaston III would not have been the only great man in his time to seek such an elevation. Most notable in their energetic pursuits were two younger sons of kings – Louis d'Anjou and John of Gaunt: the latter claimed Castile on behalf of his wife Constance, daughter of the murdered Pedro I, while the French prince coveted first Majorca, then Naples and Sicily, and sometimes entertained the hope of a hypothetical kingdom of Adria. Neither pretender was able to secure his chimerical heritage (Louis would in fact die in Italy without ever seeing Naples), but in both instances the cost of their failure was borne by their home countries, with sometimes severe consequences. Of more direct interest to Pyrenean history, Jean III d'Armagnac would, upon the death of Peter IV, attempt to make good a dubious title to Majorca, and in 1396 another Count of Foix would make an equally ineffectual lunge at the Crown of Aragon itself. But Fébus never made the slightest move to conquer a kingdom near or far.

As for the possibility of forging his several domains into a single, contiguous state, Gaston III was too much of a pragmatist to entertain a project that, had anyone seriously contemplated it, would have required a sustained effort by several generations of like-minded rulers of Foix-Béarn. He had of course achieved to a large extent the goal envisaged by his predecessors, *viz.* control of enough lands, towns and castles to open a secure corridor between Béarn and the county of Foix; and he had in fact exceeded that goal by extending his influence to the westernmost districts of Languedoc. But many fragments of the Count's inheritance – such as the Moncada and Castellbò seigniories in Catalonia – still lay outside this potential 'ensemble'. Besides its geographical dispersions, the 'ensemble' on which Fébus held sway was characterized by the great diversity of his feudal or other prerogatives. Sovereign lord in Béarn, he owed homage to England for Marsan and Gavardan, to France for Foix, Lautrec and other fiefs in Languedoc, to Aragon for the Catalan domains. In addition to these relatively substantial holdings, he enjoyed a multitude of partial seigniorial rights and interests – some inherited, some purchased – in towns and lands beyond his own domains. Then there were several different kinds of negotiated – or coerced – obligations that gave Fébus control over a vast number of individuals or communities: first, the contracts whereby Fébus held castles and maintained garrisons for the protection of towns and villages in the Basque viscounty of Soule, in Bigorre, and later in the Toulousain and Albigeois; then the money fiefs (*fiefs-rentes*) with which he bought the vassal services of nobles outside his 'natural' claims of fealty; lastly, the liens and other legal devices whereby he ensured the docility of defaulting debtors and other offenders (such as the imprudent lord of Mirepoix). All those contracts, paid homages and obligations were, of course, personal transactions of Gaston III that, unlike feudal bonds, did not necessarily pertain to his successor, so that the next Count of Foix might choose or not to renew a contract or a money fief – as indeed the other party also might. Viewed in its totality, the 'ensemble' resembled not so much the pieces of a incomplete puzzle – where a clever player might find a way to fill the gaps – as a discontinuous mosaic, made up of pieces of such very different material that they could never fit together and be a coherent whole.

Given those facts on the ground, and with the convenience of hindsight, Fébus' political and strategic moves are somewhat less enigmatic than they might first appear. His flexible and balanced use of force and diplomacy marks him as a cool-headed pragmatist who learned quickly and early from his own experience, and presumably from that of other rulers. The misfortunes of Charles of Navarre, for instance – his kingdom repeatedly invaded, his towns sacked with impunity, himself taken prisoner in his own land – made it clear that the royal dignity conferred no protection to a realm that lay in the path of contending powers. Another sad story was that of Brittany, where for more than twenty years the clash of two pretenders to the ducal succession, one pro-French, one pro-English, had made the province one of the chief battlegrounds of the Valois–Plantagenet war. Whether or not Fébus reflected on these and other cautionary examples, he remained from 1353 constant in a policy of non-alignment in that conflict, not so much as a passive bystander, but always looking for advantage to be taken of the weaknesses of either belligerent. His neutrality, bristling with defences, allowed him to focus his offensive capabilities on the other constant of his external policy, the hereditary struggle with the Armagnacs. Here again, the goal contemplated by several generations of Foix-Béarn was not the creation of a homogeneous realm according to a preconceived notion of 'state', but the practical one of secure corridors between their various domains, to ensure the economic viability and growth of the whole. This Fébus achieved in what might be seen as a makeshift solution, not by the outright acquisition of intervening lands (*e.g.* Comminges, Bigorre, etc.) but by a wide variety of stratagems – loans, contracts, *fiefs-rentes*, etc. – to control strategic places and extend his sphere of influence. If Froissart's report is true, a clear example of Gaston III's preference for this piecemeal approach may be the case of Bigorre, where Fébus, while refusing Charles V's offer of the county – an offer contingent of an homage he was still reluctant to give – nevertheless managed to acquire strategic Mauvezin, and from that base *de facto* control of the whole region.

I N any era, political stability and security are relative at best, and it was particularly so in the fourteenth century. The peace enjoyed by the lands of Foix-Béarn had to be guarded against shifts in the balance of powers and the constant risk of being drawn into the quarrels and enterprises of restless neighbours. At the same time, a crisis could present both unexpected dangers and opportunities. Such a crisis was touched off by renewed French and English interventions in the affairs of Spain.

The immediate cause of the latest peninsular conflict was the succession of Portugal, claimed by Juan I of Castile – son of the Trastamara 'usurper' Enrique II. With English support, the Portuguese resisted Juan's claim, electing as their monarch Dom Joaõ, a bastard of their late king. After his initial failure to take Lisbon, the King of Castile raised a fresh army, in part by recruiting as many knights and their followers from France, Foix and Béarn. Froissart gives a vivid (albeit probably 'reconstructed') account of Gaston III's effort to dissuade his subjects from that adventure. According to the chronicler, the Castilians went briskly about their business, raising 300 lances (*i.e.* at least 900 men with their mounts and remounts) in less than four days. Froissart names sixteen Béarnais knights, but clearly more had taken the Castilian offer, among them several barons and familiars of Fébus, including the eldest son of his kinsman Roger d'Espagne. Oddly enough, the Count of Foix did not use his considerable personal influence to prevent their departure, although he reproaches them for leaving him undefended, when 'war is at hand' with Armagnac. But the chronicler relates how Fébus harangued his vassals, before and again after dinner. In vain does he plead with them: they can only answer that they have already taken the pay of the King of Castile, and cannot now default on their contracts. Fébus then predicts the direct English intervention in Portugal – of which he undoubtedly had some advance notice – the Castilian defeat, and the fate awaiting his Béarnais:

> Either you will come back so poor and in rags that your elbows and knees will show naked, and you will be so choked with lice that you will be busy crushing them with your fingernails – and then he showed them how by putting his two thumbs together – or else you will be all killed or taken.[8]

The men laughed, amused by this demonstration of lice-hunting, but they could not be talked out of their resolve. And so before they went the Count drank with them, took their hands and wished them Godspeed.

Given Fébus' long-established policy of discreet support for the Trastamaras, it is of course possible that Froissart's is a version circulated after the events, to cover up for what may have been the Count's tacit (if not remunerated) acquiescence in the recruitment of his Béarnais. But it is also plausible that the nature of feudal bonds (vassals being free to serve another lord, so long as they did not take arms against their 'natural liege') gave him no authority

---

[8] *Chroniques*, XI, 141.

to forbid it. Be that as it may, on 14 August 1385 the Anglo-Portuguese forces routed the Castilian invaders at Aljubarrota. The swift information service that made Fébus suspect of necromancy brought him the news. According to the chronicler, he remained silent for three days, and then only opened his mind to his brother Arnaud-Guilhem, saying that '... soon we shall hear the news that never has the land of Béarn suffered so many men in one day, as it has now in Portugal.' And, indeed, ten days later, the few survivors returned to Orthez and the extent of the casualty list – 'at least three hundred esquires of Béarn piteously killed', for the 'hard-hearted' Portuguese gave no quarter – became public knowledge.[9]

The disaster of Aljubarrota was felt throughout Béarn by the many 'who had lost there their brothers, their fathers, their sons or their friends'. Then, as the country had hardly had time to recover from the shock, French preparations for direct intervention in Spain put it directly in the path of another peril. A substantial army (possibly upward of 3,000 men) was mustering near Carcassonne under the command of Duke Louis of Bourbon, for the eventual purpose of meeting the Duke of Lancaster's invasion of Galicia. This English effort was the latest in a series of campaign to wrest from the Trastamaras the crown of Castile claimed by John of Gaunt on behalf of his wife Constança, daughter of the murdered Pedro I: the joint Anglo-Portuguese success against Castilian forces now gave 'Monsieur d'Espagne' (as Lancaster now styled himself) the hope of wiping out earlier failures. In the event, the campaign of 1386–7 did not fare any better than the preceding ones: after some initial success in penetrating the outer regions of Castile and Leon, Lancaster was defeated by the same enemies as his late brother the Black Prince in 1367: drought, hunger, and sickness decimated the English army and even threatened the Pretender's own life. Moreover, pending the arrival of his French allies, the King of Castile eluded the desired battle. Lancaster resigned himself to a compromise: his daughter was to marry the son and heir of Juan I, thus putting an end to more than twenty years of dynastic strife. Although its imminence had been a factor in the outcome, the French intervention had come too late for a field encounter. The delay was due in part to the need for negotiating the movement of royal troops through Béarn, on their way to the Roncevaux pass. Gauthier de Passac, captain-general of Languedoc, was sent to Orthez with the formal request stipulating the precautions taken by the French government to avoid any damage to the viscounty – all provisions and forage were to be paid for, no plundering tolerated, etc. These instructions amounted to another tacit recognition of Béarn's independence, and of its neutral status. Nevertheless, Fébus reminded Gauthier, courteously but pointedly, of the high degree of alertness of Béarn, quoting the warning that once circulated among the English: 'Take care not to steal anything in the lands of the Count of Foix, for there is not voice in

9 *Ibid.*

a Béarnais throat but has a bacinet on its head!' The two parted in cordial understanding, Fébus going so far as to counsel prudence in the peninsular campaign, 'for all my good Béarnais died there, although I had warned them against going.'

The French contingent led by Gauthier de Passac marched through Béarn without any incident in April 1387, while the Duke of Bourbon travelled by way of Foix and Andorra. On the return journey in June or July, the Duke desired to stop at Orthez and meet the Count of Foix. This probably not fortuitous occasion was the beginning of a tentative rapprochement between Fébus and the French court, and Louis de Bourbon perhaps the best choice of an envoy. A direct descendant of Saint Louis – and Charles VI's maternal uncle – he would not have been hampered by the baggage of old grievances that his cousins Anjou and Berry had acquired in the Midi. For his part, Fébus deployed all the courtesies due to a prince of the blood, and then some more: upon entering Béarn, the Duke and Duchess were met by several of the Count's familiars (including the indispensable Espan de Lion) bringing an offering of money, fine horses and a mule. Fébus then bid them welcome at Sauveterre, and the whole household rode to Orthez under the protection of the Count's banner. Four days of sumptuous feasting ensued before Louis de Bourbon took his leave – with his purse refreshed by a loan of 15,000 *écus*. To show his appreciation – and also to give his troops, denied the pickings of Béarn, something to plunder, the Duke allowed them to attack certain rebellious vassals of Fébus whose lands lay in Aquitaine.

After this cordial beginning, Gaston III seems to have simply waited for the French government to make the next move. It came in December of the next year, when the Marshal de Sancerre was sent to Orthez to broach the topic of a royal visit. Froissart, who had arrived in the last days of November, was not present at the interview between Fébus and the Marshal, but Ernauton du Pin, his landlord and one of his prime informants at the 'ostel de la Lune', was also a trusted servant of the Count, who had in fact negotiated some of the practical aspects of the French troops transit with Gauthier de Plassac. Thus, except perhaps for rhetorical flourishes, the chronicler's report of the conversation may be taken as verbatim. The words of both men are revealing of remaining tensions, but also of a promising frankness of exchange. In answer to Sancerre's direct query, Fébus having assured him that he was willing to welcome the King, the Marshal replied:

> True, my lord Count [...] but when he comes, what the King shall want to know plainly and openly is on which side you want to be, French or English; for you have always avoided war, and never took arms [for France], whether you were only asked, or so ordered.

To which the Count is reported as having laughed – as if to show that he took

no offence at the old soldier's direct speech, but in a more serious vein, he goes
on to answer the implicit charge of disloyalty:

> If I have hitherto excused myself and refused to take up arms, I had
> reasonable cause to do so, for the war between the King of France and
> the King of England does not concern me. I hold my land of Béarn from
> God [...] And so I have no business going into service, and no quarrel
> with one king or the other.[10]

Here again, as vigorously affirmed as ever, is that fundamental, non-negotiable
tenet of Fébus' external policy, the doctrine of the sovereignty of Béarn. Brave
words, quite possibly meant to be repeated through the inns and taverns of
Orthez. But it was undoubtedly then that Fébus gave the Marshal what he had
come for, *viz.* the promise that he would not only welcome the young Charles
VI, but also acknowledge him as his liege for the county of Foix and other
lands he held from the Crown of France. The renewal of this long overdue
homage was to be a notable event, all the more so as Gaston III had never given
it directly in the hands of Charles V. But before the solemnities could take
place, two outstanding issues had to be resolved between the parties: Sancerre's
agenda therefore addressed the matters of Fébus' position in regard to the
Schism, and of his relations with the Duke of Berry.

THE Schism that rent Western Christendom of 1378 was the most dramatic
consequence of the seventy-two years of papal residence in Avignon. The
'Babylonian captivity', as many called it, had begun in 1305 when Clement V –
born Bertrand de Got in Gascony – had fled there from the strife between the
Roman factions that threatened to hijack the papacy. But during his reign and
those of the next six pontiffs – all of them Frenchmen from Languedoc or Limousin – the Holy See became instead a virtual satellite of France. While Avignon
flourished as a centre of splendid cultural achievement, the corruption of the
papacy itself became only more scandalous. Its sinful opulence denounced with
equal (and equally useless) vehemence by many, most notably by the visionary
Catherine of Siena and the humanist poet Petrarch. Moreover, as the Anglo-
French conflict grew larger, the rôle of the Holy See as the just arbiter of disputes between Christian princes was perhaps fatally compromised. Although
most of the Avignon popes were honest and conscientious men, often striving
to restore the integrity of their office, they were unable to bring the venality,
nepotism and plain partisanship of their entourage under control. Finally, after
the failure of a first attempt by Urban V, his successor Gregory XI returned to
Rome in 1377, despite the contrary advice from the French court, the protests of
his cardinals, and the tears of his own father. Gregory died only fifteen months
after entering the now decayed, still insecure Eternal City. While the majority

[10]  *Ibid.,* XIII, 299.

of the cardinals saw his death as an opportunity to come back to the luxury of their Avignon palaces, the Roman populace were equally determined to keep the papacy – and its considerable revenues – at home. The fear of a murderous uprising frightened the faction-ridden conclave into an early compromise on 8 April 1378: as a partial concession to the threatening mob, the cardinals elected, if not a Roman, at least an Italian, the low-born Bartolomeo Prignano, and then they fled the city.

Urban VI, as the new pontiff chose to be called, now disagreeably surprised his electors by launching a vigorous offensive against the corruption and der-eliction of duty that had become the ordinary culture of the papal court. The invective to which the upstart subjected the (mostly high-born) cardinals, the decrees against simony, the withholding of their customary revenues, were shocking enough; but when the hitherto docile Neapolitan refused to return to Avignon, it was more than the dominant French faction could bear. Assembled in Anagni under the protection of Breton mercenaries, they began by issuing a proclamation claiming that the election of Urban had been made under duress, and was therefore invalid; the Holy See was declared vacant, and with impec-cable logic, its vacancy was the ground invoked to reject the option of sum-moning an Ecumenical Council. Next, the cardinals sent to Paris to secure the assurance of support from Charles V. On 10 September the King convened a conference of prelates and theologians. Hoping perhaps that Urban VI might resolve it by resigning, they advised Charles against any action for the time being in a dispute of such momentous consequence for all Christendom. But if the King of France did not overtly acquiesce in the principle of a new election, he did nothing to prevent one. While the Sorbonne was still debating the issue, the conclave of cardinals met at Fondi on 20 September, and in a single day elected and crowned a French prelate and kinsman of the Valois, who chose the name of Clement VII. No man perhaps was more hated in Italy than Robert de Genève, who, as cardinal-legate, had unleashed war on Florence and the bloody repression of rebels against the absent papacy. Now, having failed to expel Urban, who, far from resigning, named a whole new College of cardinals, Clement and his followers returned in April 1379 to the safety and comforts of Avignon.

In France, Clement VII was soon acknowledged as the rightful Pope by a solemn assembly held in the presence of the King. Under pressure from the court, the Sorbonne theologians reluctantly acquiesced, but while their advo-cacy of a council to end the schism was silenced for the moment, it was by no means forgotten. Europe was soon divided by politically motivated obediences to the rival pontiffs: England, where resentment of the Avignon papacy was nothing new, naturally recognized Urban; in keeping with its traditional 'auld alliance', Scotland declared for Clement. The choices made by other powers were less predictable: the Emperor Wenceslas disappointed his cousin Charles V by opting for the Roman Pope; Peter IV of Aragon declared his neutrality, as did France's ally Juan I of Castile. Writing to Charles, the latter observed that, as the majority of his subjects were Urbanists, he could not hope to impose a contrary choice 'over public conscience supported by reason'. This lucid remark suggests that public opinion entertained a reasonable doubt about the validity of Clement's election. It also touches on the effect of the schism on all Catholics: in an age when faith entailed the literal belief that salvation depended on valid sacraments, the choice of obedience was a truly agonizing dilemma. Only one of the contending popes must have the legitimate *potestas clavium* – the keys to the kingdom of Heaven – and therefore to obey the other, or merely receive a counterfeit absolution from those priests and prelates who obeyed him, would mean certain damnation. This was a very present concern for all Christian rulers, whose decision to support either pontiff would tip the scales of judgement for all of their subjects. The attitude of the Iberian monarchs was, moreover, based on the not unreasonable prospect that a Council, or the abdication of one – or better, both – of the contenders, would soon resolve their dilemma: no one expected the Schism to last forty years. However, given the political pressures and diplomatic manipulations applied by France and England, complete neutrality was a difficult position to maintain. Despite his eloquent declaration, Juan I of Castile was the first to succumb and recognize Clement VII as the rightful Pope; in 1387 Peter IV's pro-French successor John I – married to a niece of Charles V – quickly rallied to the Avignon standard; three years later, Charles III of Navarre would also jettison his father's neutral policy.

By all accounts, none more eloquent than his *Book of Orisons*, Gaston III was a devout prince, surely aware of his responsibility for the spiritual as well as the material welfare of his people. There are good reasons to believe that, like his Spanish neighbours, he preferred not to commit himself to either pontiff. And indeed, to the extent that he refrained from any formal acknowledgment he could be seen as neutral. Often cited in support of this view is the picturesque account by Froissart of the Christmas banquet he attended. The chronicler writes that he saw the Count seated at his table, with four bishops, 'two Clementists and two Urbanists: the bishop of Pamiers and the bishop of Lescar, Clementists, – these two were seated above; and after them the bishop of Aire and the bishop of Ron [Oloron], these two were Urbanists.'[11] But somehow Froissart was utterly misinformed: the bishop of Lescar, implicated in the plot of 1380, was still in exile; while, of the two claimants to the bishopric of Aire, Fébus was certainly more likely to have received the Clementist one – a Béarnais nobleman – rather than the Urbanist nominee, an English prelate who never took possession of his see. Likewise, Oloron was firmly in the Avignon sphere of influence.[12] There are, moreover, many indications that Fébus

---

[11] *Voyage*, 112.

[12] *Vicomté*, 330, n. 29.

discreetly allowed Clement VII to exercise his authority in his domains. The fact that in August 1380 the Avignon Pope sent one of his cardinals to intercede for young Gaston, suggests that his legitimacy was already implicitly recognized at Orthez. The grant in 1378 of an ecclesiastical living to Bernard de Béarn also shows that cordial relations existed from the beginning of the Schism. For his part, the Count not only did not hinder Clement's appointments or the collection of ecclesiastical revenues by Avignon envoys, but he provided escorts for them, and in 1384 authorized the levy of an exceptional tithe. Nevertheless, Fébus did not issue the formal proclamation that Avignon and – perhaps even more so – the court of France desired, but confined himself to what a Clementist bishop called contemptuously 'lesser obedience', a recognition implicit in his dealing with the schismatic Curia, and to all appearances sufficient to satisfy Clement VII. In all practical matters, Gaston III can be said to have followed the example of Charles V, except for his toleration of Urbanist opinion. That such dissent existed in his domains was made clear enough by the case of Constance de Rabastens, the self-proclaimed prophetess who was spreading in the Albi region the news that the Count of Foix was God's chosen instrument to bring the Midi back into the obedience of the legitimate Pope Urban VI. She may have been an embarrassment, but Fébus may have had reason to fear that any attempt to silence her would provoke disorders; besides, since she was also cursing the staunchly Clementist Armagnacs as traitors and minions of Satan, her rantings were not altogether unwelcome.

O N the whole, the attitude of Fébus in regard to the Schism was consistent both with his policy of progressive rapprochement with France and with his concern to maintain at least correct relations with England. Even though it appeared that the military situation of Aquitaine had been irretrievably damaged since the resumption of the war in 1369, the diminished principality was still staunchly English, and would remain so for another half century. Apart from the desirable political balance, peaceful relations meant that trade through to the seaports of Bordeaux and Bayonne, essential to the economic life of Foix and Béarn, would continue undisturbed. True to his long established policy, Gaston III remained in constant diplomatic relations with the Duke of Lancaster throughout his negotiations with the Valois.

One of the more immediate objects of the December 1388 mission of Louis de Sancerre was to finalize the agreement regarding the marriage of Jeanne de Boulogne and the Duke of Berry. The twelve-year-old bride-to-be and potential heiress of the county of Comminges was a cousin and a ward of the Count of Foix, who had had no scruple to use the prospect of her eventual marriage as a diplomatic bargaining chip. A first offer from the recently widowed Jean de Berry was rejected out of hand, as a transparent manœuvre to make Jeanne's claim to Comminges available to the Armagnac clan. On that occasion Fébus even rattled the threat of marrying his ward to Lancaster's son, the future

Henry IV. However, by the end of 1388 the longed-for peace between Valois and Plantagenets seemed to be at hand, and therefore there was little profit to be gained from playing one party against the other. Berry had been recalled from his government of Languedoc, and was therefore less likely to be of use to his nephew of Armagnac, and this time his offer was considered. The bargain was brokered by Berry's younger brother the Duke of Burgundy – who would be handsomely thanked with the dedication of the *Livre de chasse*. The political clauses included the reciprocal restitutions of two castles wrongfully occupied by Berry and Fébus, as well as the renunciation by Jeanne and Gaston III of their rights in Comminges. There were complicated and finely timed articles regarding the return of jewels handed by the Duke in pledge of a promised annuity, and of his gift to Fébus of two trophies of five-prongers and six of his best hounds. But the most conspicuous provision was for the payment of 30,000 francs – ostensibly to repay the Count, as Froissart put it, 'for the ten years during which he had lodged and fed the damsel and maintained her household, but still not as if he wanted to sell the lady.' Despite the sarcasms of his nephew the King, the bridegroom – now nearing fifty, an advanced age by medieval reckoning – eagerly acquiesced to Fébus' demands. The agreement was signed at Orthez on 9 March 1388. A few weeks later the young Duchess-elect was escorted to Morlaàs by the inevitable familiars (Arnaud-Guilhem, Pierre de Béarn, Yvain) and 500 lances. Froissart, who had taken the opportunity to travel in style with the bride's party, reports that the cortège from Orthez was met by a French embassy also backed by 500 lances. Not only had both sides taken similar precautions to guard their respective treasures, but the exchange took place 'in an open field', to forestall any treachery. In the Count's absence the Béarnais envoys took possession of the money bags, Jeanne was instantly married by proxy, and presented with tokens of her husband's devotion: 'I want you to know', Froissart writes, 'that the Duke of Berry had sent her a whole train of carriages and carts and palfreys all laden with clothes and ornaments, both for the body and for the head, as much as if she were to be Queen of France.' After a journey interrupted punctuated everywhere by sumptuous feasts – the most notable ones at the papal court of Avignon – the marriage proper was celebrated at Riom in Auvergne on Whit Sunday.

This happy conclusion, burying the old grievances between Fébus and Jean de Berry, went a long way to expedite the negotiations between the Count and the French Crown. The young Charles VI had recalled his father's advisers, temporarily dismissed during his minority by the now late Louis d'Anjou. Mockingly dubbed *Marmousets* (*i.e.* grotesque figurines, serving for instance as door-knockers), these able lawyers and clerics set out to repair the damage done to the monarchy by the King's uncles. Few projects were more urgent than the affairs of Languedoc, where decades of ravages by the *routiers*, and of rapacious misgovernment by the dukes of Anjou and Berry, had severely strained loyalty to the Crown. To restore its prestige, the 'Marmousets' were counting on a royal progress through the Midi, with the homage of the notoriously difficult Count of Foix as its triumphal conclusion. And so it went: after stops at Montpellier and Béziers, where a kind of justice was rendered by trying and hanging a treasurer of the Duke of Berry for his master's exactions, Charles VI made his entry in Toulouse on 29 November.

The comings and goings that followed the King's arrival in the capital of Languedoc give the appearance of having been delicately balanced and choreographed to demonstrate the majesty of the Crown, without causing the Count to lose face in his own country. For his part, Fébus, avoiding the semblance of unduly obsequious haste, did not leave Orthez until at least mid-December. It was thus at Mazères, his habitual residence in the vassal county of Foix, rather than in the capital of a *de facto* independent Béarn, that he received the King's envoys, the Marshal de Sancerre and the chamberlain Bureau de la Rivière, bearing their master's invitation to attend him in Toulouse. According to Froissart's *Chroniques*, the Marshal offered the alternative that the King 'will so exert himself that he will come to see you in your country, for he wishes very much to see you.' This thoughtful offer to spare the Count the trouble of going to Toulouse – a day's ride away – may or may not have been a veiled threat of armed invasion: if it was, it may suggest that even at that late stage, a discreet push was still needed to help the negotiations cross the finish line. In the event, Fébus knew how to take the hint, replying with the expected deprecations that he would be in Toulouse within four days – time to prepare for his entry, not only the display of magnificence, and his retinue of at least 200 knights and squires, their remounts and their servants, but also the welcome of the Toulousain, as a timely demonstration of the Count's popularity.

The show was a success. Late in the afternoon, Fébus arrived in the city afternoon, greeted by a delegation of the burghers with presents 'of fine wines and other things', and then retired for the night to his quarters in the Dominican convent. The next morning, he rode with his whole entourage to the Château Narbonnais, where he was received by Charles VI with a solemnity reflected in Froissart's narrative:

> The Count of Foix, who was a handsome prince [...] entered the hall
> bareheaded, his hair floating free, for he never wore a hat; when he saw
> the French lords, brother and uncle [of the King] he knelt low on one
> knee to honour the King and no one else, then he stood up and came forward, and a second time knelt again and then stood up and came forward,
> and for the third time knelt very near the King. The King took him by
> the hand and embraced him, then made him stand up and said to him:
> 'Count of Foix, gentle cousin, you are welcome with us. Your coming and
> the sight of you please us greatly.'[13]

[13] *Chroniques*, XIV, 74–5.

This highly staged entrance was undoubtedly an event worthy of note, ranking as it does among the relatively few that are fully illustrated in the illuminated manuscripts of the *Chroniques*. Froissart's oblique comment about honour being rendered to 'the King and no one else' hints at the precautions taken to avoid humbling Fébus – who evidently was not prepared to kneel before mere princes of the blood. The three genuflexions, followed by the King's gracious reply, clearly signify reconciliation, and the Count's acknowledgment of his allegiance. The submission of the Count of Foix, in all but name a 'prince of the Pyrenees', who moreover enjoyed such popularity among the Toulousains, was reason enough to celebrate. His solemn entrance was immediately followed by a royal banquet lasting well into the afternoon, at which Fébus, seated at the first table with Charles VI and the Duke of Bourbon, was honoured with the privileged offering of sweetmeats from the King's drageoir. On the next day Fébus hosted the royal princes at an equally grand feast, served by his own knights and squires. Etiquette did not allow the King to be among the guests, but he nevertheless made an impromptu appearance at the end of the banquet, and stayed late to enjoy the entertainments, especially the music (see p. 121 above). Fébus, says Froissart, was overjoyed that the King had 'so humbled himself as to come to him', and so was the entire company. Before parting, the Count distributed lavish presents of horses and mules to his guest's retainers, as well as 200 gold crowns to their heralds and as much to the minstrels. On the fourth day of his stay in Toulouse, Fébus rode once more to the King's residence, and there, in what seems to have been a rather less fully staged ceremony, did homage to Charles VI for the county of Foix and its dependences, to the explicit exclusion of Béarn. Whether the Count swore homage simple, or the homage liege that would have required him to serve under the French banner – and thus repudiate his traditional neutrality in the Anglo-French conflict, Froissart does not say. Perhaps the issue – the same that had led to the rebellion of the Duke of Brittany – was side-stepped for the time being, for it is hardly plausible that Fébus would have either abandoned one of the basic tenets of his external relations, or blatantly perjured himself.

The Count then returned to Mazères, to prepare for the King's visit. On the day of his progress from Toulouse, Charles VI and his retinue were met, as soon as they entered the county of Foix, by various shepherds, cowherds and grooms leading choice sheep, cattle and horses which were then presented as gifts to the King. That evening at Mazères, the guests recognized the shepherds, cowherds and grooms as knights and squires of Gaston's court. This charming entertainment, that seems to anticipate the pastoral charades of the Renaissance, may have been devised by Yvain. Perhaps it was then that Fébus' favourite son came to the notice of the pleasure-loving young King; but neither of them could foresee the tragic end to which Yvain's gift as master of revels would bring him. The festivities at Mazères – music, dances, banquets and sporting competitions – lasted three days. Froissart (who, however, has him return to

Orthez directly after the ceremony of homage) asserts that the royal visit to Languedoc cost Fébus more than 60,000 francs but that 'whatever the expense, the Count of Foix, who was generous and courteous, paid it gladly.'

WHILE details of the pomp and opulence of the festivities, be they at Toulouse or Mazères, were publicized by awestruck chroniclers (not only Froissart, but the usually laconic Monk of Saint-Denis, and later Juvénal des Ursins and Michel du Bernis), the tenor of the treaty signed by Fébus and Charles VI on 5 January 1389 long remained an object of mystery or confusion. Contrary to Froissart's report – repeated by most historians before the publication of the original document by Tucoo-Chala – the treaty of Toulouse was not secret, as it was countersigned by a galaxy of French dignitaries, including the dukes of Bourbon and of Touraine, the Constable, several bishops, the Marshal de Sancerre, the lord of Coucy and the indispensable Bureau de la Rivière. It was, however, not made public, pending ratification by the many vassals of the Count of Foix who were required to guarantee its application: in the first instance, Yvain named 'our natural son', Arnaud-Guilhem, then the castellans of all major castles and cities of Foix and Béarn. Even after this time-consuming process was completed, rumours and speculations about the treaty had pre-empted the need for sober truth.

The version long accredited by Froissart's account is not, however, without historical merit, for it reflects the expectations and the apprehensions of significant segments of public opinion. According to the chronicler, the object of the pact was to settle the succession of Foix-Béarn in favour of the Count's natural sons Yvain and Gratien. Yvain was to hold the county of Foix, Gratien the viscounty of Marsan, while all other lands held and acquired by Fébus reverted to the legitimate heir, *viz.* the Viscount of Castelbon. Froissart adds that this partition was the object of 'debates and differences' between the Count, the barons and the knights of his country, and 'many said that this could not be done without the general council of all Béarn and Foix.' The rumour was informed by a certain logic, and the ground for it had long been prepared: the marked predilection of Fébus for Yvain and Gratien was a well-known fact, and the argument for the accession of a bastard – citing the precedents of William the Conqueror, Enrique II of Castile and Joaõ I of Portugal – had undoubtedly been circulated with his approval. But is was also very probable that an illegitimate succession would have met with a great deal of opposition in both Béarn and Foix.

Froissart and his informants may, however, be excused, for the treaty of Toulouse represents a radical departure from anything they had been led to expect. Stripped of its legal and feudal jargon, it provided for the lifetime grant of the county of Bigorre and of 100,000 francs in gold to Gaston III, in consideration of which the Count bequeathed all of his domains in perpetuity to the King of France. Were it not for the archival evidence published in 1960 by Tucoo-Chala, this reversal of Fébus' lifelong effort to preserve the sovereignty of Béarn and to keep royal overlords at a safe distance from his other domains could hardly be believed. But there is no possible equivocation: the list of Gaston III's possessions is quite thorough; by specifically naming the lands of Ossau, Aspe and Barétous, it even forestalls any attempt by those mountain communities of Béarn to claim exceptional status. This precaution, as well as the provision for ratification of the treaty by all the principal castellans in Foix and in Béarn, suggests that the parties to the treaty of Toulouse were conscious of going against the wishes of the Count's subjects.

The motives of the French government in this treaty are clear and simple enough: in return for a one-time payment and the *de jure* (albeit temporary) recognition of Fébus' *de facto* control of Bigorre, the Crown was to inherit not only Pyrenean domains extending almost uninterrupted between Roussillon and Navarre, as well as substantial holdings in Lautrec and Albigeois, but also the Gascon lands of Marsan and Gavardan, thus putting French garrisons within striking distance of Bordeaux. Bureau and his colleagues cannot have failed to see the disparity in the exchange, and may have wondered whether the bargain was not simply too good to be true. But from their point of view, there was little to lose, and much to be gained. But what impelled Fébus to give all in return for so little, may never be completely understood. At a single stroke of the pen, he ceded to France not only the territorial domains inherited from his predecessors of the Foix-Béarn and Moncade dynasties, but even more astonishingly his own achievement, the independence of Béarn, for which he had been striving from the beginning of his reign.

Froissart, alluding no doubt to the fabled treasure in the Moncade Tower, perceived that, despite Fébus' reputation for avarice, a grant of 100,000 francs was not enough to explain the legacy, for 'it is plain enough that the Count of Foix had no need to mortgage his lands, for he had plenty of money.' But, the chronicler continues, 'what he did, he did only to defraud his heir the Viscount of Castelbon.' The long-standing enmity between Gaston III and the junior branch of the House of Foix-Béarn – an enmity harking back to the Castelbons' opposition to the regency of Aliénor de Comminges – makes Froissart's explanation plausible. Moreover, to the old grudge could be added the fact that the legitimate heir presumptive, Mathieu de Castelbon, was not the 'valiant man at arms' needed for the defence of his lands and subjects, but a mere boy. The chronicler was, of course, well aware that Fébus had hoped instead to make his bastard sons Yvain and Gratien his heirs. That solution had merits beyond the Count's personal likes and dislikes, for Yvain at least was a grown man with substantial military experience, and had long been a member of his informal privy council.

Froissart's conversation with Espan de Lion on that topic had taken place while they were riding to Orthez in November 1388, and yet only one year later, Fébus appears to have abandoned the idea and then, having found no other

way to exclude his sole legitimate heir, sacrificed the sovereignty of Béarn. It
was a startling about-face, and yet there were perhaps compelling reasons for
it. Since first 'leaking' his intention, the Count may have been made aware of
the obstacles he would have to overcome before his natural sons were accepted
as their lords by all his subjects of Foix and Béarn. While it may not have been
very difficult to obtain their legitimation from the venal Avignon Curia, challenges from the Castelbon party supported by the disaffected barons, as well
as reticences from traditionalist communities, were only too probable. At the
time of the Orthez plot, his nobles and burghers had indeed begged the Count
to spare his son, however guilty, because 'he had no other child.' They could not
have said more clearly that they did not regard Yvain and Gratien as potential
heirs and guarantors of Béarn's sovereignty. Moreover, Fébus knew very well
that in every case invoked as precedent for the accession of a bastard – in England, Castile and Portugal – the crown had been conquered or defended on
the battlefield. Hence his dilemma, between a legitimate heir unacceptable to
himself, and an illegitimate succession unacceptable to many, if not most, of his
subjects. Either choice would almost certainly bring to the lands of Foix and
Béarn the warfare from which Gaston III had so far managed to shield them.

It is possible to imagine that Fébus, having weighed the relative damage done
to his lands and his subjects by the strife following a weak or disputed succession, or by cession to a French Crown capable of maintaining order, chose to
renounce his lifelong political ideal in order to preserve a practical reality – the
peace and prosperity of the Pyrenean estate he had assembled. Unfortunately,
there is not a single piece of evidence to support this morally attractive hypothesis. On the contrary, the activities of the Count of Foix in the less than two
years he still had to live suggest that he may well have regarded the treaty of
Toulouse only as a temporary expedient, a necessary manœuvre in that most
constant strategy of his reign, the struggle against the House of Armagnac.

✦  ✦
✦

# Death, and the Spoils

Taken at its face value, the treaty of Toulouse may appear to be the testament of a Count of Foix who, having considered his own mortality, wished to put his earthly affairs in order. In 1389 Fébus had reached an advanced age, at least by medieval reckoning. Enough of his contemporaries, friends and foes alike, had failed to reach the threescore years and ten allotted by the Psalmist: the once mighty Edward, Prince of Wales and Aquitaine, dead at the age of forty-six; Charles V 'the Wise', at forty-four; the turbulent Louis d'Anjou, at forty-five. Dead also, the great champions: Chandos, Du Guesclin, both in harness; in a French prison, Fébus' cousin and comrade-in-arms, the famed Captal de Buch; and his brother-in-law Charles of Navarre, burned to death in his own bed; but then none closer and more tragic than the son slain by his own hand.

But while Fébus had ample cause to meditate on the uncertainty of life and death, he does not seem to have had the kind of premonition that prompts men to dictate their last will and testament. For the treaty of Toulouse was not a testament, either in form or in substance, but rather a contract whereby the Count of Foix mortgaged his entire estate to the French Crown in return for 100,000 francs and the lifetime grant of Bigorre. Like most contracts of that kind, it contained a clause providing for its reversal: in the event that Gaston III had 'heir or heirs procreated and descended of [his] own body in true wedlock', his entire estate, *viz.* 'the said county of Foix, lands, countries, inheritance and aforementioned movable goods and real estate, present and to come', would be considered mortgaged – and thus redeemable upon repayment of the 100,000 francs to the King. This cannot be simply dismissed as boilerplate language: although there is no indication that Fébus intended to seek at long last an annulment of his marriage, his estranged wife was as mortal as any of their contemporaries, and he might yet find himself, as Jean de Berry had so recently done, a still vigorous and eligible widower, capable of siring another legitimate son and heir. In the immediate, the escape clause sharply distinguishes the revocable treaty from a – by its very nature irrevocable – *last* will and testament. The same clause implicitly denied Fébus' illegitimate sons any right to redeem his mortgaged estate.

The bequest of all of the Foix-Béarn holdings for a sum of money of which, as Froissart notes, the Count had no need, would be absurdly disproportionate, if it could not be seen as a pretext covering the unrecorded – perhaps even unspoken – *quid pro quo* Fébus may have expected from the transaction.

The grant of Bigorre, although only for his own lifetime, nevertheless represented a recognition of the rights of the House of Foix in the county, trumping any claim put forward by the Armagnacs. But another effect of the treaty was to make the King of France, as potential heir, a party to the interests of Foix-Béarn. In this perspective, the pact might seem to be yet another diplomatic move to isolate the Armagnacs – a strategy that had already succeeded in separating the Duke of Berry from his long-time allies.

Such was perhaps the subtext of the treaty of Toulouse and of the whole process leading to it. The overt discourse, however, was all about peace and reconciliation between the two rival houses: in the summer preceding the King's visit to Languedoc, the counts of Foix and of Armagnac had in fact met on their mutual border and concluded a peace agreement sanctioned by the reciprocal restitution of castles and lands seized in the course of past hostilities. Some accessory issues being unresolved, it was agreed that these would be subject to the arbitration of the Duke of Lancaster, whose ruling was indeed given and accepted in October. The choice of Lancaster as a referee notwithstanding, the French court could only applaud the end of a feud that had for several generations undermined royal authority in the Midi. To emphasize its importance to the Crown, Charles VI exacted from Fébus a promise to respect the peace with the Count of Armagnac – a formal document dated 10 January, the last day of the King's festive stay at Mazères.

Nevertheless, it was not long after his return to Orthez that Fébus reopened negotiations with England. The pretext – if a matter involving a large sum of money can be so qualified – was the caution that Gaston III had posted for the ransom of the Count of Denia, 75,000 florins twenty years overdue. Prompted by his uncle Lancaster, who was well aware of Fébus' fondness for florins, Richard II wrote to him on 10 March, offering to release him of his obligation, and thus allowing him to keep the substantial profit he had so far realized from that transaction (see p. 93 above). This led to an alliance in clear contradiction with the spirit, if not the letter, of Gaston III's promise to Charles VI. The treaty signed on 6 April by Fébus and the Duke called specifically for Lancaster to provide 300 men-at-arms, 'whenever the Count of Foix shall have need of them in his wars against the Count of Armagnac and the lord of Albret, be there war or truce between the two Kings of France and England.' Conversely, Fébus promised to 'serve and aid our lord the King of England against the Count of Armagnac and the lord of Albret, whenever we shall be so required by the said King, etc.', by providing a contingent of 200 men-at-arms.[1] Practical clauses stipulated that each party undertook to defray the cost of the troops engaged in his service, to the amount of 15 francs per man and per month. Two days later, the Duke promised Fébus a grant of 30,000 francs – 10,000 to be paid at once, and the balance in a year's time; and as soon as possible, he would obtain

---

[1] *Vicomté*, 365, no. XXIII.

from the King Gaston's release from his obligation regarding the ransom of the Count of Denia. In the larger context of Anglo-French relations at that time – a dormant state of war, with the uncertain prospect of peace – this treaty, besides being blatantly hostile to the Armagnac party and therefore contrary to Fébus' promise, also signified his intention to remain neutral between the two kings: clearly, he regarded his homage of fealty to Charles VI as no more than a traditional courtesy, devoid of serious obligation.

Then on 15 May Fébus signed at Pamiers another treaty with the King of Aragon. This text, countersigned on 10 June by John I and his brother Martin, replicated in a somewhat more succinct terms the Count's recent pact with Richard II and his uncle of Lancaster: by the terms of an alliance against 'the Count of Armagnac and [his brother] Bernard d'Armagnac', Aragon would place 400 men-at-arms and 400 foot soldiers (*pillarts* in the Catalan vernacular) at the Count's service, and he would provide 200 of each kind – each party paying the wages of the troops he required.[2] However similar, the two agreements suggest different motives on the part of Gaston III's allies. In the event of renewed war with France, the greatly diminished military situation of English Aquitaine made any regional alliance highly desirable, and the traditional rivalry between Foix and an Armagnac clan solidly aligned with the Valois made Fébus the ideal partner, in that he could justify *his* war as a private quarrel with the hereditary foe.

For Aragon the need for a strong ally was more urgent: the Armagnacs had for several years interfered in the quarrels between Peter IV and his son and heir. Expelled in 1387 after the accession of John I, Bernard d'Armagnac now claimed his 'rights' to the kingdom of Majorca, which he had purchased from Isabella, daughter of the dispossessed Jaume III (and briefly betrothed to the young Gaston III). However fantastic the claim, Bernard's troops and his energy were all too real, but the equally energetic response by the King's brother Martin stopped the threatened invasion of Catalonia. For its part, the French court was less than sympathetic to the Armagnacs' enterprises against the stoutly pro-French John of Aragon, who had defied his father by marrying a niece of Charles V, and now declared enthusiastically for the French-supported Avignon Pope. Nevertheless, the potential threat to his Aragonese ally gave Fébus a pretext of sorts to break his promise of peaceful coexistence with the Count of Armagnac – all the more plausible if he were to send troops, not against the Count himself, but against his brother Bernard. He may have seen in that situation an opportunity to seize part or all of the disputed county of Comminges, and thus complete the territorial bridge between Foix and Béarn. But there is no evidence, other than Froissart's assertion, that Gaston III was preparing any military all-out attack. According to the chronicler, Fébus planned to take advantage of the Count of Armagnac's departure for Italy, where he had

[2] *Ibid.*, 367, no. xxv.

become embroiled, on behalf of his sister Beatrix, in the violent feuds and vendettas of the Visconti.[3] In the event, neither of the two counts was given the time to carry out or even undertake anything decisive: Jean III d'Armagnac was killed in Italy on 25 July 1391, and death came to Gaston III Fébus on 1 August, so soon after his rival that some believed he had been overcome by 'so great a joy'.[4]

ACCORDING to Froissart's narrative of the death of the Count of Foix, Fébus had been that morning in the woods near Sauveterre-de-Béarn, 'until high noon hunting a bear, which was taken'. By the time the ritual *curée* was done, it was 'basse none', *i.e.* about 3 o'clock, when the Count decided to dine at the nearby 'hôpital d'Orion' before riding back to Orthez 'in the cool of evening'. Together with his retinue, the Count

> ... went into his chamber and found it strewn with fresh new greenery, and the walls covered with branches to make it cooler and more fragrant, for the weather and the air outside were terribly hot, as it happens in the month of August. ... [The Count] said: 'This greenery does me good, for this day has been hard and hot.' Then he sat on a chair and chatted a while with messire Espan de Lion; they talked about the dogs, which of them had given the best chase. And so as he talked, his bastard son messire Yvain came into the room, together with messire Pierre de Cabestain; and tables were already dressed in the same room. Then he asked for water to wash with; two squires came forward, Ramonnet Lane and Ramonnet de Copane; Ernaudon d'Espagne took the silver basin, and another knight named Thibault took the towel. [The Count] stood up from his chair and put his hands out to wash them. As soon as the cold water came down on his fingers – which were fine, long and straight – his face paled, his heart fluttered, his feet failed him, and he fell back on his chair, saying: 'I am dead, Lord True God have mercy!' He never said another word, but did not die right away, and went into pains and trances.[5]

Despite the efforts of Yvain and the other attendants, who 'put into his mouth bread, water and spices and all kinds of comforting things', Fébus died in less than a half hour.

Froissart's vivid narrative could easily be taken for an eyewitness account, when in fact the author of this well-wrought *page d'anthologie* was then many leagues away, in his native Hainault. Some details betray the chronicler's

---

[3] After the death of young Gaston de Foix his widow Beatrix had married Carlo Visconti, lord of Parma.

[4] *Chronique des quatre premiers Valois.*

[5] *Chroniques,* XIV, 325–6.

A bear hunt, from the *Livre de chasse*, Bibliothèque nationale de France, ms. fr. 619

inventiveness: for instance, while Fébus was plausibly stricken upon returning from the chase, it is doubtful that at that season he would have been hunting a bear in that particular district of Béarn. But Froissart the poet may have found the motif of the ill-omened bear, already encountered in the story of the accursed Pierre de Béarn, impossible to resist; likewise, the name of the mythological huntsman, resonating in that of the Hospital d'Orion, may have sounded more appropriate than the castle of Sauveterre reported by local sources as the place of death. Apart from these minor ornaments, the narrative appears very precise in its notation of the time, the sequence of events, and the identities of those present at the scene. So precise, indeed, that it reads like a deposition at a coroner's inquest, an impression reinforced by the chronicler's – or rather his informant's – eagerness to dispel any suspicion of murder:

> The two squires who had brought the water came to the basin and the ewer, lest one might think that they had poisoned it, and said: 'Here is the water. We have tested it in your presence, and we wish to do it again.' They did so, and all were satisfied with it.[6]

Poison was often suspected as the agent of sudden death, but Froissart takes great care to emphasize the details pointing to a natural cause – a massive heart attack brought on by exertion on a 'hard and hot' day, and perhaps triggered by the shock of cold water on the hands of the patient. The chronicler presumably based his account on information sent to him by an eyewitness (Espan de Lion, once his guide and chief informant, comes to mind), and this paradoxically lends greater credence to the narrative, which in this instance did not have to rely on sometimes faulty memory or dishevelled field notes. In view of the uncertainties regarding the succession of Foix-Béarn, and of the activity deployed by some of his familiars immediately after the Count's death, it was perhaps not a bad idea to put the accent on any fact that might help quell eventual rumours of foul play.

O F all those attending Fébus in his last hour, none was more shocked and aggrieved than Yvain, his favourite son, but his companions sensed that this was no time for idle tears:

> The knights who were there looked upon Yvain his son, who wept and lamented, wringing his hands. They said to him: 'Yvain, it is over. You have lost your lord and father; we know that he loved you above all; take care of yourself, mount your horse and ride to Orthez, and seize the castle and the treasure that is in it, before anyone comes and before the death of my lord is known.'[7]

[6] *Ibid.*, 327.
[7] *Ibid.*

Taking their advice, Yvain then rode to Orthez, bearing as his father's tokens a ring and his habitual table knife – perhaps the same 'petit long coustelet' that figured in the episode of young Gaston's death. With these he gained admittance to the castle and cowed the porter into obedience, only to find that the keys to the three doors guarding the treasure were in a locked steel box. Fortunately, the Count's attendants had in the meantime found a small key attached to the dead man's shirt; the chaplain Nicolle de Lescar, 'who knew all the secrets of the Count of Foix', recognized it as the key to the steel box containing the three door keys, and was dispatched at once to bring it to the now very frustrated Yvain. Although Froissart does not specify the time, the chaplain cannot have arrived at Orthez before dusk. By then the townspeople had begun to gather at the main crossroads, for rumours of the Count's death had begun to circulate; they had also seen Yvain ride by, distraught and alone, and they suspected that 'something must have happened, for he was not in the habit of riding out without his father.' When the chaplain in turn arrived, they tried to question him, but he denied the rumours of death, giving out that the Count was only taken ill, that he and Yvain had come to fetch 'certain things good for his health', and with that went up to the castle. Now thoroughly alarmed, and conscious of their responsibility lest the Count's treasure should be removed, the men of Orthez decided to arm themselves, close all the town gates and guard the castle. Yvain knew then that his attempt had failed. Speaking to them from a window overlooking the place where the militia were mustered, he tried to win the Orthésiens to his cause

> Good people of Orthez, I know why you are assembled here […] You know that my lord and father loved me above all others as his son, and that he would have made me his heir if he could. But it was God's will that he left this world without accomplishing or making any provision for it. He has left me with you, among whom I lived and was raised, and without your help and counsel, I am only a poor knight, bastard of the Count of Foix. So I beg you in God's name and for mercy, to reflect on it, and I shall be in your debt. I shall open the castle to you, for I do not want to shut it or guard it against you.[8]

The reply of the Orthez notables was no less courteous, but they made it clear that, their sympathy for Yvain notwithstanding, the Count's unrealized intentions had no real bearing on the legitimate succession. They said that they would stay with him, to guard and help him guard the castle and all it contained

> … and if the Viscount of Castelbon, *who is heir to this land of Béarn, for he is the nearest kinsman to your lord and father,* comes forth to claim the heritage and the movable goods, we shall want to know why; and we

[8] *Ibid.*, 332–3.

shall make sure that you and your brother Gratien have your rightful share. But we suppose that when the King of France was lately in Toulouse, and your father was with him, some kind of arrangements were made ...⁹

In conclusion, they proposed to write to the Count's cousin Roger d'Espagne (who had countersigned the treaty of Toulouse) for his help and advice regarding the entire inheritance. Meanwhile, Yvain opened the gates, and the Orthez militia took up their positions in the castle.

As in the case of Fébus' last moments, Froissart's narrative of this episode was almost certainly based on eyewitness accounts: such details as the location of the window from which Yvain harangues the townsmen (*viz.* in the room formerly occupied by Jeanne de Boulogne) are not gratuitous, but placed as tokens of veracity. The speeches, true to a long tradition of historiography, may well have been 'reconstructed', but their tenor is quite believable. What Yvain meant to do with the treasure if he had been able to take it is never spelled out – and perhaps he had no clear plan of further action – but the reaction of the Orthésiens is indicative of the opinion prevailing among the great majority of the subjects of Foix-Béarn. Any illegal action by anyone – including the legitimate heir Mathieu de Castelbon – would have undesirable consequences, either civil war, or foreign invasion. People were already lamenting the passing of 'the great prosperity of a peacetime that lasted as long as their lord reigned, for then there was no Englishmen nor Frenchman who dared molest them. [...] We used to live in a land of peace and freedom; now we live in a land of misery and subjection, for there is no one to [...] defend us.' The exchange between Yvain and the men of Orthez also reveals that the latter were not entirely unaware of the treaty of Toulouse – another issue that required a more expert approach, hence the decision to seek at once the help for one of Fébus' ranking political advisers.

Thus exit Yvain de Foix from the main stage, in as amicable an atmosphere as could be expected. He had appealed to those among whom he had been nurtured, and their reply, albeit guardedly negative, had not been devoid of affection. In an era that had seen so many violent confrontations between overbearing nobles and enraged mobs of commoners, the scene is a model of tactful rationality: not total candour of course, but good manners on both sides, and on the part of the Orthésiens the self-assurance of those well aware of, and ready to claim their own rights and responsibilities.

THEY acted at once. Summoned by the *jurats* of Orthez, the nobles of the *Cour majour* and the delegates of the *Cour des communautés*, convened on 8 August, only a week and a day after the death of the Count of Foix. The

⁹ *Ibid.* Italics mine.

orderly swiftness of the process clearly shows that, while their dismay at the loss of their sovereign lord was genuine enough, it was not unmixed with a sense of relief after thirty years of Fébus' autocratic rule. Significantly, the joint commission established at their first meeting by the Estates of Béarn was presided by Bishop Odon de Mendousse, one of the chief plotters of 1380, who lost no time in returning from his exile in Navarre, together with several other fugitives. The first task of that commission was to inventory the treasure of the Tour Moncade. Thanks to the strict accounting maintained by Fébus, this was quickly done; grants were made as bequests to the communities of Béarn, Marsan and Gavardan, and to the members of the Count's household; Yvain and Gratien were to have 100,000 florins and the movables goods in the castle. The balance was to be administered by a permanent delegation – in effect a provisional government of Béarn, empowered to authorize expenditures 'for the common good'. But, even though their taxes had formed a substantial part of the hoard, no share of it was set aside for Fébus' subjects in the county of Foix, the viscounty of Lautrec and other parts of Languedoc.[10]

The Estates also reaffirmed what the reply of the *jurats* to Yvain had already made plain: Mathieu de Castelbon was the legitimate heir presumptive, but they also stipulated conditions to his being accepted as rightful lord of Béarn. The first of these was to guarantee Yvain immunity from prosecution, his illegal entry into the castle being interpreted as a well-meaning move to 'protect' the Count's treasure – a politically unnecessary clause, attesting to the personal popularity of Fébus' favourite son. More substantially, the Estates swore a 'union', *i.e.* the members pledged not to enter in any separate negotiations with anyone, about anything. Mathieu and his eventual successors must swear to respect that pact, as well as the traditional liberties – the *fors* – of the land, above all its status as a freehold, vassal to none.

By acting quickly and decisively to reaffirm the sovereignty and neutrality of Béarn, the Estates upheld one of the major tenets of Gaston III's policy, which coincided with the desires and interests of his subjects in all his western domains – Béarn, Marsan and Gavardan. On the other hand, they seemed willing to abandon the other goal of the late Count's efforts, the union of Foix and Béarn in a single, continuous 'ensemble'. The appropriation for the sole benefit of Béarn and the Gascon viscounties of Fébus' entire cash reserve could be attributed merely to opportunistic greed, but a declaration to the effect that sovereign Béarn 'had nothing to do with the King of France', while the people of Foix were 'in their heart all French', made it all too clear that the Estates were ready to dissolve the 'indissoluble union' of proclaimed in 1290 by the marriage of Roger-Bernard de Foix and Marguerite de Béarn. What the Béarnais feared was the application to their land of the treaty of Toulouse, which would have made them subjects of France, thus undoing at one single stroke what

---

[10] *Prince*, 367–70.

Fébus had imposed – at least as a *de facto* situation – to all would-be suzerains. In their defiance of the French Crown, the Estates may have been encouraged by the promptness of England to react: as early as 12 September, Richard II formally acknowledged Mathieu de Castelbon as heir to Gaston III, by offering him an alliance in return for his homage.

Meanwhile, the French government had also reacted to the news of Fébus' death. Despite his uncles' opposition, Charles VI was still being guided at that time by his father's advisers, the low-born officers derisively dubbed Marmousets by their royal adversaries. The princes' party had been somewhat weakened by the death of Louis d'Anjou, allowing the Marmousets to pursue their policy of reinforcing royal authority, sometimes at the expense of the private interests of apanaged grandees. The treaty of Toulouse, promising a vast extension of the Crown's direct holdings in the Midi, had been one of their most recent successes. Now Bureau de la Rivière and his colleagues convinced the young King that, since the Count of Foix had died without a direct heir 'of his body', the county was his by right – being moreover mortgaged for the loan of 50,000 francs. They emphasized the strategic value of Foix as a strongly defended border with Catalonia, and represented to Charles that 'the people greatly desire to be in your hands.'[11] As 'quoted' by Froissart, their advice to the King makes no mention of Béarn and the other Gascon viscounties. This suggests that they may have already been aware of the probable hostility of the Béarnais and of England. Nor was there any French move in that direction, but as early as 6 August, the Lautrec and Albigeois portions of Fébus' domains were occupied, and Marshal Louis de Sancerre began to position his troops on the borders of the county of Foix. On 14 or 15 August a delegation of the royal council led by Bureau started on the journey to Toulouse. Theirs was a late start, the chronicler notes, and they took the long way, 'riding short stages, at a leisurely pace, they went by way of Avignon.'[12]

The slow progress of the French envoys gave the advisers of the new Count of Foix ample time to stake out their positions and muster political support. Mathieu de Castelbon who, at fourteen, had just attained his majority, arrived at the castle of Foix on 17 August to receive the homages of the ranking nobles of the county. The event had been staged by his mother, who appears no less capable than Aliénor de Comminges. Viscountess Géraude had secured not only powerful local support, but that of the King of Aragon – soon to become Mathieu's father-in-law. Moreover, the style of the homage named the boy 'by the grace of God Count of Foix, lord of Béarn, Viscount of Castelbon, Marsan, Gavardan, Nébouzan.', thus laying formal claim to the whole inheritance of Fébus, while preserving the all-important distinction between the vassal

---

[11] *Chroniques*, XIV, 336.

[12] *Ibid.*, 337.

county and viscounties, and the lordship of sovereign Béarn.[13] After a week's tour of the principal towns of the county, whose homages he received, Mathieu returned on 26 August to Foix, to swear to uphold the customs and liberties of the land. If Froissart's assertion that the people of Foix would have preferred to be 'governed and led by a seneschal, even as the country and city of Toulouse, and those of Carcassonne and Beaucaire' is correct, it may reflect differences of opinion – perhaps between the nobles and the commons – contrasting with the unanimous effort of all Béarnais to forestall a royal takeover. Moreover, the application of the treaty of Toulouse could still trump whatever homages Mathieu had received in Foix, and nullify his accession.

In Béarn, however, his investiture depended first upon the approval of he Estates. Towards that goal he could have had no better guide than Roger d'Espagne: as seneschal of Carcassonne – and thus an officer of the Crown – this kinsman and confidant of Fébus had the trust of both the Béarnais and the French; moreover, as the Count's lieutenant in Nébouzan, and lord of Montespan in his own right, he controlled the strategic Upper Garonne corridor between Foix and Béarn – a deterrent to any French surprise. The *jurats* of Orthez had first turned to him upon the death of their lord, and soon afterwards the Estates charged him and Espan de Lion to inform the legitimate heir of the conditions of his acceptance. Escorted by Roger and Espan, Mathieu de Castelbon arrived at Orthez on 1 September, and upon his undertaking to respect all the dispositions taken by the Estates on 8 August, was recognized as heir presumptive of Béarn. His accession being, however, contingent on the renunciation by Charles VI of the treaty of Toulouse, he was granted a large subsidy to defray his travel expenses and – more to the point – as ammunition for the forthcoming diplomatic campaign.

By then the French government commission had arrived in Toulouse, possibly unaware of the peaceful 'revolution' that had taken place in Orthez on 8 August, and of the firm resolve of the Béarnais to uphold their country's sovereignty – if necessary with English support. If that was the case, Bureau de la Rivière was quickly brought up to date when he came to Saint-Gaudens for a preliminary interview with Mathieu and Roger d'Espagne. The negotiations then continued in Toulouse, with Roger systematically developing the arguments against the application of the treaty, *viz.* that to renounce it would bring the King profit, honour and the salvation of his soul. The 100,000 francs granted to Fébus were only a loan, and the bequest of the Count's entire inheritance a pledge redeemable upon repayment of that sum – with accrued interests, he added shrewdly. Moreover, Fébus had had no need of that loan: he had mortgaged his estates only out of hatred for the Viscount of Castelbon and to frustrate his legitimate right of succession. The clear implication was that the treaty was illegal, irregular, immoral, sinful and contrary to feudal honour.

---

[13] *Prince*, 371.

These lofty arguments ought not to be regarded as mere rhetorical dressing: Charles V had been particularly sensitive to the eternal consequences of his political decisions, and there was no reason to doubt that his son would be less concerned with maintaining a state of grace. However, Roger d'Espagne did not neglect the more worldly arguments: the Crown would reap no profit from the annexation of Foix, as the cost of 'guarding' the land would be greater than the revenue collected – a discreet warning of popular resistance to a new administration. Lastly, the King could ill afford to offend and 'lose the homage of' a legitimate heir; although the lord of Montespan is not quoted as having spelled out the possible consequences, his interlocutors knew well enough that a rejection of Mathieu's claim could also alienate his other suzerain the King of Aragon, and perhaps drive both into an English alliance. In short: 'If I were like you a member of the royal council', Roger concluded, 'I would exhort the King to take back his money, to recover Bigorre, and to let the rightful heir receive his inheritance.' [14]

B EFORE the last period was played in that complex diplomatic match, time out was allowed for laying to rest the man who had endowed its trophy and established at least some of its rules. On the day after his death Gaston III Fébus had made his last entry in his capital with what solemnity could be improvised, his face uncovered (to allay suspicions of poisoning), and escorted by several barons; he had then been embalmed and placed in a lead casket in the Dominican church of Orthez, where twenty-four large tapers held by forty-eight valets burned day an night until the day of his obsequies. It was a long vigil, for the funeral service was only held on 12 October. The heraldic pomp preceding the Requiem, with knights and barons of Foix and Béarn carrying the sword of the defunct, his shield and his helmet, and leading his favourite charger around the casket, is all related in loving detail by Froissart. In the presence of Mathieu de Castelbon, and of Yvain and Gratien, Mass was said by that same bishop of Pamiers who, in his Avignon exile, had so rejoiced at the news of the Count's death. His colleague of Lescar, Odon de Mendousse, was of course present. It is fair to assume that those attending that ceremonial farewell harboured a variety of contradictory sentiments.

Mathieu de Castelbon and Roger d'Espagne then returned once more to parley with the French commissioners in Toulouse. Perhaps measuring for the first time the risks involved in applying the treaty, the latter agreed to give Mathieu and his advisers time to appeal directly to the King and the full royal council. To make the delay more acceptable, they were invited to 'stay and enjoy yourselves in the city of Toulouse, for your expenses shall be paid by the treasure in the castle of Orthez.' After a last consultation with Mathieu, Roger

---

[14] *Chroniques*, XIV, 347.

d'Espagne and Espan de Lion started on their journey to France, taking the shorter route *via* Rodez and Limoges.

The French court was then at Tours, and very preoccupied by potentially more critical issues. One was the search for an elusive peace with England, glimpsed from one extension to the next of the 1389 truce of Leulinghen; the other, even more volatile, was the effort to pacify the Duke of Brittany. Brought up at the court of Edward III, Jean IV had won the duchy after twenty years of civil war against Charles de Blois, nephew of Philippe VI of France. Having given the French Crown a most reluctant homage, he had then repudiated his allegiance, bolted to England, and joined Lancaster in his dismal 1379 chevauchée. Pardoned in the wake of the general truce, his potential for mischief was still considerable, and his mutual enmity with the Constable of France Olivier de Clisson was a constant threat to peace, capable of reigniting the dormant Anglo-French conflict. A treaty of reconciliation was in the making, to be sealed by assorted matrimonial arrangements. It was in part for the Duke's convenience that the French court had transported itself to Tours, where it was to remain 'well into the winter', wholly occupied with not one but two equally delicate negotiations.

On the face of it, this was not the best time or place to add another thorny problem to the agenda of the royal council. Roger d'Espagne and Espan de Lion arrived 'on a Wednesday'. The days, says the chronicler, 'were short, as they will be in winter, and so there was not much time for talks before dinner, nor between dinner and night.' (Even for diplomats, this was indeed 'a world lit by fire.') The city was so full of nobles and their retinues – including an English embassy and the Bretons – that the travellers had a great deal of trouble finding lodgings. Still, they were able to address the council and explain their mission, but although 'Messire Roger was heard willingly, he was not given an answer so soon.' Froissart exaggerates when he reports that the Foix-Béarn envoys were kept waiting for two months, but they were time and again put off with the same message from royal advisors: 'We shall counsel, […] but that counsel was not coming.' In the end, the chronicler attributes the mission's success to the intervention of a *deus ex machina* in the person of the Duke of Berry, with a back-room proposition: he would bring the proceedings to a satisfactory conclusion if he were given back the 30,000 francs with which he had bought Fébus' consent to the marriage of his young ward Jeanne de Boulogne. 'Upon hearing what the Duke said', Froissart writes, ' the two knights looked at each other without a word.'[15] Berry reiterated his assurance of success, adding that the Viscount of Castelbon would have no trouble finding the money, 'for the late Count had hoarded more than the King had in his treasury.'

Success was achieved when on 20 December Charles VI signed the letters patent whereby he renounced the treaty of Toulouse and recognized Mathieu

[15] *Ibid.,* 338.

de Castelbon as sole heir of Gaston III. The loan granted Gaston III was to be repaid, with an additional 40,000 francs: even counting the 30,000 francs returned to Berry, the cost was well within the 250,000 florins set aside by the Estates of Béarn for the negotiation. As for Bigorre, the lifetime grant to Fébus was naturally cancelled by his death, but in the next century, the embattled Charles VII would award it to the reigning Count of Foix. It is, of course, unlikely that the sole support of Jean de Berry had carried the decision, or for that matter that his intervention was solely motivated by the desire to recover his lost florins. The Duke and his brothers, Philip 'the Bold' of Burgundy, and the (now deceased) Louis d'Anjou, had been locked ever since the death of Charles V in a bitter struggle with the pragmatic advisers – the 'Marmousets' – the late king had bequeathed to their nephew. The resolution of the Foix-Béarn issue was another blow against the despised 'knights and clerks' whose centralizing policies often clashed with the interests of the apanaged princes. But it may well be that what prevailed was the counsel of prudence articulated by Roger d'Espagne: however tempting the prospect of extending the direct holdings of the Crown by seizing the heritage of the Count of Foix, it entailed too many predictable risks: local resistance, and the cost of keeping civil order, but also such a destabilization of the balance of power in the South as might have wrecked the hopes for peace with England – not to mention the friendly relations with Aragon.

THE new Count came to give homage for the county of Foix, the viscounty of Lautrec (which had been also given back) and other holdings within Languedoc. He then departed, not for his domains, but to join Duke Louis of Bourbon in an ongoing crusading expedition against the 'Africa' of the chroniclers – the Barbary corsair stronghold of Mahdia on the Tunisian coast. In the hindsight of history, this anticlimactic exit of a protagonist seems to leave other characters, at the denouement of the play that bound them together, to act their own absurd tragedies on a darkened stage. In August 1392, while leading a punitive expedition against the Duke of Brittany, Charles VI suffered the first attack of the madness that was to recur off and on throughout his disastrous reign. The King's uncles seized their opportunity: dismissed, arrested and charged with various malversations, the Marmousets barely escaped the block. Meanwhile, Yvain de Béarn had attached himself to the French court and become one of the favourite companions of the King, who may have remembered his part in the festivities at Mazères. As Charles VI recovered from his first attack, the Bastard of Béarn was much in demand as an impresario of revelry. Any pretext would serve to amuse the King. For the wedding of one of the Queen's ladies, Yvain thought of a new thrill: a charivari of six young gentlemen, led by the King and Yvain, bursting in on the ball. They were costumed as Savages – 'wild men', sewn up from head to foot in tight suits of linen covered with loose flaxen 'hair' glued to the cloth with pitch. It was to be the *bal des*

*Ardents*, one of the great horror stories of the time, told of course by Froissart in all its tragic details: the precautions taken to keep torches away from the flammable costumes; the arrival of the King's brother, unaware of the danger, trying to see who was behind a mask; the torch too close to the mummers; the instant conflagration. Thanks to the presence of mind of the young Duchess of Berry, who smothered his flames with her gown, the King escaped. Another mummer escaped by throwing himself in a dishwashing tub, the rest perished. Yvain, the beloved son who had once hoped to be lord of Béarn, lived two more days of agony before passing out of history, last protagonist of the Orthez mystery. His brother Gratien, of whose life so little is known, is believed to have taken part in the Barbary expedition of Louis de Bourbon, and died the following year in Sicily.

Mathieu de Foix only returned to Orthez in July 1393, there to receive at last the homage of the Estates of Béarn, and to swear in his turn to uphold the *fors* and customs of the land. In his absence, the Estates had governed Béarn unilaterally, and were now so in control that the new lord, and his successors, had no choice but to share their sovereign powers with the representatives of their subjects. Thus the autocratic rule that Fébus had progressively imposed, often by ignoring or defying ancient liberties and privileges, and especially by keeping the *Cours* dormant throughout his reign, had been quietly overthrown. Moreover Mathieu de Foix, born a Catalan magnate, soon abandoned the prudent external policy of his predecessor. Gaston III had carefully steered clear of Iberian entanglements, and never sought a royal crown; but Mathieu's marriage to the daughter of John I of Aragon exposed him to perhaps irresistible temptations. In 1396 the King – dubbed '*el Caçador*', a correspondent and admirer of Fébus – was also stricken and died suddenly while hunting. Mathieu claimed the throne on behalf of his wife, but his invasion of Catalonia was quickly routed by John's brother and successor, Martin I.

Two years after that dismal attempt, Mathieu died without issue, leaving the entire Foix-Béarn inheritance to his sister Isabelle and her husband Archambaud de Grailly. Their son Jean, a loyal supporter of Charles VII during the dark years of the 'kingdom of Bourges', was allowed to purchase the county of Bigorre, thus retrieving a lost piece of Fébus' territorial achievement. His *galant* motto 'J'ay belle dame', rather than Gaston III's proud 'Fébus me fe', adorns the lintel above the gate of Mauvezin Castle. In 1450 Gaston IV – the last to bear the dynastic name of Béarn-born heirs – transferred his capital to Pau. Married to Leonor, heiress of Navarre, his grandson François-Phoebus inherited that kingdom, but died without issue. Soon after her accession, his sister Catherine, now Queen of Navarre as well as Countess of Foix and Dame of Béarn, married Jean d'Albret. The ironies of those various successions may well have been cited as *exempla* of the caprices of Fortune: Gaston Fébus could hardly have imagined a Count of Foix wearing the crown of his murderous brother-in-law Charles 'the Bad', much less the devolution of his whole estate – augmented with Navarre – to a descendant of the upstart Albrets, in his time mere clients of the great counts of Armagnac.

The Foix-Navarre did not enjoy their trans-Pyrenean realms very long: in 1512 Ferdinand II of Aragon seized its greater, Iberian part. The court of Pau now ruled an almost nominal kingdom, reduced to the northernmost provinces of Soule and Basse-Navarre. Then, as the wind of Reformation swept through the Midi, Jeanne, last of the Albret-Navarre dynasty and a staunch Calvinist, married Antoine de Bourbon, a prince of the French royal blood and leader of the Protestant faction. In 1589, when a Catholic fanatic murdered the last of the Valois monarchs, the French throne was inherited by Henri III of Navarre, son of Jeanne d'Albret and Antoine de Bourbon. It was during his reign as Henri IV 'the Béarnais', of 'Paris is worth a Mass' fame, that the county of Foix was annexed to France, but the son of Jeanne d'Albret kept his native Béarn as a Protestant safe haven, out of the direct control of the French Crown. The formal union came only in 1620, ten years after his death. Béarn, however, retained its Estates, with many of its privileges and franchises, until the Revolution of 1789.

THE last physical remains of Gaston III were scattered and lost, probably when Huguenot troops sacked the convent churches of Orthez. In 1597 the poet Jean de Sponde recalled how he and his fellow students had finished the destruction in the tomb 'which they said was that of the great Gaston-Phoebus [...] who in his time had been the terror of Guyenne.'[16] Fébus' memory did not fare much better than his mortal parts. While during his reign his subjects had enjoyed the rare privilege of thirty years of peace, and his some of his administrative innovations endured until the Republic levelled them, his death was most frequently recorded with few expressions of regret, or worse. Thus the abbot of Moissac, writing at the end of the century, briefly relates Fébus' victory of Launac, his early conflicts with the Toulousains, his passion for the hunt, before coming to the dark side of his subject: 'He practiced hydromancy, and it was commonly said that he owned a thousand pounds of gold in coins, which he spent for his own glory, although he had violated the rights of prelates, burdened his people with taxes, and killed with his own hand his only legitimate son [...] His riches were dispersed and distributed to those he had robbed, who were many.' This obituary then subsides into a moral sermon on the familiar *topos* of capricious Fortune.[17] In the chronicle of the counts of Foix compiled in the fifteenth century by the archivist Esquerrier, the entry on Gaston III only notes that he had no legitimate son, and died intestate. Froissart's exception, his posthumous (and therefore sincere) praises, even with their occasional

---

[16] Cited in *Vicomté*, 338, n. 51.

[17] In *Prince*, 381–2.

evasions and reservations, remains the only contemporary text sympathetic to
the enigmatic Count Fébus.

After the fashion leaders of the French Renaissance had censured medieval
poetry and music as primitive and uncouth, the cultural achievements of the
fourteenth-century court of Orthez remained buried in libraries for more than
300 years. Moreover, under the absolute monarchy that culminated with the
triumph of Louis XIV over fractious grandees, Gaston III and such feudal
magnates of old could only be regarded as best forgotten relics of a politically
incorrect past. For centuries to come, Fébus would be known only to the more
methodical enthusiasts of the hunt, as the author of the *Livre de chasse*, for his
manual remained one of the indispensable references for later treatises and
was even cited as a source by Buffon. In the even more rarefied circles of biblio-
philes, the great illuminated manuscripts collected by royal amateurs preserved
the dormant memory of a Count of Foix increasingly surrounded by an aura of
gothic mystery. Some recognition came towards the end of the Ancien Régime,
when a heroic notion of chivalry was promoted, an idealized example of the
rôle the nobility ought to assume in defence of the tottering monarchy. The
Comte de Tressan adapted medieval romances and epics to the *style galant*, and
Voltaire himself joined the parade with his *Adelaïde du Guesclin*, a patriotic
tragedy hastily refurbished to exploit the name of the legendary Constable. On
the eve of the Revolution, Fébus came in for a share of the nostalgic feast, with
the *Éloge de Gaston-Phébus, Prince Souverain de Béarn*, a Discourse delivered on
11 March 1789 in the grand lecture hall of the University of Pau by Dom Maris,
Professeur de Rhétorique.[18]

After the Bourbon Restoration, in the pell-mell medievalist revival that
accompanied the Romantic movement, the strong figure of Fébus did not fail
to attract the attention of writers in search of the picturesque. The first modern
edition of Froissart's *Chroniques*, published by Buchon in 1826, was the chief
source of the first extensive biography of Gaston III, published by H. Gauche-
rot in 1834. Froissart's narrative of his voyage to Béarn also provided material
for a number of novels and plays, usually focused on the tragic enigmas of the
Count's private life. Most of these efforts have fallen into oblivion. One exception, notable for the later achievement of its author, is a short novel published
by Alexandre Dumas in 1839 – five years before his *Three Musketeers*. This
fantastic tale weaves together the stories of Horton, the familiar imp of the
baron de Coarraze, Pierre de Béarn's hunt of the infernal bear (now a malefic
sow), and the death of Fébus, stricken in the obligatory enchanted castle when
the ghost of his dead son brings him the fatal ewer. Some of the contemporary
scholarship was no less imaginative than the works of fiction: in 1856 Prosper
Tarbé identified Agnès de Navarre as the rather cruelly flirting damsel that the
elderly Guillaume de Machaut does not name in his *Voir Dit*, and published a

[18] *Ibid.*, 388.

collection of poems he attributed to that princess. For his part Buchon, editor of Froissart's *Chroniques*, accredited the legend naming Fébus as the author of the traditional ballad *Aqueras montanhas*. Since it was generally assumed that the marriage to Gaston III and Agnès was a love match, the song was taken literally as the expression of his longing for his absent fiancée. It is easy enough to deride the scholars whose enthusiasm led them into uncritical acceptance of romantic legends as history – but perhaps better to note that, wrong-headed though it was, their antiquarian enthusiasm rescued from oblivion the mass of documents that allowed scholarship to proceed beyond their speculations.

Since the 1950s especially, academic studies grounded in painstaking archival research and critical reading of Froissart's and other medieval chronicles have contributed to a better informed consideration of the Count of Foix. As the prince of a marginal but strategic state, his actions are necessarily viewed in the context of the larger political issues of his time, with their attendant constraints and opportunities; as feudal lord of lands and people whose ancient laws and customs clearly delineated his powers and his obligations, his rule is necessarily viewed in terms of his relations to his subjects. Thanks to half a century of scholarship (largely dominated by the monumental work of Pierre Tucoo-Chala), it is now easier to weigh objectively the relative merits of Fébus' external policy – peace and prosperity lasting long past the thirty years of his reign – against the adverse aspects of his despotism: as it now stands poised, the balance on the whole is more positive than not. This is of course not to say that future research, or new trends in the interpretation of history, will not alter it again; but in any event the rôle of Gaston III as an important participant in the affairs of his time, rather than as the romantic protagonist of a domestic tragedy, is certain to be acknowledged.

Nevertheless, a certain image of Fébus has continued to flourish in the Pyrenean folklore, in association with the vigorous resurgence of regionalist pride. Although his *Book of the Hunt* and *Book of Orisons* were written in French, the attribution of the ballad *Aqueras montanhas* and the Count's undoubted authorship of the canso *Aras can vey del boy …*, made him the tutelary hero of those nineteenth-century promoters of a literary revival of the *langues d'oc*, from Provence to Gascony, the *félibres*. In 1897 a cultural association dedicated to that effort was named *Escole Gastou Fébus*, as one of its founding members figuratively picked up the banner of the legendary Count: 'The time has come to revive the old battle cry of the Gascons: *Fébus abant!*'[19] That organization, still active after more than a century, has acquired the castle of Mauvezin and undertaken its restoration. As the Fifth Republic acknowledged the economic advantages of decentralization, cultural diversity was also encouraged, in part as an incentive to the development of 'historical tourism'. With the support of local governments, an 'Association Route Historique Gaston Fébus' promotes

---

[19] *Ibid.*, 393.

an itinerary across the former fiefs of Foix-Béarn, highlighting, from the Jacobins church in Toulouse, to Bellocq in Béarn, every site more or less intimately associated with the 'Sun Prince', as the twelfth Count of Foix is dubbed in their handsome brochure. The name of Fébus has been appropriated by a number of institutions – a pensioners' home in Mazères, a lycée in Orthez – and not a few commercial establishments.

In an age where celebrity has become so much to depend on visual stimuli, the effigy – albeit imaginary – of Gaston III was given nationwide exposure on the occasion of the 'Année Fébus' commemorating the 600th anniversary of his death, with the issuance of a postage stamp and the poster saluting the arrival at Orthez of the high-speed rail line – the TGV-Atlantique. Juvenile popular culture was, however, ahead of these official recognition, with the bande dessinée *Gaston Fébus et le Prince Noir*, published in 1985 with a text by Pierre Tucoo-Chala. In this graphic album, the artist José de Huescar portrays the Count as a youthful, athletic knight in full plate armour, with the obligatory mass of unruly blond locks and facial features reminiscent of other cloaked super-heroes of the genre. A more durable image of Fébus overlooks the gardens below the castle of Pau. This sedately idealized statue, installed in 1866, shows Gaston III in the guise of a young huntsman leaning lightly on his spear and accompanied by a greyhound. It is the work of Triqueti, the sculptor once commissioned by Prince Albert and later retained by Queen Victoria to decorate her Consort's funeral chapel at Windsor. The ensemble is fraught with symbolic and fittingly contradictory homages to Fébus: the indirect English connexion, an ironic coda to the ambiguous relations between the lord of Béarn and his Plantagenet neighbours; the soft features and relaxed pose of the statue, contrasting with the severity of the square keep; and the brick tower in its turn superseded and enveloped by the elegance of the – now royal – Renaissance castle. Thus, the diverse aspects of the elusive Count: bold and prudent, lavish and avaricious, devout and lustful, erudite naturalist and avid hunter, galant troubadour and slayer of his son, conscientious defender of his people and harsh autocrat – and yet there are still missing pieces of this picture, pieces that may yet some day bring coherence to the whole.

✦  ✦

✦

The Renaissance castle at Pau, with Triqueti's statue of Fébus

# Bernard de Béarn, Count of Medinaceli

I N September 1367 the pretender Enrique de Trastamara began his reconquest of the Castilian throne by crossing the Pyrenees, by way of the Val
d'Aran, with a force of 400 lances. One of his principal followers was Bernard,
called 'the Bastard of Béarn'. Upon reaching Calahorra, where the small army
was increased by such distinguished recruits as the Archbishop of Toledo and
the Master of Alcantara, Bernard was knighted by Enrique's own hand. When
the invasion, with the eventual help of the Breton captain Bertrand du Guesclin, had achieved its goal, and Enrique II, having killed his half-brother Pedro
I 'the Cruel', once again wore the crown of Castile, the Bastard of Béarn was
one of the first recipients of the royal largesse wryly known in Spanish annals
as *las mercedes enriqueñas*. In July 1369 Bernard was created Viscount of Medinaceli, with considerable landed estates and privileges. Soon elevated to the
rank of Count, he was given the hand of Isabel de la Cerda, a granddaughter
of Alfonso X 'el Sabio' of Castile. This marriage of a Béarnais bastard with a
lady of the royal blood of Castile was the origin of the still extant ducal house
of Medinaceli.

Most modern authors – including Kervyn de Lettenhove, editor of Froissart's *Chroniques* – identify this Bernard de Béarn as a son of Gaston III Fébus;
Pierre Tucoo-Chala, Fébus' most thorough and scholarly biographer, concurs.
Russell inexplicably identifies Bernard with 'Arnaud-Guillaume' [*sic*] de Béarn,
bastard brother' of Gaston III.[1] There are puzzling variations: in the Index
to the Pléiade edition of *Historiens et Chroniqueurs du Moyen Âge* [p. 1469],
Bernard is assimilated to another bastard of Fébus, Gratien de Foix; following
perhaps the lead of that anthology, Gunnar Tilander states in his Introduction
to the *Livre de chasse* that it was Gratien who married Isabel de la Cerda and
founded the house of Medinaceli. And Tucoo-Chala goes so far as to suggest
that Gaston III Fébus, foreseeing the favour that the pretender Enrique de
Trastamara, himself of irregular birth, would extend to a fellow-bastard, had
'seized the opportunity' of the Castilian civil war to advance the fortune of 'his
first-born'.[2]

Unfortunately, no document – notarial record, correspondence, etc. – has
been exhibited to confirm without any doubt the paternity of Gaston III. Even
Froissart, who gives us the most detailed account of the Count's family life, fails

[1] Russell, 50, n. 2.

[2] *Prince*, 128–30.

to mention Bernard. More precisely, his informant Espan de Lion, whom he questions with some insistence about Gaston's progeny, only mentions the 'two fine bastard knights' Yvain and Gratien. One might expect that such an illustrious connection as the marriage of a son of Fébus with a princess of Castile would not have escaped the notice of a chronicler anxious to show his host in the most prestigious light. However, Schwennicke's *Europaische Stammtafeln* indicate that Bernard de Béarn, first Count of Medinaceli, had died in 1383, five years before Froissart's conversation with Espan, which touched on the issue of the eventual succession of Foix-Béarn in the absence of a legitimate heir.[3] Because of Fébus' known predilection for them, Yvain and Gratien clearly had to be discussed, but in 1388 the Count's degree of relationship to the deceased Bernard was no longer relevant to the issue of succession. While one might have expected Espan, who clearly approved of his master's 'irregular' family, to mention the connection of Gaston III with the royal blood of Castile, his omission cannot be conclusive.

A more serious objection to the identification of Bernard de Béarn as a son of Fébus may be found in Lopez de Ayala's narrative of Enrique de Trastamara's return to Spain in 1367. The Castilian chronicler and standard-bearer to the exiled pretender, who was present on the scene, names several of the most prominent mercenary captains in Enrique's following – such as the Bègue de Villaines – but he states unequivocally that the largest contingent was led by 'the Bastard of Béarn' ('... e venieron con el rey el vegue de Villanes, e el bastardo de Bearne, *como quier que las mas compannas destas tenia el bastardo de Bearne*').[4] This suggests that Bernard was by 1367 a seasoned military entrepreneur, in effective command of a substantial company, rather than the very young man he would have been if sired by Gaston III, himself born in 1331. Nor does the fact that he was knighted by Don Enrique during that same campaign imply necessarily that the Bastard of Béarn was only then entering the career of arms: Bertrand du Guesclin was knighted in his mid-thirties, after many years of hard fighting. And yet, given Fébus' subsequent 'confession' of a depraved, lustful youth, the possibility of a precocious Gaston fathering a bastard son while still in his 'teens cannot be totally excluded. As for Bernard's ability to command a mercenary company, military history is replete with examples of youthful leadership: the example of the sixteen-year-old Edward Prince of Wales comes to mind. It is therefore not unthinkable that a twenty- or even eighteen-year-old Bastard of Béarn, perhaps seconded by a veteran officer, and with Fébus' gold guaranteeing the pay of his men, may have commanded 'las mas compannas' in Don Enrique's small army.

The House of Medinaceli documents selected for publication by Paz y Melia

3 Detlev Schwennicke (ed.), *Europäische Stammtafeln, Neue Folge* (Frankfurt am Main, c.1998–), Band III, Tafel 123, III, 2.

4 Pero Lopez de Ayala, *Cronica*, year 1367, cap. 33. Italics mine.

shed no light on the parentage of Bernard de Béarn. They include the often cited donations by Enrique II, as well as the King's letter to Isabel de la Cerda, expressing his wish that she marry the Count of Medinaceli. A particularly interesting entry is that of the act of legitimation of Bernard, a curious 'privilege' founded on the authority delegated, not by the Pope, but by the Emperor (in the event, Charles IV) to the Count Palatine. The act in effect removes all the legal (and presumably, canonical) disabilities inherent to bastardy, with explicit reference to rights of inheritance, honours, prerogatives, and public offices – but it is a legitimation without any acknowledgment of a lineage, in that it does not name either of the beneficiary's parents.[5]

The *Europaische Stammtafeln* entry already cited would appear to answer the question of Bernard parentage, by making him the son of Roger-Bernard I de Castelbon, whose grandson Matthieu would succeed Fébus as Count of Foix. At first glance, this relationship fits well with Bernard's known career: given the trans-Pyrenean situation of the Castelbons, it would have been the obvious course for their bastard to seek his fortune in Spain. Born *c.* 1330, he would also have been of an age consonant with substantial military experience. But Schwennicke's credibility is undermined by the mention of Constance de Luna – Roger-Bernard's legitimate wife – as Bernard's mother. It may be possible to regard Constance's paradoxical maternity as an *ex post facto* reintegration of Bernard in the Castelbon genealogy on account of the 'blank' legitimation act of 1381, but this is a matter of so far unsupported conjecture.

Moreover, even if we take the mention of Constance de Luna as a mere *lapsus*, and accept Roger-Bernard's paternity as fact, it is difficult to see why his presumed offspring should have routinely been called 'the Bastard of Béarn', rather than 'of Castelbon' or 'of Foix'. But more than any of the documents published to date, the testament of the first Count of Medinaceli strongly suggest that his relationship was with the elder branch of the Foix-Béarn. Dated from Badajoz, on 3 August 1381, Bernard's will names as his heir 'my son, Don Gastón'. There follow various bequests to his followers, and provisions for his other (and probably natural) children: Juan, who is being brought up by the Infanta of Castile (*que cria la Infanta de Castilla*), should be made a priest; and to Juana, 'the daughter I have in Orthez' (*mi fija, que tengo in Ortes*), he leaves a dowry of 40,000 *maravedis*.[6] This last item provides credible evidence of Bernard's attendance at the court of Gaston Fébus, where he was received as an envoy from Enrique II to Gaston III.[7] Moreover, his diplomatic rôle as a Castilian grandee did not preclude his military service to the Count of Foix

[5] See A. Paz y Mélia, *Series de los mas importantes documentos etc.* (Madrid, 1915), 28.

[6] *Ibid.*, 27.

[7] In 1377 Peter IV, suspecting him of complicity with Louis d'Anjou's hostile plans, refused Bernard safe-conduct through Aragon while travelling to Orthez. Russell, 253, n. 3.

– notably during the 'War of Comminges', and his presence as witness to the 1379 treaty of Tarbes. But perhaps the most eloquent exhibit is the dynastic name of Gaston given to the second Count of Medinaceli (d. 1404) – a name hitherto reserved for the heirs to the viscounts of Béarn, born in Béarn.

This is, however, as near as we come to discerning a definite link between the – soon to be extinct – elder branch of Foix-Béarn and the nascent House of Medinaceli. Many questions remain unanswered; some of them giving rise to tantalizing suggestions. Thus, it may be pure coincidence that Bernard was legitimized soon after the tragic events of 1380, which had left Fébus with Matthieu de Castelbon as his only legitimate heir, but it is also conceivable that an act removing the bar to the accession of his 'first-born' was secured in order to forestall that of Gaston III's despised cousin. If this were the case, however, the death of Bernard in 1383 would have aborted that plan and made it not worth mentioning, even by the talkative Espan de Lion. In the event, whether or not they had rights to the succession of Fébus, the descendants of Bernard de Béarn chose not to claim them. Instead, they prefer to emphasize their royal Castilian lineage, and it is under the family name of La Cerda that Count Luis II was elevated 1479 to the dukedom of Medinaceli.

✦  ✦
✦

# Bibliography

## 1. Medieval Sources

*La Chanson de la Croisade albigeoise. Texte original; préface de Georges Duby; adaptation de Henri Gougaud.* Paris: Le Livre de Poche, 1989.

*Chronique des quatre premiers Valois (1327–1393). Publiée pour la première fois pour la Société de l'histoire de France par M. Siméon Luce.* Paris: V. J. Renouard, 1862.

Edward of Norwich, Duke of York. *The Master of Game: the Oldest English Book on Hunting, by Edward, Second Duke of York.* Edited by Wm A. and F. Baillie-Grohman. With a foreword by Theodore Roosevelt. London: Chatto & Windus, 1909.

Esquerrier, Arnaud. *Chroniques romanes des Comtes de Foix. Composées au XVe siècle par Arnaud Esquerrier et Miégeville et publiées pour la première fois par Félix Pasquier et Henri Courteault.* Nîmes: C. Lacour, 1999 (1895).

*Five Ballades for the House of Foix.* Music score and lyrics, edited by Peter Lefferts & Sylvia Huot. Newton Abbot: Antico Edition, 1989.

Froissart, Jean. *Chroniques.* In *Œuvres*, edited by Baron Kervyn de Lettenhove. 28 vols. Brussels: Académie Royale des Sciences, des Lettres et des Beaux-Arts de Belgique, 1867–77.

—— *'Dits' et 'Débats'. Introduction, édition, notes, glossaire par Anthime Fourrier.* Geneva: Librairie Droz, 1979.

—— *Méliador, par Jean Froisart. Roman comprenant les poésies lyriques de Wenceslas de Bohême, duc de Luxembourg et de Brabant, pub. pour la première fois par Auguste Longnon.* 3 vols. Paris: Firmin-Didot, 1895–9.

—— *Poésies. Publiées par Auguste Scheler.* 3 vols. Brussels: Devaux, 1870–2.

——*Voyage en Béarn.* Edited by A. H. Diverres. Manchester: Manchester University Press, 1953.

Gaston III Phébus. *Livre de chasse. Édité avec introduction, glossaire et reproduction des 87 miniatures du manuscrit 616 de la Bibliothèque nationale de Paris par Gunnar Tilander.* Stockholm: Almqvist & Wiksell, 1971.

—— *Livre des oraisons: les prières d'un chasseur. Edité avec introduction, glossaire et reproduction d'une miniature du manuscrit 616 de la Bibliothèque nationale de Paris par Gunnar Tilander.* Stockholm: Almqvist & Wiksell; Paris: Crepin-Leblond, 1975.

—— *The Hunting Book of Gaston Phébus. Manuscrit français 616. Paris, Bibliothèque nationale. Introduction by Marcel Thomas and François Avril. Commentary by Wilhelm Schlag.* London: Harvey Miller Publishers, 1998.

Jean de Venette. *The Chronicle of Jean de Venette.* Translated by Jean Birdsall. Edited, with an introduction and notes, by Richard A. Newhall. New York: Columbia University Press, 1953.

Juvénal des Ursins, Jean. *Histoire de Charles VI, roy de France … Augmentée, etc. Par Denis Godefroy.* Paris: Imprimerie royale, 1653.

Le Baker de Swinbroke, Galfridus. *Chronicon Galfridi Le Baker de Swynebroke.* Edited with notes by Edward Maunde Thompson. Oxford: Clarendon Press, 1889.

*Les Livres du roy Modus et de la royne Ratio. Publiés avec introduction, notes et glossaire par Gunnar Tilander.* Paris: Société des anciens textes français, 1932.

Machaut, Guillaume de. *Le Livre du voir-dit, où sont contées les amours de Messire Guillaume de Machaut et de Peronnelle, dame d'Armentières, etc.* Edited by Paulin Paris. Geneva: Slatkine Reprints, 1969 [reprint of the Paris edition of 1875].

—— *Les Poésies d'Agnès de Navarre-Champagne, dame de Foix.* Edited by Prosper Tarbé. Collection des poètes de Champagne antérieurs au XVIè siècle, vol. 16. Paris: A. Aubry, 1856.

Petrarca, Francesco. *Letters on Familiar Matters*, vol. 3. Translated by Aldo S. Bernardo. Baltimore: Johns Hopkins University Press, 1985.

## 2. Modern Sources

Ainsworth, Peter F. *Jean Froissart and the Fabric of History: Truth, Myth and Fiction in the Chroniques.* Oxford: Clarendon Press, 1990.

Castéret, Jean-Jacques. 'Musique et Musiciens à la Cour de Gaston Fébus'. [Unpublished thesis.] Mémoire de maîtrise. Paris: Université de Paris-Sorbonne, 1992.

—— 'Panorama musical de la cour de Gaston Fébus'. In *L'Amour courtois des troubadours à Fébus / Flamenca. Actes des rencontres-communications de Image / Imatge 94 à Orthez.* Orthez: Éditions Per Noste, 1995. pp. 125–42.

—— 'Les Musiciens de Gaston Fébus' in *Actes du 118ème congrès des sociétés historiques et scientifiques.* Pau, 25–29 Octobre 1993. pp. 165–74.

Contamine, Philippe. *La France au XIVe et XV siècles: hommes, mentalités, guerre et paix.* London: Variorum Reprints, 1981.

—— *War in the Middle Ages.* Translated by Michael Jones. Oxford: Blackwell, 1984.

Cosman, Marjorie Pelner. *Fabulous Feasts: Medieval Cookery and Ceremony.* New York: George Braziller, 1976.

Delachenal, Roland. *Histoire de Charles V.* 5 vols. Paris: Auguste Picard et Fils, 1909–31.

Dembowski, Peter F. *Jean Froissart and his Meliador: Context, Craft and Sense.* Lexington, KY: French Forum Publishers, 1983.

Dumas, Alexandre. *Monseigneur Gaston Phoebus: chronique dans laquelle est racontée l'histoire du démon familier du sire de Corasse [sic].* Avec des extraits des *Chroniques* de Froissart, transcrits en français moderne. Présentation et commentaire par Pierre Tucoo-Chala. Biarritz: Atlantica, 2000.

*Les Fastes du Gothique: le siècle de Charles V. (Grand Palais, 9 octobre 1981 – 1er février 1982)*. [Exhibition catalogue.] Paris: Éditions de la Réunion des Musées Nationaux. 1981.

Fowler, Kenneth. *Medieval Mercenaries*, vol. 1: *The Great Companies*. Oxford: Blackwell, 2001.

Gómez Muntané, M. C. *La música en la casa real catalano-aragonesa durante los años 1336–1442*. vol. 1: *Historia y documentos*. Barcelona: Antoni Bosch, 1979.

Harvey, L. P. *Islamic Spain, 1250 to 1500*. Chicago: University of Chicago Press, 1990.

Hewitt, H. J. *The Black Prince's Expedition of 1355–1357*. Manchester: Manchester University Press, 1957.

Higounet, Charles. *Le Comté de Comminges de ses origines à son annexion à la couronne*. 1932. 2 vols. Toulouse: Privat, 1949.

—— *Histoire de l'Aquitaine*. Toulouse: Privat, 1971.

*Histoire de Foix et de la Haute-Ariège*. [Sous la direction de Claudine Pailhès.] Toulouse: Privat, 1996.

Hoppin, Richard H. *Medieval Music*. New York: W. W. Norton, 1978.

Lamazou-Duplan, Véronique. 'Froissart et le drame d'Orthez: chronique ou roman'. In *Actes du colloque international Jehan Froissart, Lille-Valenciennes, 2004*, ed. Marie-Madeleine Castellani and Jean-Charles Herbin. Paris, 2006. pp. 111–41.

——'Duo politique: Charles II de Navarre et Gaston Fébus (1349–1364)'. In *Minorités juives, pouvoirs, littérature politique en péninsule ibérique, France et Italie au Moyen Âge*, ed. Jean-Pierre Barraqué et Véronique Lamazou-Duplan. Biarritz: Atlantica, 2006. 81–98.

Leroy-Ladurie, Emmanuel. *Montaillou, The Promised Land of Error*. Translated by Barbara Bray. New York: George Braziller, 1978.

López de Ayala, Pero. *Crónica del rey don Pedro y del rey don Enrique, su hermano, hijos del rey don Alfonso onceno. Edición crítica y notas de Germán Orduna*. Buenos Aires: Secrit; Ediciones Incipit, 1994–7.

Lot, Ferdinand, and R. Fawtier. *Histoire des Institutions françaises au Moyen Age*, vol. 1: *Les Institutions seigneuriales*. Paris, 1957–.

Marca, Pierre de. *Histoire de Béarn, contenant l'origine des rois de Navarre, des ducs de Gascogne, marquis de Gothie, princes de Béarn, comtes de Carcassonne, de Foix et de Bigorre* [...] Par Me Pierre de Marca. Paris: la veuve Camusat, 1640.

Pagès, Amédée. *La 'Vesio' de Bernat de Sò*. Toulouse: Privat, 1945.

Pailhès, Claudine. *Gaston Fébus, le Prince et le diable*. Paris: Perrin, 2007.

Paterson, Linda M. *The World of the Troubadours: Medieval Occitan Society, c. 1100–c. 1300*. Cambridge: Cambridge University Press, 1993.

Paz y Mélia, A. Antonio. *Series de los mas importantes documentos del archivo y biblioteca del Exmo. señor Duque de Medinaceli, eligidos por su gargo y publicados a sus expenses. 1a series historica por A. Paz y Mélia. Años 860–1814*. Madrid, 1915.

Rougemont, Denis de. *Love in the Western World*. New York, 1940.

Russell, P. E. *The English Intervention in Spain and Portugal in the Time of Edward III and Richard II*. Oxford: Clarendon Press, 1955.

Schwennicke, Detlev (ed.). *Europäische Stammtafeln, Neue Folge*. Frankfurt am Main: V. Klostermann, *c*. 1998–.

Strayer, Joseph R. *The Albigensian Crusades*. With a New Epilogue by Carol Lansing. Ann Arbor: University of Michigan Press, 1992 (1971).

Sumption, Jonathan. *The Hundred Years War*, vol. 1:*Trial by Battle*. Philadelphia: University of Pennsylvania Press, 1990.

—— *The Hundred Years War*, vol. 2:*Trial by Fire*. Philadelphia: University of Pennsylvania Press, 1999.

Tuchman, Barbara W. *A Distant Mirror: The Calamitous 14th Century*. New York: Knopf, 1978.

Tucoo-Chala, Pierre. *Gaston Fébus et la Vicomté de Béarn (1343–1391)*. Bordeaux: Imprimerie Bière, 1959.

—— *La Vicomté de Béarn et le problème de sa souveraineté des origines à 1620*. Bordeaux: Imprimerie Bière, 1961.

—— *Gaston Fébus, prince des Pyrénées (1331–1391)*. Pau: J & D Éditions / Bordeaux: Deucalion, 1991.

—— *Le Livre des Hommages de Gaston Fébus (1343–1391)*. Saragossa: Universidad de Zaragoza, 1976.

—— *Les Forteresses pyrénéennes de Gaston Fébus*. Toulouse: Loubatières, 1997.

——'Forêts et landes en Béarn au XIVème siècle'. *Annales du Midi*, vol. 67 (1957), 247.

——'Productions et commerce en Béarn au XIVème siècle'. *Annales du Midi*, vol. 69 (1957), 39–58.

—— and Patrick Amblevert. *La Jeunesse de Fébus*. [Bande dessinée.] Toulouse: Loubatières, 1996.

—— and José de Huescar. *Gaston Fébus et le Prince Noir*. [Bande dessinée.] Toulouse: Loubatières, 1985.

—— and Jacques Staes. *Notaire de Prince: Le registre de Bernard de Luntz, notaire de Béarn sous Gaston Fébus*. Pau: Laboratoire de Recherche en Langues et Littératures Romanes & Editions Covedi, 1996.

Vidal de La Blache, Paul. *Tableau de la géographie de la France*. Paris: Tallandier, 1979.

Warren, W. L. *King John*. Berkeley: University of California Press, 1961.

Wolff, Philippe. *Commerce et marchands de Toulouse (vers 1350 – vers 1450)*. Paris: Plon, 1954.

Zink, Michel. *Froissart et le temps*. Paris: Presses Universitaires de France, 1998.

✦  ✦

✦

# Index

✦  ✦

✦